W9-CFO-255

Men Own the Fields,
Women Own the Crops

Miriam Goheen

Men Own the Fields, Women Own the Crops

Gender and Power in the Cameroon Grassfields

The University of Wisconsin Press

The University of Wisconsin Press
114 North Murray Street
Madison, Wisconsin 53715

3 Henrietta Street
London WC2E 8LU, England

DT
571
N74
G64
1996

5   4   3   2   1

Printed in the United States of America

Library of Congress Cataloging-in-Publication Data
Goheen, Miriam.
    Men own the fields, women own the crops: gender and power in the
Camerooon grassfields / Miriam Goheen.
    252 p.   cm.
    Includes bibliographical references (p. 234) and index.
    ISBN 0-299-14670-7 (alk. paper).
    ISBN 0-299-14674-X (pbk. : alk. paper)
    1. Nso (african people)—Social conditions.   2. Sex role—
Cameroon.   3. Cameroon—Social conditions—1960–
4. Cameroon—Politics and government—1982–   I. Title.
DT571.N74G64   1996
305.3'096711—dc20   95-25275

To Sally Chilver and Molly Goheen,
with love and appreciation

Contents

Illustrations

Maps

Prologue

We are just arriving back in Kimbo' after accompanying the *fon* to Foumban to celebrate "600 years of Tikari history." The dry season has now set in in earnest. The dry winds of the Harmattan whirl the red dust around us like a giant brush stirring the very core of the Earth. The landscape changes from green to red. I am travelling along with one prince and two princesses (*won nto'*) as part of the palace entourage. We are carrying the *fon*'s elephant tusk—crucial in symbolizing his power—along with the sacra and instruments of Lale, the dance society of the royal women to which I now belong. A *kikeŋ* plant is attached to the front of the car, denoting the fact that we are travelling with the *fon;* while we ride through the far reaches of the Nso' countryside, women bend down in respect and men stop and salute in recognition of the importance of these "things of the palace." During the time we spent in Foumban and for a good deal of the trip back, conversation has centered on comparing the traditions of Nso' and Bamum, with the latter characterized as all show with fancy clothes but no correct "country fashion"; people talk angrily about the fact that the *fon*'s entourage, which includes his top councillors and two *vikiy nto'* (wives) as well as ourselves, was not received with correct dignity and respect on arrival in Foumban. There is a lively discussion of whether or not it is the fact that Foumban is Muslim (as are two of the *won nto'* with us) or Francophone or a combination of these which has eroded "correct fashion" of the Bamum, who are both brothers and, in the past, the most important rival of the Nso' in the region.

It is now a decade and a half since I first arrived in Nso' as a graduate student with a clearer understanding of Hegel, Marx, and Weber than of the reality of African life. In the past 16 years I have become literate if not fluent in Lam Nso', and many of the people here have become friends and even family. Recently, I was installed as *Yaa Nso'*, a position which carries significant responsibility; I have experienced firsthand the respect as well as the burden and expense of Nso' traditional titles. The scene is familiar.

Life in Nso' has remained deeply rooted in what is locally referred to as tradition or country fashion. When one sits in the Squares in Kimbo', one is struck by the seeming paradox of the juxtaposition of timelessness and movement—of "development." The Squares area remains the center of traditional Nso', of Nto' (the palace), and of the people of the palace, which include a host of citizens of different ages, professions, and statuses. Many of the stores and off-licenses and their proprietors have persisted essentially unchanged for the past two decades. Periodically the population of Nso' gathers along the perimeter of the main square and lines the road to Nto', kneeling in the wake of the masked jujus of the ŋweroŋ and ŋgiri, the palace societies, who dance, display, perform, and generally terrorize the crowd.

The center of Nso' political and cultural life, Nto' remains the heart of the Nso' people. The current national political and economic situation has reinforced the Nso' sense of identity and the political role of the *fon* and the palace. The current Fon Nso', Səm Minglo I, enstooled in 1993, has more local power, both because of current national politics and because of personality, than Ŋga' Bi'fon II had in 1979, and clearly more than Ŋga' Bi'fon III, Səm Minglo's immediate predecessor. While the state has become a symbol of corruption and its role one of repression, the local political discourse organized around the *fon* and his notables has increasingly come to be the voice of reason and the source of order and organization in Nso'. Nso' people remain staunchly committed to local identity; Kimbo' is the largest ethnic town in Cameroon, and outsiders constantly complain that, when you get two Nso' people together, they will refuse to speak anything but Lam Nso'. A main center of the Social Democratic Front, Kimbo' has become known nationally as Baghdad because of its tough opposition politics. In the current economic crisis and national political situation, in which Anglophone Cameroonians feel disenfranchised by the national center, local and national politics have become even more intertwined. The current *fon* was chosen at least partly, if not in fact wholly, because of his strong support of the SDF. The national center has tried in vain to tighten its control in opposition areas. In many ways Nso' has withdrawn from the state. People and businesses have refused to pay taxes and have put enough pressure on national law enforcement personnel locally to get away with this, albeit aided by some bribery. When the national government tries to shut down shops for nonpayment of taxes, people just laugh, take down the notice of closure, and business continues as usual. Taxis are painted blue and red instead of the official yellow, and most are running "*clando*," or off the record, so to speak.

Within this context, the power of the Fon Nso' has been augmented, not lessened. Hoodlums and harassers are regularly brought to the palace, rather than to the police, for punishment. It is widely believed that the police take bribes rather than deal honestly with the problem of theft, harassment, and other crime. Traditional courts and the *fon* adjudicate these cases and mete out punishment, and community work on roads and bridges is organized through the palace societies.

But life in Nso' today, while familiar, is lived in a context that is very different from the one of even a decade ago—economically, politically, and, yes, socially, if not culturally. The economic boom which provided the background to life in the late 1970s and the early 1980s has turned into a downward spiral of ever-increasing economic crisis; unemployment and inflation are two of the main topics of conversation. And the rather dreary economic situation does not seem to have prospects of changing for the better, at least not in the near future. It is all too likely, and no secret, that things will get worse, even much worse. Many highly educated young people are leaving if they can—for the United States, Canada, England, France, Holland; for Saudi Arabia and the former Yugoslavia; for Zambia and South Africa.

Today the dreams have changed from the boom time of the 1970s and 1980s, which created an atmosphere of hope that the future would be better for the young, a hope that did not seem farfetched at that point. Cameroon was an African success story. Ahidjo, the first president of Cameroon, encouraged agricultural production, and Cameroon was at that time almost entirely self-sufficient in food production. Ahidjo was a master at cooptation. And he had the oil. Autocratic, but not as out of touch or perceived to be as corrupt as the current president, Paul Biya, is widely thought to be by most Cameroonians, Ahidjo created at least an illusion of continuing economic growth and future prosperity. Today, after almost a decade of life under Biya, people are disillusioned, angry, frustrated, perplexed, and anxious. With far more formal education as a group, they have fewer prospects as individuals, and many if not most face an uncertain future.

The four most striking changes over the past two decades are found in the age structure of the population, in shifts in gender and power, in the commodification of absolutely everything, and in the increasing internationalization of culture. All of these are in turn connected to a growing gap, primarily in terms of access to knowledge of the wider world and consequent changes in style of dress and living, between elites and their less fortunate relatives. Although this gap is bridged somewhat by the obligation of wealthy kin to their dependents and clients, it has nevertheless widened in the most critical factors—access to higher education, often outside Cameroon, and knowledge of and access to the national and international cultural and political discourse outside Nso'. Young people from elite fami-

lies are aware of and often have access to the international communica-
tions highway—telephones, faxes, e-mail. They speak knowledgeably
about the latest computers as well as the latest adventures of Steve Urkle on
"Family Matters" or of "The Fresh Prince of Bel-Air." Many go to the
United States or Great Britain to the university, and even more aspire to do
so. This is in contrast with the majority of the population, especially those
living in smaller villages, most of whom don't own or have access to a
television set and few of whom have seen or even heard of computers.
Elites can (and do) purchase "traditional culture" in the form of titles,
donations to the palace, and membership in palace societies. The reverse is
not true; nonelites do not have the purchasing power to gain access to the
knowledge necessary to operate effectively in the world outside Nso'. Nso'
tradition has tended to become owned and dominated by the new elites,
who often use their local, traditional, political status to gain access to the
national political arena.

In the course of everyday life, visiting compounds, and hanging out in
the market, I am often struck by the number of children in compounds and
the proportion of young people in public gatherings. This is not only because I am fifteen years older than when I first came to Nso'; it is also
because over 45 percent of the population is under the age of 15. Many of
these young people have had parents who have struggled to put them
through primary and secondary school. Others have no knowledge of
"book." There is perhaps more of an unbridgeable knowledge gap within
and between generations today than ever before in the past. There has been
little gender discrimination in educating children; the deciding factor in
who does or does not become educated is today who has or does not have
money. The children in families with resources become educated; their
poorer neighbors and relatives do not. By the time children reach secondary school it is clear which families are "middle class." Young people
today, with few exceptions, are able to make their own decisions about
marriage; level of education, and even which secondary school one attends, has become a primary factor in determining marriage partners. Children of unmarried women in families with money are simply incorporated
into the family while their mothers continue their education. In the better
secondary schools there has been a broadening knowledge of the world
outside Nso' and outside Cameroon.

Nso' has, of course, always been connected to an international network through trade. The awareness, and power, of this connection grew
exponentially with the advent of colonial rule in the early twentieth century. It increased again in the 1950s with coffee's addition to kola as important export crops. Decisions made in Washington or Winnipeg—or more
often Paris or London—have had important effects on Nso' for over half a

century. The difference today is a growing emphasis on international culture. Beginning approximately in the mid-1970s, this has been a cultural rather than a political or economic change per se. But the result of differential access to an international cultural discourse has been both a generation gap and a widening cultural and economic breach between elites and nonelites in the younger generation.

In Nso' public life, conversation is often centered on national politics and the Social Democratic Front, the primary opposition party. People in off-licenses discuss the wars in Bosnia and Rwanda, the relative merits of Italian and Brazilian soccer players, the Cairo conference on population, and winners of the latest Paris horse races. But this knowledge of an international cultural world has been added to, not displaced, whatever else already existed in Nso'. Local life and local knowledge may be discussed in terms relative to these events, but discussions of them have not been replaced by discussions of these events. On the contrary, many events, such as wars in distant places and blue movies on television, are relegated to the realm of "them" rather than "us." Other events, as Christianity and Islam were in the past, have been integrated into and become part of Nso' everyday reality.

This then is the Nso' world today: a people who have become increasingly and acutely aware of national and international political and cultural worlds, and whose own identity remains locally centered; a people held together by a pride of place and of language; a world in which alliances shift and the balance of power is constantly negotiated in complex ways but one in which the Fon Nso' is central and focal in this dialogic interplay; a people conscious of their identity and aware of the ways in which their lives are connected and intertwined with worlds and peoples outside Nso'. Yet as we arrive back at Nso' Nto', the Nso' palace, after the trip to Foumban, it is obvious from the large and enthusiastic crowds of Nso' people from Kimbo', Bamenda, Douala, and Yaounde who have made the long trek to Foumban to support their *fon*, and who are waiting to greet him at home, that these are people who are first and foremost "*wiri* Nso' "—people of Nso'.

I cannot begin to thank all the people who have helped me and had input into this work over the past 16 years. I owe a great debt to all the people of Nso'; especially to Fon Ŋga' Bi'fon II and Fon Səm Minglo I, to Faay Kiŋga' and Faay Lii Wong, to Shuufaay Chem Langhəə, and to Sheey Joseph Landze, Michael Siryi, Stephen and Victorine Shang, Dede Kande, Emmanuel Wirsey, Edith Lukong, Ben Wirsey, and Kingsley Njoka.

Many people have read and commented on earlier versions of this manuscript. I have profited greatly from discussions with Jane Guyer,

Parker Shipton, Pauline Peters, Lila Abu-Lughod, Steve Fjellman, Mary Jo and Byron Good, Corky White, Jean Jackson, Genie Shanklin, Rhonda Cobham-Sander, Margaret Hunt, Jerry Himmelstein, Sean Redding, Deborah Gewertz, Fred Errington, Peter Geschiere, Nantang Jua, and Achille Mbembe. Dan Rosenberg edited various narrations of the manuscript and provided invaluable comment and criticism. Susan Urquhart patiently and with great style and wit typed and retyped many versions. To Stanley Tambiah, whose own eclectic and powerful interpretation of the world gave me inspiration and whose constant faith in me kept me trying to "get it right," I owe a great debt of gratitude.

Then there is the matter of funding for fieldwork and time to write. I would like to thank Amherst College, whose faculty research grants have been more than generous; the Social Science Research Council; the Mary Ingraham Bunting Institute of Radcliffe College; and the Council on the International Exchange of Scholars, for their support over the past decade.

I am grateful to the staff at the University of Wisconsin Press, whose professionalism and patience are much appreciated. Special thanks to Barbara Hanrahan, whose faith in this manuscript kept me going; to Robin Whitaker for her tolerance and keen editorial skills; and to Raphael Kadushin for his help with the maps and photos.

My greatest debt is to Elizabeth "Sally" Chilver. Her keen mind, vast knowledge of Nso', and generosity of spirit have contributed immensely to my life, intellectual and otherwise; whatever contribution this book may make to the literature would not have been possible without her. Any mistakes in the work are, of course, my own. It is to Sally Chilver, and to my mother, Molly Goheen, both women of insight, knowledge, and substance, that this book is dedicated.

Kimbo', Nso'

December 1994

A Note on Orthography

The orthography of Lam Nso' that I have used derives from the general alphabet adopted by the Cameroon government for the transliteration of Cameroonian languages and the preparation of reading materials after a meeting of authors in March 1979. I have made use of a word list kindly supplied by Mr. Alfred Vensu of the Societe Internationale de Linguistique, Yaounde, and of *A Guide to Lam Nso' Orthography*, by William Banboye, issued by the Permanent Secretariat for Catholic Education, Yaounde, in 1980.

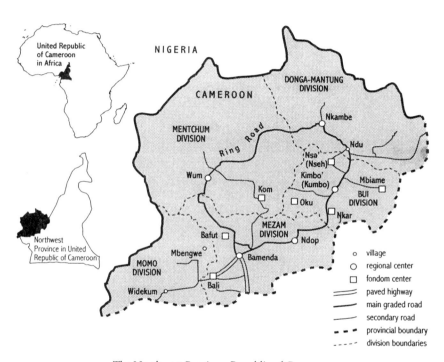

The Northwest Province, Republic of Cameroon

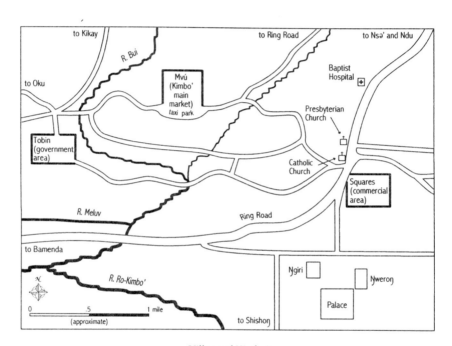

Village of Kimbo'

Men Own the Fields,
Women Own the Crops

1
Introduction

In the mid-1940s, the British anthropologist Phyllis Kaberry travelled to
the Nso' chiefdom in the highlands of western Cameroon, commissioned
by the International African Institute to write a report on women for the
Nigerian government. The result of this study was *Women of the
Grassfields*, a comprehensive historical ethnography in a regional setting
describing the structure of Nso' politics and kinship as well as the texture
of both men's and women's lives. Three decades later, inspired by
Kaberry's detailed work, I journeyed to the same region to investigate the
relationship between local and national politics within the postcolonial
state. The Nso' I entered had changed significantly from the one Kaberry
first encountered. Yet the continuities are at least as obvious as the
discontinuities. The changes brought about by the intensification of the
marketplace and the increasing embeddedness of the lives of Nso' people
within the capitalist system are ones which are recognizable. As Jean
Comaroff has emphasized, the transformation of modes of production in
Africa has seldom been a smooth, unidirectional process; nor has the
penetration of capital simply swept everything in front of it to replace
"indigenous cultural forms with its own social and ideological structures."[1] Instead, the current context and the ways in which capitalist relations are locally incorporated are significantly shaped by indigenous cultural systems.

Nso' today is contained within the independent postcolonial state of
Cameroon rather than constituted as part of a trust territory under United
Kingdom administration, effectively that of the Nigerian arm of the Colonial Service. Yet in significant respects Nso' has retained a distinct cultural
and political integrity. The Fon Nso', who is now paid a monthly salary by
the national government instead of receiving a modest stipend from local
revenues and a percentage of taxes collected on behalf of the colonial administration, continues to practice a version of indirect rule. Palace politics
and the palace-based secret societies hold their importance in the local
political discourse, and titles and offices in these societies are important as
symbolic capital. The division of labor remains gendered, with women's

labor allocated to food farming and provisioning the household while men work in the wage-labor sector, grow coffee, and engage in a variety of entrepreneurial activities. Although the meaning of these continuing relationships has clearly shifted, what has not changed is the complexity of the Nso' social world as people negotiate their universe to synthesize precolonial, colonial, and postcolonial experience and meaning.

Phyllis Kaberry demonstrated that women's lives could not be described adequately without placing them within a broader ethnographic and historical context. Conversely, starting from an investigation of local and national politics, I found that the articulation between regional politics and the *"recherche hégémonique"*[2] of the postcolonial state cannot be understood without reference to gender: gender relations lie at the very heart of both the precolonial and the postcolonial political discourse. Gender relations are thus central to an understanding of the complicated interconnections between Nso' and the national state today. None of these relationships can be grasped outside the contours of the colonial and precolonial histories which have produced this complex present.

This book takes as its central problem the issue of internal power relations within the Nso' chiefdom of the western Grassfields of Cameroon, and the ways in which these political networks articulate with national power. Its eight chapters are connected by several themes, all related by an emphasis on history, gender relations, and the articulation of local political processes with the hegemonic project of the state. Together they call into question the adequacy of the commonly applied terms "hegemony" and "counterhegemony" in national studies. These terms are too limited to elucidate completely the actual distribution of power and authority between the Cameroon state and its constitutive regions and chiefdoms. A corollary of this is found too in the questioning of the use of resistance as an all-encompassing category, which includes all forms of cultural expression of dissatisfaction with the current social order.[3]

After this introductory chapter and chapter 2, describing the geography and social setting, four chapters discuss the hegemonic discourse in Nso'. Chapter 3 outlines the ways in which the Nso' established regional hegemony in the nineteenth century to create the largest and most powerful chiefdom in the northeastern Grassfields. Chapters 4 and 5 analyze various strategies men have used from precolonial times to the present to create and maintain a gendered hierarchy through control of access to productive resources. Chapter 6 is a study of the articulation of local and national power by elite men, who appropriate the symbols and practices of traditional leadership, allowing them then to graft new relations of domination onto the existing hierarchy. The two concluding chapters look at voices of dissent and counterhegemony. Chapter 7 explores the relationship between Nso' and one of its subchiefdoms, Nsə', by describing a land dispute between the paramount Fon Nso' and the Fon Nsə'. It analyzes the outcome in terms of their historical relationship to each other and to the postcolonial state. Chapter 8 assesses various women's voices and life strategies as an important form of counterhegemony This analysis of women's resistance to traditional patterns of marriage contemplates the place of this resistance in the "hegemony-counterhegemony" dichotomy, and suggests that what appears as counterhegemony from one vantage point may be seen as constitutive of class formation from another.

The reconstruction of Nso' history is based on a collection of Phyllis Kaberry's unpublished fieldnotes (deposited at the London School of Economics),[4] oral histories, and colonial documents. Between about 1820 and 1906, when their expansion was halted by German conquest, the Nso' established dominion over the northeastern Grassfields by attracting immigrants and refugees and conquering and subjugating a number of smaller chiefdoms. The Nso' also created a regional political and cultural hegemony which has remained powerful up to the present. First German and then British policies of indirect rule divested the chiefdom of some of its autonomy, but the colonial officials supported many of the institutions of the chiefdom and left the regional hegemony of the Fon Nso' in place. When this formerly British-administered region joined the Francophone national state in 1961, the Nso' were distanced from the centers of national power, and sought to maintain cultural distinctiveness and regional control. Nso' history since the mid-nineteenth century has been shaped by the struggle to establish regional hegemony and the effort to maintain that hegemony in the context of the colonial and postcolonial states.

Much of the stability which exists today despite economic decline and extreme dissatisfaction with the current administration, headed by President Paul Biya, can be attributed to the methods of state building employed by Ahmadou Ahidjo, the first president of Cameroon, in the immediate postcolonial period. Cognizant of the diversity of the citizenry of Cameroon, as well as sensitive to the power of various local elites, Ahidjo became adept at coopting elders and chiefs as well as the Western-educated elite into the center. In the more firmly entrenched arenas of power such as those dominated by the *afon* in the western Grassfields, the ways in which state power was allocated resembled a continuation of British indirect rule, with the Francophone government in Yaounde replacing the colonial government. No political slouches themselves, the *afon* in the Grassfields very early on saw the need to incorporate state power through the new elite into the domain of their own authority. In order to incorporate the new (mostly Western-educated) elites into traditional government, the Fon Nso' consciously expanded the traditional title system to make it available and attractive as an investment for the emerging Nso' elite. This acted to facilitate an articulation between local and national levels of political discourse.

The interaction between these two systems of authority—the Cameroonian postcolonial state on the one hand and the chiefdom of Nso' on the other—is paradigmatic of many national-regional relationships in sub-Saharan Africa. Local and national political discourse is interconnected in important ways; however, the discourse contains many strands of opposition and resistance to the central government in Yaounde. Capitalist relationships promoted by the state have become an arena of contestation, for capitalism brings cultural as well as material changes. The majority of these are expressed in cultural themes such as disputes over the meaning of landownership; or the obligations of people (especially the new elites) to their kin; or whether inheritance should be lateral (as was often the case in precolonial Nso') or lineal (as it is according to the national legal code); or the right of the Nso' people (symbolized by the *fon*), rather than the national government, to control the local water system, a gift to Nso' in the 1970s from the Canadian government. Nso' has become a contested arena of power within which two multilayered, multifaceted forms of hegemony interpenetrate and compete with each other for control of the dominant discourse. This process is complicated by the fact that both of these attempts to forge hegemony contain within them forms of counterhegemony. People use whatever tools they have at their disposal to support their actions of resistance on the local level, including access to the state level. For example, subchiefs and women both use the national discourse and access to capitalist relationships (which are in many ways isomorphic with the state's *recherche hégémonique*) pertaining to control over land on the one hand and to access to wage labor and education on the other to oppose the dominant hegemonic discourse in Nso'. Local resistance then becomes a larger move within a larger arena, and local action taken out of local logic has repercussions in the larger system. We can see this in chapter 7 in the discussion of the land conflict between the Fon Nso' and the Fon Nsǝ', one of his subchiefs, and in the dialogue surrounding women, work, and marriage in chapter 8. At times the goals of the dominant elite in Nso' are isomorphic with those of the postcolonial state, as argued in chapter 6 regarding elite men and traditional titles; at others the relationship between the Nso' elite and the state is more opaque and contested, as can be seen in current political discourse in Cameroon, which is often couched in terms of Anglophone-Francophone opposition. While these can be seen from one vantage point as competing hegemonic projects, ultimately the two forms of hegemony, although of different historical

and structural origin, are mutually supportive and even mutually constitutive. And both are subject to a number of oppositional arguments we
can label counterhegemonic. This creates a context within which different forms of hegemonic process exist in varied and shifting relationships
to one another. These cannot easily be captured by a dichotomous concept of hegemony and counterhegemony. Nor can acts such as resistance
to traditional marriage patterns on the part of women—an example of
cultural and individual statements of dissatisfaction—necessarily be labelled resistance in the sense of true potential for transformation. There
has recently been a shift in scholarly attention from collective efforts to
change economic, political, and cultural conditions of oppression to a
focus on popular culture and individual words and actions. In describing
such cultural and individual practices, many of which bring no discernible change in the structure of domination within which people live their
lives, recent scholars have applied the blanket term "resistance." They
have also used words such as "recognition," "self-determination," and
"reconstruction" to describe, for example, the rituals of the Zionist
church in South Africa, gossip among villagers in rural Malaysia, and
incidents of spirit possession among young women factory workers in
Malaysia.[5] In some of these analyses, large claims are made for personal,
often small, acts of defiance, and such resistance is seen as key to reproducing power and to challenging and transforming power. This perspective sees conceptions of power and hegemony as multifaceted, contested,
and rooted as much in culture and practice as in economy. This shift in
perspective, and the concomitant widespread use of the work "resistance" with regard to personal and localized decisions and actions can, I
argue, be viewed as problematic if such cultural and individual response
to oppression is not linked to a material reality and looked at dialectically as a response to oppressive and often-changing material conditions.
I argue here that for "resistance" to be indeed truly resistant in the sense
that it creates a transformative power shift, it need not be *consciously*
collective, but must ultimately be collectively transformative.

The articulation between local and national arenas in Cameroon is
thus shifting, elusive, and often fraught with contradictions. This is especially true for societies like Nso', whose separate political identity from the
national center is reinforced by a British rather than a French colonial
history. For people in Nso', legitimacy is associated, not with the national
center, but with relations among kin and neighbors and the political institutions of their indigenous chiefdom. Yet the internal cohesion and hegemony of the Nso' are not now, nor have they ever been, without voices of
dissent. Power within the chiefdom has always been shifting and contextual. Nso' today constitutes a state within a state, a complex society where

the multiple strands of chieftaincy, secret societies, titles, kinship, gender, and seniority are interwoven into an intricate multivocal, multicultural pattern, informed by national politics and the market economy.

Women play a key role in this study because control of their productive and reproductive labor in Nso' has always been central to maintaining the hierarchies of male power and status. This is as true today as it was in the past, when men controlled large networks through polygamous marriage alliances. This is not merely a philosophical concern, but also a crucial political and economic issue. I would argue that, along with changes in the structure of the age pyramid in the overall population, where over 43 percent of the population is currently under 25 with a growth rate of 3 percent, gender is the most critical variable when looking at change in Cameroon (indeed in all sub-Saharan Africa). In combination, shifts in the meaning of age and gender are bound to create far-reaching consequences for African societies. This is especially true in Nso' because women produce virtually all the food crops, and women in Cameroon supply the national centers as well as feeding their own families. Women have always supported men's investments outside the domestic sphere by assuming responsibility for food production, provisioning the household, and producing children, who form the basis of symbolic and material wealth.

Gender is thus a critical dimension of both power and dissent in the study of local-national articulation. Women's voices and strategies of resistance are critical in Nso', in Cameroon, and indeed throughout Africa. Yet they have been largely excluded from both traditional and national power within the modern state. This study demonstrates the ways in which women are protesting their political and economic positions. Women's resistance to men's current monopoly of political power is expressed in a variety of ways. Their resistance cannot be ignored, since the male hierarchy is dependent on women's agricultural production and social complicity for its very survival.

From another vantage point, it becomes clear that the restructuring of gender relationships, especially those surrounding marriage, is at the very center of elite class formation in Nso'. Bridewealth, brideservice, and marriage prestations, found in various patterns in different sectors and subchiefdoms of Nso',[6] have in many ways taken on the structure usually associated with dowry, matching people of the same social and economic status. Women's marriage strategies have moved to the center of power shifts and class formation. This is very different from the previous function of various marriage prestations, including bridewealth, which usually served to integrate rather than isolate status groups. Women's resistance and their growing reluctance to continue their support of male hierarchies without more substantial contributions from men, and the changes in women's marriage patterns, have created not only a local but also a national controversy with their potential threat to undermine the male hegemony over both traditional societies and the postcolonial state.

Theoretical Ambience

The word "ambience" is used advisedly. The theoretical contours and vistas of this study all directly or indirectly share ancestry in Marxist thought, primarily through Antonio Gramsci and Raymond Williams. Gender was not the main focus of this study at its inception. The primary conclusions of this book are the result of a decade of fieldwork, of thinking and rethinking the connections between local and national politics from the micro- to the macrolevel in Cameroon. The centrality of gender emerged from this empirical investigation. However, over time it became increasingly obvious that gender and the negotiations over the meaning and relationship of gender categories and roles hold the key to an understanding of power, hierarchy, and the historical process in Nso'.

I began conceptualizing the data which form the basis of this study within a more or less classic structural-Marxist paradigm. This became radically reshaped, "culturized," and recast over the course of investigation and writing. Just as gender emerged as primary in my analysis of the interaction between Nso' local hegemony and the national *recherche hégémonique*, so too did culture and ideology come to the fore in the historical processes that have reproduced and transformed the Nso' present.

This book owes another scholarly debt to the work of Jean-François Bayart, Pierre Bourdieu, Peter Geschiere, and Jane Guyer, all of which to a greater or lesser extent can be fitted within a cultural Marxist paradigm.[7] Other scholars whose work has informed my thinking about and understanding of gender are too numerous to list here, and they are acknowledged instead where appropriate in the course of my analysis.

The following chapters are connected by four themes. First, women in Nso', at least from the inception of the chiefdom in the nineteenth century, have been the most important source of male power, status, and accumulation. Second, the meaning of power relations including gender has been, throughout Nso' history, contextual, shifting, and the subject of negotiation. Third, national-local practices, legal systems, and cultural institutions within the postcolonial state have served to articulate male power in the local arena with power at the national level. This has served to reinforce male hegemony and control of the dominant discourse by male elites. Fourth, women in Nso' have asserted power by virtue of being female. For as long as can be remembered or documented, women's protests have been concerned with asserting a gender complementarity, a gendered balance of power, rather than with appropriating or negating male power so as to create a nongendered category of power.

The theoretical assumptions connecting these themes share a Marxist affinity. However, these do not constitute a conventionally constructed paradigm, but rather are juxtaposed to form a theoretical *bricolage* which I, perhaps optimistically, see as logically connected. In order to clarify the connections between them, these assumptions require some further explication.

General Analytic Issues

The central question becomes one of categories and application: How can we talk about hegemony and counterhegemony in the context of two hegemonic projects, each with a number of discursive themes—themes which had and continue to have diverse and elusive relationships? Where do we locate civil society and "popular modes of political action"; that is, where is resistance, both to the state and to the hegemony of the paramount Fon Nso'? Are these identical? Are they completely separate? Can we in fact even use the terms "hegemony" and "counterhegemony," which were developed to talk about the bourgeois state, to talk about systems of interaction which have deep historical roots in the precolonial era? I argue that such terms provide a useful heuristic model for examining the ways in which local and national powers articulate in Africa today, and the ways in which both of these ultimately are effectively challenged by a counterhegemonic discourse of gender. The struggle to establish a legitimate state on the basis of the bourgeois model and the search for civil society and "popular modes of political action" in the postcolonial state have been at the center of much of the current work on the state in Cameroon.[8] Yet ultimately these must be part of a larger theoretical *bricolage* if they are to elucidate the current Nso' reality.

The core interests of this study bring it within the range and influence of a number of central concerns in anthropology and African studies. Key to all of these at the broadest level is the integral interdependence between anthropology and history.[9] This historical emphasis has been central to anthropological investigation for long enough to have become virtually a truism, especially so among scholars working in Africa.[10] For the purposes of this introduction it is sufficient to emphasize that the Nso' present needs to be understood as the outcome of a continuous and changing relationship between the local system and the "external" world of the postcolonial state of Cameroon embedded in turn within a world capitalist system. The local system and the postcolonial state both share a history and have separate histories. These histories are each fraught with contradiction and struggles over power and meaning. These historical contradictions and struggles are brought to bear in current negotiations over the construction of power and the meaning of cultural categories. Local meanings and practices are thus informed by and molded in interaction with the larger external world of the postcolonial state, but these in turn also exert a pivotal influence on the construction and configuration of national power.

A second analytic focus of this study is the relationship between practice and discourse, between the material and the ideological, between base and superstructure in the ways that these are articulated and reproduced in and by the contours of history. Following Donham, I argue that Nso', like human societies everywhere, has always been organized by systems of material domination and that these systems have been socially problematic since its inception. When Nso' culture and society becomes transnational at one level, at another there is a core set of Nso' beliefs and practices which inform this transnational focus. This is not an argument for privileging the material base in analysis. On the contrary, in order to understand these power relations I have tried to locate not only the ways that effective power differences over material production are reflected in varying control over necessary products, but also the ways in which these power relations are produced and reproduced through culturally specific meaning and practice. Local forms of domination then are exactly that: forms reproduced in their own particular practices and encoded in their own cultural terms. We see this demonstrated in the following chapters in numerous ways, from the respect behavior given to the *fon* and other men of title, to the mystification of power exhibited by the belief that women will fall sick and even die if they see the inside of the lodges of the most important men's secret societies, to the beliefs about the connection between the Earth and the ancestors which forms much of the basis of Nso' belief and practice regarding land use and access. From this purview, it is the superstructure that often makes the base what it is, so that ideology is not simply an epiphenomenon of a fixed base that legitimates power but instead provides exactly the terms in which power is reproduced as power.[11] Critical here is what Bourdieu[12] has called symbolic power, that is, the power to impose the categories of social reality, a major dimension of political power.

Conceptualizing Hegemony and Counterhegemony

If the relationship between discourse and practice, the material and the ideological, base and superstructure within a historically specific process is one master theme of this book, then a focus on hegemony and the state (i.e., on the relationship between local hegemony and the *recherche hégémonique* of the postcolonial state) is another. It is here that the historical struggles over power and meaning central to this analysis—the relationship between experience as it is lived and ideology as explicit discourse—take place. Here the theories of hegemony and counterhegemony and the relationship of these to the state become central to this study.

Gramsci uses "hegemony" to mean the ways in which a governing power wins consent from those it subjugates; it is carried in cultural, political, and economic forms, in nondiscursive as well as in theoretical utterances.[13] To win hegemony is to establish moral, political, and intellectual dominance in social life by disseminating one's own world view throughout the total social configuration, thus equating one's own interests with those of the society as a whole. In order for a hegemonic process to work effectively, individuals in society need to internalize the dominant discourse and make it spontaneously their own; they need to carry it around as a principle inseparable from individual identity. Hegemony then is the common sense of the whole social order. It is reproduced through both material conditions and ideological pronouncements. And it is maintained and reproduced through the workings of everyday life—through practice as well as ideas, through form as well as content.

The most powerful way to maintain hegemony is to naturalize and internalize, and thus legitimate, forms of domination. These internalized systems act to produce a sense of spontaneity in habitual behavior, which in turn produces deeply held and deeply tacit norms, meanings, and values. The question then becomes, How is this accomplished by what Bourdieu calls "the mundane workings of everyday life"? In order to explain this, he develops the concept of *habitus*.[14] By this he means the infusion and internalization in individuals of a set of enduring ideals or dispositions which generate particular practices. The habitus has been characterized by Eagleton as ." . . the relay mechanism by which mental and social structures become incarnate in daily social activity."[15] Thus "the habitus, rather like human language itself, is an open-ended system which enables individuals to cope with unforeseen, ever-changing situations; it is a 'strategy-generating principle' which permits ceaseless innovation, rather than a rigid blueprint."[16] Social life contains a number of different habitués; each system is relevant to what Bourdieu calls a field. In *Questions de sociologie* Bourdieu argues that a field is a "competitive system of social relations which functions according to its own internal logic, composed of institutions or individuals who are competing for the same state . . . the attainment of maximum dominance within them—a dominance which allows those who achieve it to confer legitimacy on other participants or to withdraw it from them."[17] For such power to become legitimate, it must be masked or misrecognized. The set of unspoken rules which are not conscious or articulated but are instead tacit and part of the "collective unconscious" operates as a mode of symbolic violence. Those who control or set the rules are dominant; they are able to maintain and reproduce their dominance through control of symbolic and cultural capital. In Nso', forms of symbolic and cultural capital have included such things as credit in the form of granting access to the factors of production, especially but not exclusively to land; ritual knowledge and *səm* or power; the right to control marriage alliances and long-distance trade; titles and offices in lineages and access to regulatory societies. The hierarchy in Nso' has attached to it explicit and highly institutionalized modes of behavior which structure all personal interaction. These operate on the dual hierarchies of age and gender, both of which are dominated by the status hierarchy. Terms and forms of address and the physical behaviors associated with these, such as bending down, averting one's eyes, clapping hands, and talking through one's hands, are strictly prescribed in virtually all contexts in ways which reproduce the status hierarchy in daily social interaction. In Nso', such symbolic and cultural capital has been dominated by men; thus the hegemonic discourse in Nso' has been gendered in ways which have privileged "male" as a category.

Bourdieu's notion of symbolic violence is very similar to, although not isomorphic with, Gramsci's use of hegemony. The unspoken rules which structure any social field operate as a mode of symbolic violence; this is a legitimate and legitimated form of power which most often goes unrecognized *as* violence. Symbolic violence is, as Bourdieu explains in *Outline of a Theory of Practice*, "the gentle, invisible form of violence, which is never recognized as such, and is not so much undergone as chosen, the violence of credit, confidence, obligation, personal loyalty, hospitality, gifts, gratitude, piety . . ."[18] Symbolic violence maintains the same phenomena as the hegemonic discourse does: it is most powerful when it is part of what Bourdieu calls doxa, within which the ideas and practices that support the dominant discourse are naturalized and unquestionable. The rights of men, especially lineage heads, to control land, male exclusivity of membership in the central secret societies, the political (and ritual) power of men over women, the reservation to males of important forms of esoteric knowledge, the rights of fathers to own children in the case of divorce, the divinity of the office of *fon*—all of these have been part of a doxa in Nso' which has privileged men, especially men of title. While most of these notions have today become in Bourdieu's terms orthodox or even heterodox (that is, they are privileged in the dominant discourse but subject to discussion and even resistance), they remain as powerful modes or pieces of symbolic and cultural capital. Bourdieu's categories too must be used heuristically rather than as analytic fact, not least of all because he tends to essentialize the notions he uses in describing the Kabyle of Algeria as belonging to an unchanging, stable, and tradition-bound universe, and by extension all "tribal peoples" who inhabit this space reside there too.[19] His claim that doxa has characterized the lives of kin-based societies more than it has those living in advanced capitalist ones is problematic and remains open to question. Clearly such societies as the chiefdom of Nso', built on the conquest and incorporation of diverse peoples, cannot ever have been without voices of contestation and dissent. Most of what is "taken for granted" in Nso' today is ideologically based, sometimes consciously so. Much of the Nso' orthodox discourse is resistant both consciously and unconsciously to the *recherche hégémonique* of the postcolonial state.

Hegemony and the State

As Weber stressed, the *idea* of the state is a *claim* to legitimacy, a means by which politically organized subjection is simultaneously accomplished and concealed.[20] While African states possess international legitimacy, internal legitimacy is a more elusive goal. Hyden attributes this lack of internal cohesion to "clan politics," and to the failure of the bourgeoisie to develop a state culture which would allow the state to "capture" the peasantry.[21] In the Western bourgeois state, moral regulation is coextensive with state formation. State forms are also cultural forms, and the state, epitomized as the nation, claims people's primary social identification and loyalty.[22] To paraphrase Durkheim, the bourgeois state is the organ of social thought.[23] The point is that, although Western bourgeois states have had significant internal national problems, they have solved them sufficiently to complete the state building process and construct hegemony in the form of a legitimized national culture.

In Cameroon, on the contrary, there is no common cultural frame of reference between dominant and dominated groups.[24] Regional politics, ethnic loyalties, and differing colonial experiences have militated against national cultural hegemony.[25] Thus the Cameroonian state has been unable to incorporate the diverse political and cultural practices of its multiethnic population into a collective conscience. Nor has there developed a common cultural discourse. Indeed, the bulk of the population, some 70–80 percent, is a rural peasantry whose cultures articulate only tangentially with those of the more nationalized and cosmopolitan urban centers.[26] State formation in Cameroon has not been successful as a totalizing project representing all Cameroonians as a particular community (in Marx's words, an illusory community), nor has it been successful in individualizing its citizens to the same extent as this has happened in Europe and North America.

For most Cameroonians, legitimacy stems, not from identity with the national center, but rather from participating in the moral virtues of communal life. This legitimacy flows not only from relations with kin and neighbors but also from the institutions of the indigenous chiefdom which surround the *fon* and the palace. But this legitimacy is itself the result of a process of state building and the creation of regional hegemony. This was evident in the local reaction to "Operation Ghost Town," the general strike during 1991–92 called by the national opposition. Bamenda, the capital of the Northwest Province, was (and is) seen as one of the strongholds of the national opposition. Nso' too has been a center of opposition to the national government, and people in Nso' strongly supported Operation Ghost Town. The Fon Nso', in a number of public statements and moves, made it clear that he too sided with the people in their discontent with the national government. During this general strike no business was conducted during the week. As might be expected this had a profoundly negative influence on the local economy. Yet things continued to work; goods and services flowed through the system in ways which looked like magic to the outside observer. The office of the national water company was moved to the *fon*'s palace; the informal economy grew; smuggling to and from Nigeria became the norm; and more often than not barter replaced the exchange of cash for goods and services. Although the past several years have not been particularly easy in Nso', the economy has continued to run, largely because of the relationships between kin and neighbors and the legitimacy maintained by the *fon* and traditional government. The opposition movement has both reinforced regional hegemony and strengthened ties of local leaders to national political parties.

Bayart has argued that the degree to which the postcolonial state in Cameroon was successful in establishing a coalition between the center and its constituent parts has depended on a hegemonic alliance (*alliance hégémonique*) between regional and national elites.[27] This in turn has served to reinforce the regional hegemony of local elites and to articulate their power with that of the national center. National political relations have been based on a merging of old and new relations of domination, and the national alliance has consisted both of different factions from the new educated elite and of power groups from older local patterns of organization.[28] Geschiere maintains that in order to understand this alliance one must look at it in terms of the articulation of differing modes of production with an emphasis on regional histories and regional variation.[29] This study attempts to do just that, situating this understanding not only in political and economic articulation but also in the local hegemonic discourse.

As Williams argues, hegemony is best seen as "a lived system of meanings and values—constitutive and constituting—which as they are experienced as practices appear as reciprocally confirming." What becomes decisive then is not only this "conscious system of beliefs, values and ideas," but the "whole lived social process as practically organized by specific and dominant meanings and values."[30] This system of meanings and values is, as Bourdieu points out, the product of a double structuring.[31] First, it is objectively structured by outward appearances so that properties assigned to particular persons correlate with social position. The second meaning of this double structuring is a subjective one. The world is structured not only by practices, through human action, but also by schemes of perception about these practices. I argue that in Nso' the structure of practice and the structure of meaning have created and reproduced a unique Nso' identity. At the same time they have promoted a gendered hierarchy which privileges male titleholders and have assigned to women the task of producing food and reproducing children. This gendered hierarchy, created in the precolonial past, has been maintained and reinforced within the postcolonial state by the coalition between regional and national male elites. A third analytic focus of this work then is the connection between gender and power and the relationship of this connection to the state.

If the integral relationship between history and anthropology has become central to much of anthropological discourse, so too has the axiom that gender relations are largely products of social and cultural practices.[32] These practices and the resulting construction of male and female at the level of ideology are intrinsically related to the social organization of production and reproduction.[33] Gender categories are thus culturally and historically specific, and their meaning and relationship to power have to be explored and not assumed. In looking at gender, this study attempts to focus on the connections between the symbolic or cultural aspects of social existence—the cultural representation of gender—and the shifting social and economic conditions under which people live their lives.

A number of theorists have demonstrated that control over women's productive and reproductive labor has been central to precolonial male hierarchies.[34] Kinship relations and the manipulation of marriage payments and alliances have been key variables with regard to control over labor in precolonial African states. Gender relationships have thus been at the center of power in African state formation.[35] Available evidence suggests that this was the case in precolonial Nso'. The kinship and marriage system was controlled by titled men, who then regulated access to resources and managed the allocation of labor. Although this hierarchy was gendered, there was a cultural emphasis on the complementarity of power between male and female qualities. Women were seen as powerful in their own right by virtue of being female rather than by virtue of being the wives of powerful men. They had unalienable rights to productive resources and were often important political actors within a context in which the boundaries between public and private were elusive and permeable.

In the colonial state and subsequently the postcolonial state, the boundaries between public and private became less fluid and more institutionalized, with the public domain associated with male and the private domain with female.[36] The incorporation of men has progressed differently from that of women in African nations,[37] and Cameroon is no exception. National laws and practices have facilitated a collusion between local and national elite men to the detriment of female power. At the same time the structures and institutions of the postcolonial state have afforded at least some women opportunities outside their traditional role as farmers, and women have actively taken advantage of these.

The relationship between gender and power has been significantly altered in the context of the postcolonial state. Yet women are using their cultural right to protest this shift in the balance of power between male and female. This study investigates women's protests and marriage strategies and suggests that these hold the key to understanding class formation. The precise outcome of the current articulation between women's resistance to traditional marriage, class formation, and shifts in gendered power is neither obvious nor perhaps uniform. However, this study argues that it is in this process and ultimately in the articulation between gender and class, the role of gender in the relationship between what Bayart has termed the *dominants* and the *dominés*,[38] that we can locate a counterhegemony which is likely to be truly transformative of the structures of the postcolonial state.

A Note on Method

The data on which this study is based were gathered over the course of a dozen years. From 1979 to 1981 I lived half of the time in Kimbo', the capital of Nso', and half in Nsə', a subchiefdom. In Kimbo' I lived in the compound of Faay Kiŋga', a titled palace retainer, in Jem Quarter. While in Nsə' I lived with two different families, one headed by a son and another by a grandson of the previous Fon Nsə'. During this period I was truly a "participant observer," participating in the daily life of the people with whom I lived, with all the problems and satisfactions one derives from living in an intensively interactive family situation. At first I was treated more or less as a guest and an oddity (with all the neighborhood children following me around snickering and calling me *kimbaŋ*—literally "redman," which is the Lam Nso' word for whites). After about six months I was assigned chores (mostly cooking and shopping, since I obviously was not strong enough to farm, nor if truth be known was I thought of as competent enough). People began reproaching me for committing obvious faux pas (obvious to everyone but me, that is). This included handing things to people with my left hand or talking to someone with my hands in my pockets, or wearing blue jeans, or walking around eating in public—all of which are, at best, interpreted as bad manners and crude behavior.

By living in a family one becomes conversant with those intimate details of daily life about which we cannot politely inquire. The women with whom I lived began really opening up to me and talking about men and children after ascertaining that I indeed had a son. They did so by asking if they could see the stretch marks from my pregnancy. Before this time, although I had shown them pictures of my son, they shook their heads in disbelief and asked, "He don come out from your own belly so?" not believing someone as small (and seemingly young) could have an almost grown child. In the normal give and take of daily life many patterns and details emerged about family life, about child care, about sexuality, about division of the household tasks and budget, and about gender in general—details which would have been impossible even to begin to conceptualize if I had lived alone. When people became used to my presence it became easier to collect life histories as well as opinions on a variety of subjects.

From 1979 to 1980 I gathered data for an interdisciplinary marketing study of the Northwest Province, concentrating on the division of labor, women's cooperatives, and land tenure.[39] While working on this project I combined more formal methods (questionnaires and market surveys) with personal interviews, both formal and informal. More formal or structured interviews were conducted with the lineage heads, who control land; with local representatives of the national government, such as those in the offices dealing with lands, finance, and agriculture; and with sellers in various markets. Less formal interviews were conducted with a wide variety of people: the Fon Nso', the Fon Nsə', cooperative officials, taxi drivers, market women, school children, hospital workers, and women of all ages and stations in life.

During 1981 I was the field director for a study of production and nutrition in the region. Eight villages in Nso' were surveyed, during the course of which formal questionnaires on household budgets were used to collect data from both men and women, 180 fields were measured, food consumption was measured, nutrition levels were analyzed, and production figures were estimated for 72 households.[40] Ten questionnaires were administered in each household; men and woman were interviewed separately regarding income, expenditures, and crop yields. Male research assistants interviewed the men, and female research assistants interviewed the women whenever possible. Between four and six days were spent in each village surveyed. We would try to arrive in a village the night before the market day so we could get settled and pick a random sample to interview. (Markets in Nso', as in much of West Africa, occur in each village once in eight days in a rotating cycle). We would first go to greet the *fon* (in larger villages) or the village head (in smaller villages). We picked a sample by ascertaining the different quarters in each village and selecting two or three households from each quarter, thus trying to get as random and diverse a sample as possible. Nine households were selected in each village. After the sample households had been picked we would gather the whole group together and try to explain why we were conducting this survey. My head research assistant, a *wan nto'* (a member of the royal family of Nsə', in this case a son), would explain in Lam Nso', "These people are going to ask you a lot of childish questions, but they mean no harm, and the information will be used to help better farming and marketing conditions, so you should answer them!" Late on the afternoon of market day when people had returned home we would question them about expenditures made that day. By market night people were more or less used to seeing us around. With our reggae tapes, "boom boxes," and gossip from Kimbo' and beyond we were a big hit on market night at the local "off-licenses" (bars selling beer, mimbo, soft drinks, and sometimes pieces of cooked chicken, goat, and beef).

We then spent the next three days appearing at the selected households at mealtime in order to measure the food consumed. We spent most evenings in the off-licenses getting to know the local people and the local gossip. (More often than not we all had some acquaintances in even the most remote villages; my Nso' research assistants invariably had relatives.) Using formal questionnaires in these villages gave me an opportunity to bring up a variety of topics for discussion. Some of these were quite structured and consistent, such as asking about the defining or distinguishing features of "male" and "female." Others were more conversational, such as how people felt about the local schools, problems they had with transport, the condition of the roads (and who should be blamed for these), what the *fon* was up to, what market prices were in various bush markets, and why the Bamileke and the Ibo were such good businessmen (and why people felt one should be wary of them), as well as a variety of topics of local gossip and concern. Between 1981 and 1993 I returned to Nso' six times to update the data.

In 1990 I duplicated the 1981 survey, hiring the same Nso' people who had worked for me in 1981. During this time I rented a house in Tobin, the bureaucratic quarter of Nso', and had all the people I hired live together under one roof. I thought this would expedite the work and make my life simpler. It did expedite the data collection. But make my life simpler it did not. Altogether there were seven of us: a cook called Bobe (literally, "a big man") from the neighboring chiefdom of Kom; a driver, the son of Faay Kiŋga', a young man I had known from the time he was 15 (now in his mid-20s); two research assistants, a man of 40 from Nsə' who was a *wan nto'*, and a man in his 40s who was from Nso' and had a PhD from an Ivy League university and had spent 20 years in the United States before returning to live in Kimbo'; and two young male high school students from Kiŋga', the compound where I have lived during most of the previous time I had spent in Kimbo'. The two boys moved in with us to be close to the government high school—and probably too out of a sense of curiosity and adventure. With the exception of Bobe from Kom, all these people were related in complex ways. The complications were staggering. Bobe thought it beneath him to cook for people of lower status (which he considered everyone to be, except for myself and possibly my research assistant from Nsə'). The research assistant with the degree from Brown had status in a world the cook did not recognize. Meanwhile, this man thought the cook should show *him* more respect. Family problems over school fees, hospital expenses, the use of our vehicle, washing clothes, whose compound we should go "salute" during the holidays—in general over who should do what for whom—all arose, and I became the center of most disputes, the person expected to make judgments and keep the peace. I ended up doing a lot of cooking and a lot of cajoling, even begging. At the end of this time I had great respect for senior wives and lineage heads. This living situation, which lasted six months, was invaluable in showing me the divisiveness as well as the cooperation that kin and kinship relationships create. It also gave me on-the-spot insight into the problems which can arise when two different systems of status and hierarchy come into play in the same context. In very important ways this living experience, combined with previous experience in Nso', brought home to me the complicated and enigmatic contradictions and paradoxes which are present in extremely close kin ties. Nso' people are absolutely hospitable and affable in daily social interaction. Yet they are also extremely judgmental, reading meaning into others' actions which often baffled me. People are completely interdependent, yet there is often extreme jealousy and competition. I was constantly told not to listen to gossip, that "local people are malicious gossips and just like to get other people in trouble." Bobe from Kom delighted in pointing out breaches of etiquette on the part of Nso' people, stating with each incidence of what he deemed incorrect behavior, "Miss, Nso' people get [have] bad fashion."

Kin and others who are close expect, and get, a lot from each other, and there is often a seeming contradiction between extreme hospitality and people trying to "get over" on each other.

People, especially those who are successful, use the term "buying your head," *yun kitu*, also meaning to beg. Here the meaning suggests that you must give away enough of your wealth to "get people off your back." The point is that people really believe that the actions of others can have serious effects on their own well-being, even their life—hence the veneer of politeness and the complex rules of etiquette in Nso' society. Even when people have good intentions it is believed that their acts can have unintended consequences and adversely affect the lives of those who are close to them. And the threat of witchcraft is an omnipresent part of daily life. While there is a lot of affect between people there is also a lot of suspicion. Let me give a few examples:

1. A wealthy man in Nso' had a son who died of spinal meningitis. This man was well educated and in fact had attended college in the United States; he understood very well the etiology of the disease. Yet he was convinced that his son had died because he (the father) had taken some kola nuts from the tree of his lineage head and sold them without permission.

2. My driver was continually making references to how other people's actions were causing particular events to take place. Anytime we had a problem with the car, he would think out loud about who was jealous or unhappy with us. One day when the car slipped out of gear on a particularly steep and muddy hill, he looked at me and announced, "Those women back there be don bad heart me." Although I expressed doubts about his interpretation, and pointed out that the rains had been particularly heavy the night before, he was unshakable in his belief that the women in the compound we had visited were angry with him because he was marrying someone from outside of Kimbo'. Meanwhile, I had promised him my radio when I left Nso'. When I was getting ready to leave I started to hand him the radio. He hesitated and then said that maybe I should give it to my research assistant from Nsə' instead. Surprised, I asked why he no longer wanted the radio. He assured me that he did in fact want the radio but that the other man, not knowing that I had already promised the radio, had told my driver that he was going to ask me for the radio when I left. As my driver put it, "I don't want to feel his eyes in the back of my head." I assured him that I would explain that the radio was already promised and if necessary even buy another one to give to my Nsə' research assistant. Only then would the driver take the radio (which he indeed wanted very much).

3. We were doing a survey in a small village in Nsə' which was quite off the beaten track. During the survey we were invited to drink palm wine in the compound of a lineage head. As described below in chapter 2, in Nso' there are normally two categories of lineage head: *faay*, which denotes the ritual and political head of a large lineage, and *sheey*, a title which is given to sublineage heads as well as to princes and a number of

other prominent men. It is not particularly common for a *sheey* to be a lineage head, but it happens with regularity for a variety of reasons. When we entered the room where the lineage head was to receive us, my Nsə' research assistant brought out two stools, one for me and one for my driver. At this point my driver got quite agitated and headed for a bench in the corner. He was obviously angry. When we were getting ready to leave I pulled him aside and asked him what the problem was. "That man [my Nsə' research assistant] is just trying to get me in trouble," he told me. Since the two men up to this point had had a very amicable relationship, I was surprised and pressed further. "He knows I am a man from this place [Nso']! How can he give me a stool to sit on when he knows it is not proper for an untitled man to sit on a stool in a *faay*'s compound? He is only trying to make trouble for me." I explained to the driver that in fact this was the compound of a *sheey*, not a *faay*, and he immediately calmed down. The two men resumed their usual friendly behavior towards each other. But even given their amicable relationship there was immediate distrust and suspicion both on this occasion and in the incident regarding the radio.

There are countless examples like the three I have given here; these kinds of events are very much a part of Nso' everyday life. We will examine the cultural beliefs behind much of this behavior in the discussion of the ambiguity of power, or səm, in chapter 6. But the significance of emphasis on both the positive and the negative side of acute interdependence, the intense responsibility people feel for each other—especially the moral obligation of leaders to their dependents—and a deeply held sense of the efficacy of human action pervades Nso' belief and practice in such profound ways that one must understand this if one is even to begin to understand Nso' culture and society. Altogether I spent about six years in Nso' gathering both quantitative and qualitative data, going to farms with the women, hanging out in the market, in compounds, in the palace of both the Fon Nso' and the Fon Nsə', and generally participating in village life. The data upon which this work is based are thus quite various, including formal quantitative data and a structured collection of qualitative data as well as 12 years of experience working and living with a variety of people in a multiplicity of situations. I have tried to be as objective as possible, fully knowing that I am not able to remove my own categories and subjectivity from the analysis. Where appropriate in the work that follows I have tried to locate and position myself in the discourse. In order to make the work as accessible as possible I have located much of the theoretical commentary in the endnotes rather than in the narrative. My hope is that this will act to clarify rather than obscure the argument and that it will make the material accessible to a wider range of readers than would have been the case if the discussion and conceptual definition had been pitched at a higher or more abstract theoretical level within the text.

In this work I use the words "traditional" and "modern": the former to indicate indigenous beliefs, practices, and institutions which were established prior to those of the latter, which in the following work is equated with capitalism, nationalism, commodification, and the nation-state. This is ultimately a false dichotomy, and I spent a good deal of time wrestling with alternative solutions but could not find one which was semantically clear and acceptable. I realize that for some people the use of these terms has connotations of evolutionary thinking, with an equation of "traditional" with stagnation, and "modern" with progress. Nothing could be further from my mind. Since these are the terms used by Nso' people themselves when speaking of "traditional" lineage leaders and "traditional" politics when talking of those things they equate with indigenous Nso' culture and practice, and "modern" big men and the "modern" sector in reference to capitalist relationships and the state, I decided to follow their example; to do otherwise would have been semantically clumsy at best. If I have offended anyone by doing so, I apologize.

Nso' has been at the center of opposition politics in Cameroon for almost a decade. As this book goes to press, there is a growing Anglophone opposition movement, one which calls for secession and a return to a separate state. The Southern Cameroons National Committee, led by two formerly prominent Anglophone politicians, Dr. Foncha and Mr. Muna, has won a hearing at the United Nations regarding the legitimacy and the legality of the original fusion between Anglophone and Francophone Cameroons. This movement has strong support in Nso'. When I talk in this book about "national politics," "national elite," and the "state," I am not necessarily talking about support for *this* particular organization of state power. "National elite" refers to those persons who may currently be in opposition to the government in power in Cameroon, and even to the organization of the nation-state of Cameroon as it is presently constituted, but who are active in national politics, whether in support of, or in opposition to, the present configuration of national power.

Finally, a note on the etiquette of ethnographic writing. I have used accurate given names and titles for persons who are either past or present public figures. I have used pseudonyms when writing about private citizens in Nso' in order to protect their identities and privacy, and have taken liberty with ethnographic facts as much as possible in order to disguise identities, while continuing to stay true to the contexts and arguments.

2
Nso' Geography and Social Setting
A Background

Introduction

The Nso' say that "before foreigners came Nso' was in the earth (*nsay*) and the earth was at peace."[1] This may not be precisely accurate in historical terms, but it is suggestive of the connection the Nso' make between their physical and social environments. The Nso' belong to the Earth just as the Earth belongs to them; it is the place of the important dead, the ancestors, who are believed to have power over the living. The Earth can become "hot" and punish those who transgress against the moral code, and can be called upon to make judgment in disputes. This association of the Earth with the ancestors is an important piece of Nso' doxa, as will be seen in the following chapters on land and the relationship of land and gender. For our purposes in the following discussion the important point to keep in mind is that the Nso' physical and social worlds are inextricably interconnected. It is impossible to understand one without considering the other. The purpose of this chapter is to set the scene and provide the reader with a geographic and social framework from which to approach the rest of the book. Particular points will be elaborated in subsequent chapters. This chapter is not meant to be totally comprehensive or analytic but rather to provide a background from which to interpret the multiple realities and competing images which constitute Nso' life today.[2]

Physical Setting: Geography and Demography

Leaving the humid closeness of the Ndop Plain behind, one begins the slow ascent of the steep escarpment towards Nso'. It is almost automatic to breathe a sigh of relief at the clean coolness of the high Grassfields. This is an area of proud beauty and sweeping landscape. Mountains loom up ahead, rising to heights of 1700 meters, plunging into deep valleys and ravines. During the rains, outcroppings of granite and dark thunder clouds stand in stark contrast to the sun shafts dancing on the tall grass while it bends and sways in the winds of the gathering storm. In the dry months a thin layer of red dust hangs heavily in the air and colors the countryside. Waterfalls cascade down the sides of the steep hills, racing with the rains and becoming more sedate with the changing season. The spectrum of greens covering the hills and valleys is various, from the light green of the high grass and maize growing on the hillsides to the deep, rich, forest green of the raffia bushes lining the streams in low-lying ravines. In the distance, farms lie in checkerboard patterns on the hillsides, zinc roofs wink in the sunlight, and the red and white zebu cows of Fulani herders dot the landscape. Stopping and breathing deeply, one can detect the smell of wood smoke from cooking fires, clean and distinct against the fresh highland air.

Bui Division straddles the southeast arc of the Ring Road, the laterite-surface road connecting the main towns of Cameroon's Northwest Province to the provincial capital of Bamenda. From Bamenda, a well-paved highway connects the province with Bafoussam, Yaounde, and Douala, Cameroon's major commercial city, on the Atlantic coast. Bui Division is the home of the Nso', a large and powerful group which established dominion over this mountainous region during the last century. By the latter half of the nineteenth century, Səm II, Fon Nso',[3] had consolidated his power to form the largest chiefdom in the Bamenda Grassfields.[4] Renowned as fierce warriors and described by their German conquerors as greatly feared slave hunters, the Nso' are today often spoken of by their neighbors as arrogant and stiff-necked. The emphasis of local peoples on regional cultural identity, common in Cameroon, reaches its most pronounced expression in Nso'. Precolonial as well as colonial histories have sharpened the differences between the Anglophone Grassfields, an area with complex and hierarchic chiefdoms, and the Francophone center, most of whose peoples lived in much less centralized, segmentary, lineage-based societies.[5] Nso' elites in the national capital in Yaounde can be heard telling their Francophone colleagues that they (the colleagues) are fortunate that the Germans came, because otherwise Nso' would have conquered them.

With a population of some 217,000 and an area of 2300 square kilometers, Nso' is heavily populated for an agricultural region, with an average density of 87 per square kilometer (compared with an average of 20 per square kilometer nationwide; the national population is between 9.5 million and 13 million[6]). The Grassfields in which Nso' is situated constitute a distinct culture area composed of a number of chiefdoms of varying size and complexity. Bui Division includes the smaller chiefdoms of Oku and Mbiame, considered "brothers" of Nso', the first well known in the past for its metallurgic and carving skills.[7] Overall the Grassfield chiefdoms range from the small village chiefdoms of Widekum to the expanding conquest-states such as Nso', whose population was estimated at 60,000 by the Germans, who fought and finally subdued them in the early twentieth century.[8] While these chiefdoms are linguistically and ethnically diverse, they share a number of features, including the centrality of chieftaincy, the importance of men's secret societies, and an emphasis on title and rank as significant political attributes. The Nso' also share the region with two groups of Fulani graziers, the Mbororo, who are mainly Jafun and arrived in the early 1900s, and the Aku'en, originally occupants of the high Jos Plateau, who migrated into the area in the 1950s in the wake of a cattle epidemic from what was then the Benue Province of Nigeria.

At one time in the distant past[9] the Grassfields were a forest zone occupied by hunting and gathering peoples. Many cultural features of the current populations indicate a historical connection with the forest peoples south of the highlands. Today the forests have almost disappeared and the most distinctive vegetation is the tall savannah grass after which the region is named.

The Grassfields lie east to west between the 4th and 7th parallels. The area is essentially a high lava plateau surrounded by a series of lower plains and valleys broken by volcanic peaks. Ecological conditions are diverse, encouraging production of both temperate and tropical zone crops. Altitude within the Grassfields varies substantially, ranging from a low of 500 meters in the Mentchem Valley and on the Donga Plain along the border of Nigeria to the north, to a high of 1400–1700 meters on the high plateaus around Bamenda and Nso'. The plateaus are traversed by mountains with steep slopes, often cut by deep valleys. Temperature and rainfall vary widely, mostly as an effect of altitude. The high plateau around Nso' receives over 3000 milliliters of rainfall annually, while lower regions in the Grassfields average between 1000 and 2500 milliliters. Average temperatures around Nso' range from a mean maximum of 66°F to a mean minimum of 51°F. The cold damp nights during the rainy season can chill even Europeans who are used to cold, almost Arctic, northern winters. Lower-lying areas are much hotter and less pleasant to trek around or travel through in a crowded taxi, with a mean annual maximum of 95.5°F and a minimum of 72°F. There is generally a six- to seven-month rainy season from April to October, a cool dry season from October to December, and a hot dry season from January to March. Nso' lies in the fertile crescent extending from Bamenda northeast to Nkambe and south to Bafoussam in the neighboring Ouest Province. This region is targeted by the national government for development as a breadbasket for the growing national urban centers.

Themes of Nso' Political Economy

With some minor caveats, a description of the structure of Nso' political and social organization serves for both Nso' proper (Kimbo', the Nso' capital, and its immediate environs) and the subchiefdoms.[10] The basic difference is one of scale. Kimbo' is a very complex place. The articulation of the various strands and threads (all changing in relative importance but none disappearing) that make up the traditional social net bears evidence of the ability of the Nso' social system to remain flexibly recalcitrant in the face of changes brought by colonialism, the marketplace, and national independence.[11] For analytic purposes I will distinguish five categories: (1) the *fon*, (2) major categories of people, (3) the secret societies, (4) rank and title, and (5) the lineage system.

The Fon

In Nso', as in Grassfield chiefdoms in general, the *fon* is the center of a complex political system. He is seen as the "father of his people" and as a symbol of their unity. The language used to describe him is one which stresses his generosity rather than his repressive functions. The Nso' say, "The *fon* has everything; the *fon* is a poor man," and the *fon* asks, "What is a *fon* without his people? I am in the hands of my people." The *fon* is viewed as possessing sacred attributes bestowed by the office he occupies. It is the office, not the person, which is sacred. Nevertheless, an elaborate etiquette surrounds his person. He is the intermediary between the living and the ancestors, and is responsible for negotiating and ensuring the health and well-being of the Nso' people. He is the chief officiant of the dynastic ancestral cult, in which he has a male deputy, the *taawoŋ*, who may act on his behalf and who is a prince, chosen for each reign. The *taawoŋ*'s female counterpart, the *yeewoŋ*, a princess, plays a major role in the installation and burial of *afon*.[12] She is also chosen at the start of each reign. While all the *afon* of Nso' have had a great deal of power, they have never been despotic, nor have they been able to make many political decisions on their own. There have always existed a number of checks and balances on the power of these rulers. The men's secret societies and military associations that form an integral part of the organization composed by an elaborate palace bureaucracy, in combination with the *fon*'s primary councillors, the *vibay*, and various lineage heads, provide a check on his traditional power.

Major Categories of People

The Nso' distinguish two main categories of people. These are the *mtaar* (free commoners) and *wirfon* ("people of the *fon*"). *Wirfon* are divided into *wan nto'* (royals, literally, "children of the palace"), *duy* (what Kaberry called royal cadet lineages[13]), and *nshiylavsi* (palace retainers; sing. *nshiylav*).[14] The *mtaar*, also called free lineages, the true people of Nso', and the people of the Nso' earth, are members of those lineages whose ancestors are said to have welcomed the Fon Nso' as their leader during the movement of the Nso' dynasty into the area. The *mtaar* exchanged fealty to the Fon Nso' for a number of privileges, including the right to keep the pelt and head of leopards they killed,[15] and freedom from the obligation to give women to the *fon*, only doing so voluntarily. Yet the Fon Nso' must have a mother who is a *mtaar* woman. Therefore, the Fon Nso' must bargain with the *mtaar* for wives, and he is in a sense both the son and the son-in-law of the *mtaar* lineage heads and must take their advice seriously.

The royal lineages proper (the *won nto'*; sing. *wan nto'*) include descendants of the *fon* down to the fourth generation in the case of men and the third in the case of women. After that, as is true of many peoples who have put a lid on the numbers of royalty in their polity, such people become *duy* (from the verb *du*, "to go") and join the ranks of subsidiary, or cadet, royal lineages. *Won nto'* and *duy* are eligible for membership in *ŋgiri*, the royal men's secret society. A subset of royal men forms the pool of those eligible for the *fon*ship. Royal daughters are available for marriages that create or reproduce political alliances between the *fon* and others, both within the chiefdom and in alliance networks with important men and *afon* of the various Grassfield chiefdoms.[16] Princesses also fill certain ritual or honorific incumbencies.

The traditional palace stewards are recruited from the *nshiylavsi*, who are required to give boys to the palace as retainers and girls as wives. Important palace stewards (*ataanto'*), who have been responsible for managing the *fon*'s political and domestic affairs, and officers (*asheey*) of *ŋweroŋ* the Nso' regulatory society, the most powerful men's secret society, are recruited from the *nshiylavsi*. A number of *nshiylavsi* are brought to the palace as young boys for a period of time (at present, nine years) and trained both as retainers to the *fon* and as officers in *ŋweroŋ*. This society is not only a check and balance of the *fon*, but now its senior house has also acquired an important voice in selecting a *fon* and retains the right to withhold political support from a particular *fon* who is found to be acting incorrectly.

During their training years, *nshiylavsi* leave the palace only as masked messengers. At the end of their allotted stay, they leave the palace and settle throughout the chiefdom, where they become the *fon*'s eyes and ears. A number of them settle near the palace in Kimbo', where they continue to perform their duties in *ŋweroŋ*, where some of them hold high office. They may be given a wife by the *fon*. Particularly talented *nshiylavsi* serve as secretaries to the *fon*, official spokesmen for the public in the *fon*'s court, and sometimes as Nso' representatives to agencies of the national government. The term "retainer," which Kaberry used to describe these men, stressed their relationship to the palace and to the *fon*. Perhaps in the present context it is more to the point to stress the connection of the *nshiylavsi* with *ŋweroŋ*, and note their complex mediating position between the *fon* and *ŋweroŋ*, whose functions and meaning have changed within a rapidly shifting social field.

The social categories in Nso' are neither exclusive nor endogamous. The various groups have certain rights and certain responsibilities vis-à-vis each other and the *fon*, and are culturally significant, but they are not in fact hierarchic in any measurable sense. For reasons which will be discussed in Chapter 3, the *mtaar* have lost the political power they had in precolonial Nso' while the political influence of the *ŋshiylav* seems to have expanded. Yet the cultural importance of the *mtaar* remains salient. It is the *mtaar* who are called upon to remove pollution from the *fon* and the palace; partly because they remain outside the on-going dispute between *ŋgiri* and *ŋweroŋ*, the *mtaar* lineage heads remain perhaps the most trusted and respected people in Nso'. One's membership in a particular social category is most often through the patriline, although, as noted above, the descendants of the daughter of a *fon* remain *won nto'* for three generations. Since it is more common than not that people of various social categories intermarry, it is sometimes possible to manipulate one's genealogy and move from one category to another. This is especially true today for *duy* or *mtaar* who want to become members of *ŋweron*.

There are cultural stereotypes, both positive and negative, of the various groups; this is especially true for *won nto'* and *ŋshiylav*, two groups who each claim to "own" the *fon* and the palace. *Won nto'* are characterized as drunkards who constantly "humbug" people to extract gifts and mimbo, and people say that if you lend anything, money or goods, to a *won nto'*, you should consider it a donation since they are notoriously unreliable at repaying debts. It is also said that *won nto'* are without guile; they grow up in the palace and never have to scramble for food or mimbo so they never learn to become devious. While not actually characterized as stupid, *won nto'* are seen as not able to deal with the more complex problems of daily life. The *ŋshilyav*, on the other hand, are viewed as shrewd and cunning; it is said that they are never completely straightforward in word or deed. *Ŋshiylav* are also believed to be clever and intelligent. These qualities are attributed to the fact that it is the *ŋshiylav* who are responsible for running the complex palace bureaucracy, a somewhat machiavellian task which requires a good deal of negotiation for status and position.

Men's Secret Societies

Although there are a number of men's societies and fraternal organizations in Nso', *ŋweroŋ* and *ŋgiri* are the two major secret societies. *Ŋweroŋ* is the regulatory society, the *fon*'s right hand and his eyes and ears, while *ŋgiri* is the society of royals. All non-*mtaar* males are eligible for membership in either *ŋweroŋ* or *ŋgiri*, although these are not universalistic societies. Once a member, a man may embark on a career in which, through "correct fashion" and the accumulation of resources, he moves up the ladder of ranked houses. A man's death is marked by the public showing of the jujus (the powerful masked figures) of the houses to which he belongs, which move about town in their characteristic ways in order of precedence over a period of days. During various traditional public ceremonies, the jujus of both societies will appear, with the lowest-ranking houses followed by higher-ranking houses until the highest and most powerful jujus have made their public rounds. Jujus of both societies come out to perform during mortuary ceremonies honoring the death of important titleholders.

Of the two societies *ŋweroŋ* is the more powerful. Both are internally differentiated into ranked "houses," each associated with particular rights, responsibilities, ritual knowledge, and the *shiv* ("medicine") that represents these, embodied in the masks, sacra, costumes, musical instruments, and noisemakers that constitute the house jujus.

The organization of *ŋweroŋ* is extremely complex and is shrouded in secrecy.[17] In the past it has had crucial executive functions and exists today as an important pressure group within Nso' traditional government. The executive house of *ŋweroŋ*, *yeeŋweroŋ* (the powerful inner lodge of *ŋweroŋ*; literally, "the mother of *ŋweroŋ*"), requires extensive payments of goats, fowls, raffia or palm wine, baskets of corn *fufu* (porridge), and the "*fon*'s bag," which consists of a large sum of money. Membership is open only to members of the senior *ŋweroŋ* rank who are titleholders and who are deemed worthy by the *fon* and *yeeŋweroŋ* members.[18]

In addition to the men's secret societies, whose membership is restrictive and requires payments, there is *manjoŋ*, or the warriors' organization of local clubs, which in the past universally conscripted all able-bodied men over the age of 18. *Manjoŋ* cuts horizontally across all Nso' lineages and creates ties between men of the same age that are similar to, although less institutionalized than, those described by Evans-Pritchard for the Nuer.[19] In the late nineteenth century, Fon Taamanjoŋ, son of Səm I, is credited with having reorganized the original *manjoŋ* into two sections, *ba'* and *gham*, creating a defensive and offensive militia which could be called out. The Nso' army thus created developed rapidly into an army of conquest, the most powerful in the northeastern Grassfields. *Manjoŋ* was critical in Nso' state building and in the defeat of the Bamum in the 1880s. *Manjoŋ* also conducted the royal hunt, where young men sought to make a name for themselves through bravery in the hunt or by killing special animals for the *fon*, such as leopards or elephant. When the Nso' were defeated by the Germans in 1906, *manjoŋ* lost its function as a warriors' society. During the colonial period, *manjoŋ* was used for tax collection. Today, the *manjoŋ* houses in each village are places of communication where messages from meetings or *manjoŋ* leaders outside Nso' are received. They are also social clubs (*mfu* lodges) where young men gather to gossip, drink, and dance.

Women's Secret Societies

Earlier in the century there were several women's palace societies.[20] The most widespread of these was *coŋ*, which was organized around feasting and promoting women's position as farmers. *Coŋ* provided harvest prestations to the palace and had its own *shiv*, or medicine, forbidden to men and regarded as a royal medicine (*shiv se afon*). The ritual objects of the society are also known as *shiv fon*, or "the medicine of the *fon*," categorized also as *vifa ve nsay*, or "things of the earth."[21] There is a myth surrounding *coŋ* which is said to justify the hierarchic relationship between men and women. At some point in the distant past, men had small *shiv* which they kept secret from the women. Women had *shinduyen*, which was much more powerful. Moved by curiosity the women agreed to exchange medicines, thus losing their more powerful position. Women's own curiosity led them to be less powerful than men. This is a variant on a familiar theme in foundation myths found throughout the world, which argue that, in the (usually distant) past, women were more powerful than men, but, because of some negative attribute of their own, women lost their superior position.

In the past when the harvest was ready, women would have a meeting, each bringing some food from her own farm for a feast, and they would dance the dance of *coŋ* or *shinduyen*. Men were precluded from seeing this dance, and if a man gave women trouble when they were dancing, the women could grab him and take him to the palace, where he would be fined. Usually he would be required to provide food for all the women in the group. Women of *coŋ* used to go to the palace, and the *fon* would give them palm wine and kola nuts, oil and salt, and bless them. At the harvest, it was customary for the *fon* to summon the medicine of *coŋ* and give the women food. This custom ended by the 1950s, and *coŋ* has been replaced substantially by *njaŋgi*, or savings and loan club meetings and women's church associations, at least one of which, the early Catholic Women's Association, styled itself after *coŋ* and took the same name.[22] The founders of this group called themselves the Mamma Fourteen, signifying that they were born before or around 1914. The current Catholic Women's Association is powerful not only locally but also throughout the province and is known as the Mothers of the Church.

When they feel their rights have been trampled, women have been able to reprimand the *fon* publicly without fear of reprisal. Judging from evidence of numerous women's protests in the 1950s and 1960s, it is likely that women have had a collective political voice for a long time and have been able to use it often and successfully to secure their rights.

Male Rank and Titles

Aside from the titles available only to high-ranking members of the secret societies of the retainers and royals, there are three important grades of titles in Nso': *sheey*, *faay*, and *shuufaay*. The most powerful *ashuufaay*, once supposedly seven, are also *vibay* (sing. *kibay*), councillors to the *fon*. Given the practice by which people may not use a proper name to address anyone of an equal or higher public status than himself or herself, and given the finely tuned system of deference by which titleholders are given public recognition, it is crucial in everyday life that people know what individuals belong to which ranks.

Five kinds of people may be given the title *sheey*. First, princes or men of the royal family who have founded a large family are given the title. Second, *sheey* designates sublineage heads. Third, those who serve or have served as pages in the palace are awarded the title after they serve in either *ŋweroŋ* or *ŋgiri*. Fourth, all those who have completed all the necessary ceremonies and are admitted into the inner circle of *ŋweroŋ* are known as *sheey*. Fifth, persons characterized by outstanding personal achievement (political, professional, social, or economic) are awarded the title. This last group was created and has expanded in the past several decades because of an increasing number of men having been able to achieve or "buy" (*taŋ*) the title.[23]

A lineage head is known as a *faay*. While lineage elders can recommend a candidate for the office, only the *fon* through his representatives can install a *faay*. This office not only carries considerable public prestige and political power within the traditional structures but also brings with it great responsibilities, and men have been known to "run from the stool" for that reason. The title *faay* can also be bestowed by the *fon* on a particularly successful man who is not a lineage head, one who has brought honor and prestige to Nso' and/or given outstanding service to the palace, although this is a rare occurrence.

Above the *afaay* (plur.) nowadays are the *ashuufaay*. These are the heads of large lineages or sometimes former clan heads whose ancestors pledged allegiance to the Fon Nso'. They are the truly "big men," or men of renown, in the chiefdom. A number of the *ashuufaay* (traditionally seven), the *vibay*, form the *fon*'s council of state, which assists the *fon* in *taakibu'* (the courtyard at the palace where cases are heard) for all important public and semipublic deliberations affecting the Nso' people. The title *shuufaay* will also be conferred by the *fon* on a truly outstanding son of Nso', although very rarely.[24]

Female Rank and Title

Women do not stand in line of succession to the "stool" (throne), nor are they eligible for lineage office, although there have been cases where a woman held the stool for a short interregnum, and sisters' sons are sometimes chosen as heads of their father's lineage. Daughters of the *fon* act as important court ambassadors when they are married into foreign chiefdoms, and important position of political intrigue in the past and one not without power in the present.[25] One of the princesses is appointed *yeewoŋ*. This is the most important ritual position held by a woman; the *yeewoŋ* takes a major part in both the installation and burial of the *fon*. Besides the informal title "mother of the farm" (*yee sum*), applied to all adult women, formal institutionalized titles are given to various women within the palace. These titles are held almost exclusively by the *vikiy nto'*, wives (past and present) of the *fon*.

The highest formal female title is *yeefon*, or queen mother. If a newly installed *fon*'s mother is still living, she is appointed *yeefon*. If she is dead, which is usually the case (since men are not often selected as *fon* at a young age), the *fon* appoints one of his daughters as his queen mother. The title is inherited; for three generations those who succeed a *yeefon* are called *afeŋgay* (of or belonging to the royal hall), and after this they are known as *yaa*. The *yeefon* has no official duties, although in the past she could offer political asylum. She takes precedence in protocol over the *vibay*, the *fon*'s councillors, and is given a funeral of state when she dies.

Within the palace, the *fon*'s wives are grouped into four "houses" (*lavsi*).[26] Each of these houses is headed by a leader called *yee sum*, the official "mothers of the farm" (*asee sum*) of Nso'. The *ayee sum* are installed as a *faay* is and can publicly greet (*bun*) the *fon*, but, unlike a *faay*, the *ayee sum* do not offer sacrifices or wear any insignia of the office. The title is for life. *Ayee sum* supervise the wives and daughters of the *fon* and organize work on his farms (*sum fon*).

Apart from the four *ayee sum*, two of the *fon*'s wives have high rank: the *yaa woo nto'* (queen of the palace) and *yee la'* (mother of the compound). They arrange for the preparation of food for official sacrifices, and shave the *fon* and collect his hair, which is kept until his death and then buried with him. They also serve as a link between the *fon* and the *ayee sum* and as a conduit of information to the *fon* from all his wives. They choose the *fon*'s sleeping partners, which, at least in the past, was a position with a good deal of political clout. By controlling sexual access to the *fon*, these two women can, in effect, choose the women who will bear sons who might become the next Fon Nso'. These two wives know who has and who has not been sexually involved with the *fon*, and have the opportunity to scrutinize the sexual lives of the palace women; they therefore have been important witnesses in cases of adultery with the *fon*'s wives.[27]

Power politics today have by and large moved away from palace intrigue, and relationships between chiefdoms have a different political meaning from what they had in the past. All these female titles, although not without a share of distinction and power, gave women more political power in the past than they do now. Wives of the Fon Nso', as well as the various *afon* in the subchiefdoms, have become somewhat impoverished with the increasing importance of making a cash income and the heavier demands on women's incomes. The *fon*'s wives are not allowed to go to market; if they want to sell any of the food crops they grow, they have to send their children. Moreover, none of them can become directly involved in petty trade, and they are less likely to have a surplus to sell, since they have to work on the *fon*'s coffee farms as well as cultivate their own food crops. In cases where the *fon* has so many wives he cannot afford to pay school fees for all his children, the burden falls on his wives. Girls are often used as pawns in their father's political games; currying favor with the palace by giving a daughter to the palace is not an uncommon occurrence.[28] Hence, being a wife of a *fon* today is not an enviable position. Women say that "when the *fon* takes a new wife that is when you hear much wailing in the palace."

During the reign of Ŋga' Bi' fon III (July 1983–September 1993) at least five young women escaped from the palace and went into self-imposed exile rather than stay in the palace as *vikiy nto'*, or wives of the *fon*.

The Lineage System

Descent in Nso' is patrilineal and is composed of four important levels of social organization: the family, the sublineage, the lineage, and the clan. The first three are exogamous and in some senses corporate. The clans are dispersed membership groups, whose main local import is a kind of identity based on folk histories of group movement to Kimbo' and the surrounding area.

The lineage head (*faay*) is the economic, political, and spiritual leader, the big man, of a group belonging to up to five generations in depth. A *faay* is selected from the pool of eligible adult men in a lineage by a lineage council of elders. His name is then taken to the *fon* for ratification. The *fon* reserves the political and symbolic right to name and depose *afaay*, whatever their lineage type, for serious offenses or on strong complaints from lineage members and affines.

One of the five types of *sheey* is a sublineage head. As a lineage grows over time and sublineages become large enough, a *faay* may name someone as *sheey* for that sublineage. After four generations, the successor to the *sheey* usually becomes a *faay* in his own right, but until that time he is ritually subordinate to the *faay* of the parent lineage. A *faay* may name a *sheey*, but the *faay* must report this to the *fon* for ratification.

Household and Economic Organization

Although descent is patrilineal, most people also maintain close ties to their maternal relatives. Matrikin play crucial political, ritual, and economic roles in an individual's life.[29] Occasionally a sister's son can become a lineage head in the compound of his mother's father, although at this son's death his son does not succeed him and the line reverts to the patrikin. The ideal is polygyny; the current Fon Nso' has over 80 wives (including inherited wives)—far fewer than the number who were married to the *afon* in the nineteenth century. Important councillors and subchiefs have between 8 and 15 wives. About a third of all village men have more than one wife,[30] although few men are married to more than two women. Even the most devout Christian men who intend to stay monogamous will often hesitate to state this intention officially. To do so would be thought by many men to deny one's sense of self as an Nso' male and as a man of substance.

Residence too throughout Nso' is ideally patrilocal, although it can vary. For example, people like to live near important maternal relatives, and temperaments and personal relations influence residence choice as well. The compound, usually composed of a compound head, his wives, his adult sons and their families, children, and other dependents, is the basic unit of economic and political cooperation.

Women in Nso' have been farmers for as long as can be remembered. They produce virtually all the food crops. Men's primary identification is as warriors and hunters, two occupations in which most of them have never been engaged. Since the 1950s they have instead been coffee farmers. This cash crop, like kola nuts and the raffia bush and palm trees from which local wine (*mimbo*) is tapped, is a man's crop. Decisions about planting, picking, delivering to the Nso' Cooperative Union, smuggling around National Coffee Board check points, and spending received income are made by men, although a fair amount of coffee-related labor is performed by wives, daughters, and young sons.

Most people are dependent on agriculture for their livelihood; over 90 percent of food consumed is home grown, and 85 percent of the cash income available to the household is generated within the agricultural economy from the sale of food and small livestock rather than from salaries or wages. Eighty-five percent of all households are classified as "rural" (as compared with 72 percent nationwide), and virtually all households have farms and are self-sufficient in food production.

Long before the Europeans arrived, the ecological diversity and a high population density encouraged the development of well-organized and lively commercial networks in the Grassfields. An established center of regional and long-distance trade for nearly two centuries, Nso' is today a rich agricultural region, producing substantial amounts of the national harvest of maize, beans, and Irish potatoes. The region is self-sufficient in food production, importing only palm oil and small amounts of wheat. Again, women produce virtually all food crops and provision the household, while men grow coffee and engage in a variety of entrepreneurial activities.

Land is held both individually and communally. While the *fon* has been the symbolic or titular owner of land, de facto control has been in varying degrees in the hands of a number of lineage heads, the *ataaŋven* ("the fathers who own the fields"), and family heads, the *ataala'*. Until recently, all people have had the right to use land by virtue of their citizenship in Nso'. Although this right has lately been called into question, free access to farmland is still an important piece of Nso' ideology; indeed, until very recently it was essentially part of local doxa. Within the last decade land has become increasingly privatized. This, in combination with population growth and increases in the cattle herds of the Fulani, who share the region with the Nso', has led to extreme pressure on land, with the result that women are farming up to the tops of the steepest hills and are walking long distances to their farms. With a relatively undeveloped infrastructure, few year-round farm-to-market roads exist in these steep hilly regions, and food must be head-loaded to market, a time-consuming and arduous task—and almost always women's work.

The impact of the market economy has not been uniform throughout Nso'. Kimbo', as the traditional capital of the chiefdom as well as the capital of Bui Division today, has grown at a different pace and changed in ways different from those of the surrounding villages, which constitute the major portion of the division and of the Nso' population. Kimbo' and its immediate environs have a population of approximately 60,000, while the population of the chiefdom as a whole is estimated at around 220,000 persons.[31] The view of Nso' differs depending on one's vantage point and social position, and thus the angle of the lens through which it is seen.

Life in the Capital: Kimbo'

Kimbo' was probably established as the capital of Nso' before the 1820s.[32] At that time, Fon Səm I, under pressure from Chamba raiders from Banyo to the east, moved his capital to Kimbo' from Kovvifəm (forest of old settlements), some 12 miles to the northeast. Built on the sides of steep hills, Kimbo' offered considerable military advantage rather than ease of settlement. Apart from the market and the *fon*'s courtyard there are few flat places in Kimbo'. To walk about on the slippery clay paths and roads in rainy season (or to drive the Ring Road, for that matter) is to assault one's ankles and knees and, at times, to put one's life in jeopardy. With astute accuracy, Nso' people speak of walking as "trekking."

Travelling north on the Ring Road, the pace of life quickly begins to pick up on the outskirts of Kimbo'. Titled men with distinctive crocheted caps (the cap is the title, the Nso' say) and long black gowns embroidered in red and gold stride purposefully along on their way to the palace, dane guns in hand, cutlasses slung over their shoulders. Faces as proudly mysterious as the carved masks of their palace societies, they seldom give passersby a second glance. Women with brightly patterned *lapas* tied tautly over their hips balance blue plastic buckets on their heads and babies on their backs. Grabbing their curious children by the hand, they admonish them to get out of the way, reprimanding them sternly, "Can't you hear the dust?" when vehicles drive past.

The signs of habitation become more frequent. Alongside the road, groundnuts, avocado pears, and puff-puffs (fried dough) are displayed in flowered enamel bowls on dusty bamboo tables, a battered cigarette cup set hopefully alongside for travellers to pay and make change. Elderly women, bent over under the weight of large loads, trudge along the sides of the road, their skin worn by time and hard work to the color and texture of the wood they carry on their backs. Young boys sell groundhog, a favorite local delicacy (these animals are locally called cutting grass, because they are hunted during the dry season when the tall grass is cut down). Groups of young men in jeans and tee-shirts with the slogan "Guinness is good for you" kick up the red dust and cry greetings back and forth while they swagger along the road, going to Kimbo' to work or just to hang out in the market. In the recent past, one could see donkeys laden with plantains, bananas, and palm wine for sale in the market and distribution in the palace.

Small yellow Toyota taxis dart between Kimbo' and nearby villages. Larger taxi vans, with names like God Only Knows, Why Worry, Good

Luck, God's Own, and James Bond, career precariously up and down the hilly thoroughfare, loaded down with people and cargo travelling to and from Bamenda and points south. Cadging a free trip in exchange for protection from police shakedowns on the road, a gendarme sits in the front seat, red beret tipped jauntily on his head. Petrol trucks slosh along too rapidly for safety. Twelve-ton Brasserie beer trucks, bottles rattling, travel almost daily between Kimbo' and Bamenda. Even during the heavy rains of late August, when the roads are almost impassable, these trucks make it through.

During the rainy season it is almost impossible to make the trip from Bamenda to Kimbo' without an event: sliding off the road onto the soft shoulders, getting stuck in the deep muddy ruts, or simply waiting for the flood waters covering the road on the Ndop Plain to run off. There are a few hair-raising bends where vehicles can easily slip off the steep embankments. Here you begin to understand the meaning of the names displayed on the taxis. When a vehicle slides off the road or gets stuck in the mud, groups of young boys appear as if by magic. After much negotiation they help push the vehicle or even pick it up and put it back on the road. If the wait is long and the rains unending, there are always people around to laugh with, share food and drink, and commiserate over your mutual plight.

The seat of divisional administration as well as the traditional capital of Nso', Kimbo' today is a bustling town, the focal point of commerce and government in the area. Divisional offices of various national ministries as well as the district officer and senior district officer have headquarters here. As capital of the chiefdom and home of the paramount Fon Nso', Kimbo' is also the center of Nso' politics. The Fon Nso' is the most important local political figure, and little gets done without his knowledge and approval. "Father" and symbol of the Nso' people, he reigns from his palace, down the hill from the Squares, the name given the small commercial area in Kimbo'. He is the paramount traditional leader in Bui Division and one of the four Grassfield *afon* who receive a salary from the national government of Cameroon. The Fon Nso' is at the center of the traditional Nso' system of redistribution. Goods and services pass into the palace as the material realization of public and symbolic fealty. Some of these goods and services (for example, the firewood delivered to the palace in frequent pubic paradelike displays by various descent, neighborhood, school, and sodality groups) remain in the palace to help supply and reproduce the large palace infrastructure, with its wives, children, and retainers; others pass out to the populace in the form of public and private "dashes" and in palm wine and bottled beer offered to visitors in a cycle of ongoing, conspicuous, and mandatory hospitality.

Fon Ŋga' Bi'fon II was an expansive, generous-hearted (and generous-figured) man who liked nothing more than to conduct court with a full house. During his reign, wine and conversation flowed freely at the palace, and he encouraged me to sit and socialize with him while he entertained his numerous guests. He could often be found in the palace courtyard, cup in hand and children on his knee, hearing requests and petitions for favors while dispensing advice and palm wine. One unusually hot afternoon, when each breath meant a fight with the red dust for air, I became light-headed and queasy from the continual flow of palm wine and schnapps. I turned to the *fon* and said, "I cannot drink so much because I have gastric" (a common Nso' ailment). He looked at me, smiled widely, and without missing a beat said, "No problem, we have doctors. Drink." It was a long afternoon.

With the enstoolment of Səhm Mbinglo I, the current *fon*, the office has become even more central to local events. The two former Anglophone provinces of Cameroon: the Northwest, and the Southwest, have gone from political opposition demanding reforms from Yaounde, to a seces-sionist movement aimed at recreating an Anglophone state composed of the former Southern Cameroon. For most intents and purposes, Nso' has exited the state, and the *fon*'s role has been augmented rather than attenu-ated by this turn of events. Long a center of opposition politics, Kimbo' is called "Baghdad" throughout Cameroon because of the tough political stance of its inhabitants. During the reign of the late *fon*, Ŋga' Bi'fon III, many young people had used opposition politics as an excuse to steal and generally harass people. Chosen for the throne while in his late 30s, the current *fon* is the youngest man in living memory to be enstooled as *fon*; he was not only young when chosen, he was also an active member of the main opposition party, the Social Democratic Front. His selection was a smart political move on the part of the kingmakers of Nso'. By selecting a young man whose national political leanings coincided with the majority of the population, and with virtually all the younger generation, they en-sured loyalty to, and cooperation with the palace throught Nso', won the hearts and minds of the younger generation, and revitalized the continuity of the political leadership of Nso' traditional government. Because Səhm Mbinglo I was himself one of them, he knows the identity of most of the young troublemakers. He is preventing theft and other forms of antisocial behavior in Nso' by instituting fines and public beatings, some which he administers himself, and others he leaves to officers of ŋweroŋ. Nso' peo-ple, including those who have experienced the judgment of the *fon*, ap-plaud this action, and point proudly to the fact that unlike Bamenda, Kimbo' is safe after dark. The senior district officer, a man from the South-west Province who is no fan of the Social Democratic Front, was angry with the *fon* because at large public meetings the crowd would all stand when the *fon* entered, but Nso' people gave no respect to the officer. When he heard about the *fon*'s justice at the palace, the officer wrote the *fon* a letter saying that the *fon* was "overstepping his authority." The *fon* wrote back, saying that he was *fon* in Nso' before the officer arrived, and would be *fon* after the officer left; that the Nso' people belonged to the *fon*, and that the officer should mind his own busiiness. When it became patently clear that all Nso' people, regardless of their national political allegiance, supported the *fon*, the senior district officer backed down. The officer has since begun to drink heavily, and reputedly is trying, unsuccessfully, to obtain a transfer. It is rumored also that the *fon*, who now has the SDO where he wants him, has effectively blocked his transfer.

The Fon Nso' is quite clearly an important symbol for all the Nso' people. Outsiders, whether non-Nso' residents of Bui Division or representatives of the provincial, national, or international communities, find it politically wise to pay symbolic fealty to the *fon*, if only to come to the palace and publicly "greet" him during one of his triweekly open court days. A snub to the *fon* is a snub to the Nso' people, and it generates recalcitrance and other obstructionist displays of bad feeling. The public symbolism of the palace is based on a very finely honed system of precedence. This system, revealed through complex rules of speaking, seating, and other placement in the *taakibu'* (*fon*'s courtyard), marks the comparative political status of various social and political groups in the chiefdom.

As the divisional capital and regional commercial center, Kimbo' offers economic opportunities to the people of Nso', in addition to farming. Although there are no paved roads and only part of the town has electricity, Kimbo' nevertheless is a modern town, boasting an impressive Catholic cathedral, a substantial commercial center, and one of the most important markets in the Northwest Province. The market area at Mvu' contains well over 100 permanent stalls from which cloth, household and hardware items, and packaged food are sold daily and in which such services as tailoring are available. The open-air market meets each eighth day of the regional market cycle. Here, produce from the countryside is bought and sold for domestic consumption and, in bulk quantities, for shipment south to the coast and north to Nigeria. Thousands of tons of agricultural produce—beans, corn, Irish potatoes, and hot peppers, or *pepe*—are exported yearly. Coffee is sold through the Nso' Cooperative Union and is exported from the area at the rate of 2400 tons annually, making it in value terms, over the last two decades, the most important export from the area.[33]

Most of the medium- to large-scale, permanent marketing business establishments and all the transportation are in the hands of men, each of whom would probably claim to be a coffee farmer as well. A number of off-licenses are owned by women, usually widowed or divorced, who have been able in one way or another to secure enough initial capital for supplies and a beer license. Small commercial areas are found in the Squares and Tobin and along the road from the Squares to Mvu'.

Spreading out west and north of the market area proper are larger shops, bars, restaurants, provision stores, hardware stores, hotels, and other relatively permanent establishments. Just south of the market area, on one of the rare semiflat spaces, is the taxi park, where transportation of people and goods is available to nearby villages and to towns north, west, and south on the Ring Road. Here youngsters, hawking groundnuts and cigarettes from enamelled trays balanced on their heads, vie for attention with taxi drivers soliciting passengers and with the loud beat of Salle John's Congo Highlife. The sweet odor of palm oil cooking and the smoke from roasting corn mix with the smell of exhaust fumes and rotting vegetables.

Kimbo' presents a picture of a town in transition. Tobin, the administrative section of town, expanded rapidly in the early 1980s during Cameroon's economic boom. During this time absentee landlords built modern houses here with amenities like electricity and running water to be rented out to government functionaries. There are two categories of absentee landlords. Some are Nso' men who have left the area for better jobs in national urban centers or outside the country and who have built houses to rent out until they come home to retire. The rest are men who themselves live in much less auspicious circumstances, usually in the smaller villages outside of Kimbo', and who have earned a substantial amount of money and want to invest in but not live in Kimbo'. Until recently, most absentee landlords invested in properties in Bamenda, where they could realize a higher return on their investment. Because of rising land and building costs in Bamenda, as well as the growing demand for modern housing in Kimbo', investments in urban properties in Kimbo' during the 1980s increased substantially. The economic decline which began in the mid-1980s is evident in the number of houses sitting empty in the early 1990s, with grass growing through cracks on the veranda and the main inhabitants, goats and chickens, foraging in the front yards.

The majority of local people live in mud block houses in more traditional compounds. Zinc roofs have replaced thatching grass; cement floors and glass windows have replaced dirt floors and wooden shutters. The more modern compounds have cement sidewalks around the houses and are plastered inside and out and painted or whitewashed. But many compounds appear remarkably the same as Kaberry described them in the late 1940s.[34]

Compounds vary substantially in size, depending on the status of the compound head and the number of people in residence. Younger male dependents living in the compounds of their more traditional lineage heads have often built substantial modern houses, so that the larger compounds are a mix of modern and traditional structures. The large compounds near the palace and belonging to the traditional notables may cover over an acre of land and contain over 100 houses. These compounds are usually thought of as wards, sections, and quarters of Kimbo'.

The number of separate structures found in a compound varies according to the number of residents and the orientation, "conservative" or "modern" of the compound head. In more traditional, or conservative, compounds, the head of the compound has a separate house where he sleeps, eats, and entertains guests. Usually he will have at least one structure with a thatched roof, which he says he keeps mostly because of its sentimental value. Each adult woman has her own kitchen with a granary in the rafters and sleeping quarters attached, where she sleeps with her younger children. In more modern households, family members sleep and live in the same building, but often husband and wife share neither bedroom nor mealtime. Women and children eat in the kitchen while men and their guests eat in the living room of the main house.

Life on the Periphery: Nsə'

Nsə' is one of the smaller subchiefdoms in Nso', located near the border between Bui and Donga-Mantung divisions towards the outer fringe of the political and economic grasp of Kimbo'. During the latter half of the nineteenth century, the Nso' extended their hegemony outward from Kimbo' to include what is today Bui Division. Some groups, such as the Ŋkar, when defeated in battle retained their leader as *fon*; other groups, such as the Nsə', seeing the handwriting on the wall, pledged allegiance to the Fon Nso' before any blood was shed in exchange for the right of retaining their leader as *fon*. At the time the Germans arrived in the early twentieth century, the situation was still quite fluid. Histories from the center speak of the progressive and inevitable process of incorporation of peoples at the periphery of Nso'. Histories from the periphery recount resistance and shifting attempts at alliance with other groups. The Nsə' completed their move south from what is now Donga-Mantung Division to their present location well before the Germans arrived. Although social ties and marriage alliances to the north remain, the incidence of political alliances across divisional borders has been reduced over the years, and Lam Nso', the language of Nso', has in most contexts replaced Limbum, the original language, as a primary language for most Nsə'. While there is more or less mutual acknowledgement of strong ties between Nso' and Nsə', over the past several decades the meaning of these ties has been shifting and often contested, with Nso' claiming sovereignty over Nsə' and Nsə' denying these claims.[35]

Daily life in Nsə' presents a marked contrast to the hubbub of commercial and administrative activity in Kimbo'. Situated in a rolling valley surrounded by steep hills some 20 miles northwest of Kimbo', Nsə' is a quiet village of around 4000 people. Two roads, negotiable in rainy season only by four-wheel drive vehicles and even then with difficulty, link Nsə' with the Ring Road. One road leads north through Ndu, and the other leads southeast to Kimbo'.

Living arrangements in Nsə' follow a similar pattern to those in Kimbo', although compounds in Nsə' are more spread out and are often separated by large fields. Raffia bushes and kola trees line the streams at the bottom of the valley. There is little piped water in Nsə', and these streams provide water for household use, for washing both people and clothes, and for cattle to quench their thirst during the dry season. Nsə' borders true cattle country, and all around the village cows can be seen grazing up to the tops of the steeper hills. Partly because of these large herds around Nsə', a great deal of pressure on land exists, and here, too, farms extend in checkerboard patterns up the sides of even the steepest hills.

Nsə' is a sleepy village and, depending on one's mood, feels either idyllic or stultifying. Several times a day the silence is broken by taxis making a quick run through town, soliciting passengers for Kimbo' or Ndu. There are no local administrative offices, and the coffee cooperative here is a small depot where coffee is brought for shipment to Kimbo'. There are few local employment opportunities. Some men trek two or three hours to pick tea at the nearby Ndu Tea Estate. With the exception of a few schoolteachers and cooperative officials there are no salaried jobs in the village.

The Nsə' market square is a grassy knoll located on the one motorable road running through the village. Surrounding it are a couple of provision stores selling basic necessities—soap, salt, sugar—and a handful of off-licenses and *mimbo* (palm wine and raffia wine) houses, which, with the exception of market day, are more often closed than not. Market day is essentially a social occasion, providing an opportunity for local people to come together to share a few drinks and exchange the weekly gossip. Few goods and little money change hands. A small number of petty traders from Kimbo' display their wares on raffia mats spread out on the grass: cloth, used clothes, patent medicines, cigarettes, matches, toiletries. Perhaps 20 local women sell *njama-njama*, the leafy green vegetable which, as a mainstay of the daily diet, is always in demand. A few women sell palm oil from old kerosene tins, measuring it by the cigarette cup. A variety of cooked finger foods—boiled yams and sweet potatoes, groundnuts, and puff-puffs—tempt hungry passersby. Local people do not buy staple foods, and traders from outside don't often attend Nsə' market. Some women head-load corn, beans, and Irish potatoes to the Ndu market for sale, and a small number of local men act as middlemen, buying small amounts of produce from women until they have several bags to take to Ndu to sell. Several of these men have semipermanent trading partners they supply in Ndu.

The only thriving business on market day is conducted in the off-licenses and *mimbo* houses surrounding the market square. Sometimes a messenger from the palace, carrying a stalk of the *kikeŋ* (*Dracaena*) plant as a symbol of the authority of the Fon Nsə', will make announcements in the marketplace, usually recruiting labor for public work on the roads or announcing a village meeting at the palace.

The palace is the real center of social activity and interactions. Most Nsə' men gather at the secret societies outside the palace several times a week to drink raffia wine and discuss village politics. Visiting dignitaries, often representatives of the national or divisional government, are accepted in the outside courtyard of the palace with considerable pomp and circumstance. During these visits, traditional dances are performed and a seemingly endless number of long speeches are given by the *fon* and local political leaders praising the national party, the visiting dignitaries, development in general, and agricultural development in particular. In 1992, the late Fon Nsə', by this time a man in his 90s held a large public ceremony to end a 10-year dispute with Shuufaay Mborinyor, whom he had essentially ostracized from the palace on the grounds that the *shuufaay* had been selling land to outsiders. The Nsə' gathered en masse to witness this historic event. A tin trumpet announced the *fon*'s arrival with a few notes, more or less in tune. Sitting under a multicolored large umbrella, the *fon* proceeded to hold forth for almost an hour, regal to the end in his royal robes and a felt hat studded with tin stars on which was written "State of Texas." His senior councillor, Faay Mbaraŋ, brought in to repeat the words of the elder man, could not speak as loudly as the *fon*, nor could he keep up with the *fon*. In control to the end, Fon Nsə' carried the day with his words of reconciliation.[36]

Surrounding the front courtyard are the various men's society clubhouses. The living quarters of the *fon*'s wives and children take up the left wing of the palace. Two entryways lined with carved gateposts lead into the palace from the outside courtyard. One leads into an inside throne room, and the other is the entrance to a large inside courtyard where the Fon Nsə', seated on a raised dias with carved gateposts, receives visitors and judges disputes. On the wall behind his stool Guinness posters and official village photo calendars vie for attention. These calendars, put out by each village and each division, portray outside political figures as well as prominent local men (and once in a while a few women). Photographs of local leaders of the national party, cooperative officials, successful entrepreneurs and local bureaucrats, President Biya, the provincial governor, district officers, divisional heads of ministries, and traditional notables are placed around the borders of the calendars. At the center of each calendar is a large photograph of the *fon*. Carvings on the gateposts of the *fon*'s throne platform portray important animals—spiders, leopards, lizards— and, a more recent addition, a man in a Western suit with the initials of the national party carved above his head.

The Fon Nsə', a man of extreme dignity and sharp perception, is "father" of Nsə' and enjoys uncontested authority in the village. Visitors to Nsə' must pay their respects to him. If they are to stay for any length of time, it is wise to solicit his permission first. He spends a good deal of his time receiving visitors, judging cases, hearing individual requests and complaints, and settling disputes between landlords, farmers, and graziers. While it is possible to take cases to the administration in Kimbo', most local people defer instead to the judgments of the *fon* and his court.

Formal rituals surrounding the Fon Nsə', as with the Fon Nso', are strictly followed. When he walks by, women and young men bend down, hands on knees, eyes on the ground. No one remains seated when the *fon* is standing. Women and young men bend down, hands on knees; older men clap three times, bow slightly, and greet him (*nsoon*) through cupped hands. To approach the *fon*'s stool or throne, one should bend over and walk in a zigzag path. Direct messages are relayed and requests made through the *fon*'s interpreters, who squat by the throne and whisper into the *fon*'s ear through cupped hands. Formality and informality combine in the palace. Chickens scratch in the courtyard, children peer through the latticed wood shutters on the palace windows, and, more often than not, the Fon Nsə' holds court with a small child sitting on his lap or leaning against his knee.

The authority of the Fon Nsə' is reinforced locally by kinship ties to a large number of his subjects. As previously stated, all descendants of the *fon* for four generations in the male line and three in the female line are *won nto'*, or "children of the palace." Given the disproportionate number of women married to the *fon* and the relatively small population of Nsə', a substantial proportion of local people claim kinship with the palace. Royal princes in Nsə', unlike Nso', attend both *ŋweroŋ*, the regulatory society, and *ŋgiri*, the society of princes. This acts to reinforce the political power of the royal lineage.

Despite his significant local authority, the Fon Nsə' has little political clout outside the village. While the Nso' fill up most of the political horizon of the Nsə', the view from Kimbo' is quite different. The Nsə', although never conquered by the Nso' in battle, form one of the many groups that ring the territory surrounding the Nso' capital. When Europeans such as Kaberry asked about the different local groups that were included in the domain of the Fon Nso', the Nsə' were just one name on a list. As a political group, the Nsə' have continued to insist on their independence from Nso', and the Fon Nsə' has successfully retained his ability to fine any Nsə' person who, upon being given a substantial gift or title by the Fon Nso', does not return to the Fon Nsə' personally to report that award. Yet some of the more or less collective acts the Nsə' have taken, such as welcoming Presbyterian missionaries at a time when Catholicism was clearly becoming the major new religion in Kimbo', have reproduced multistranded cleavages between them and Nso', to the present political and economic detriment of their village.[37]

The chiefdom of Nso' is today a state within a state, a complicated place where the multiple strands of chieftaincy, secret societies, titles, lineage and clan politics, gender, and seniority—all informed by national politics and the marketplace—are interwoven into complex multivocal, multiethnic patterns. Categories are far from fixed; they merge and dissolve into each other only to become distinct and disaggregated when their meaning is negotiated and boundaries shift. What appears as hegemony from one vantage point appears as counterhegemony from another. The orthodox discourse appears as doxa to some, who are surprised to hear certain things even enter the discourse for discussion, such as the validity of the judgments of the Earth, yet the same orthodoxy may appear as heterodox resistance to others. What appears as "traditional" to some, others see as newly invented. While the center of the Cameroon state in Yaounde competes with the center of the Nso' chiefdom in Kimbo' today to control local events, each seeks to impose its own version of hegemony. In the process new forms of resistance and counterhegemony are created, forms which often must appeal to the alternate hegemonic discourse to become truly oppositional. As we shall see in chapter 7, the modern state has provided the subchiefs with at least the illusion that they can bypass the authority of the Fon Nso'. Clearly, nothing in Nso' today can be understood without reference to history. The Nso' past was fluid, shifting, and complex. The Nso' present has been created in and by the history whose patterns and processes are recounted in the next chapter.

3
The Forging of Hegemony*

Fon Səm II in 1905, pressured on pain of military sanction to make an act of submission to the Germans, is said to have picked up a handful of finger millet (*saar*) and, letting the tiny seeds run through his fingers, replied, "What have I to fear? My people are as uncountable as these."[1] Unfortunately, Səm had more to fear from the German intruders than he had imagined, for even the numerous and well-trained Nso' warriors could not defend the chiefdom against machine guns. But given the military victories Səm II and his two immediate predecessors had achieved, it is not surprising that the *fon* answered as he did. When the Germans first arrived in 1902, Nso' was a powerful and prosperous chiefdom, the largest in the Bamenda Grassfields, with a population variously estimated at between 25,000 and 60,000.[2] And the Nso' were on the move militarily. Between circa 1820, when Səm I had already established his capital at Kimbo', and 1890, the Nso' had conquered the large Ŋkar chiefdom to the south, and later subjugated six neighboring Nooni village chiefdoms and made them tributary, and accomplished a major victory over their powerful neighbors, the Bamum, taking the head of Nsa'ŋgu, the *fon* of Bamum, in a hard-fought and bloody battle in the late 1880s. From the 1890s until the Germans halted the expansion of their chiefdom in 1906, the Nso' harassed Bamum settlements on their eastern frontier, warded off Fulani raids in the north, and were expanding their control north and northwest into Nsungli territory.[3]

Official German reports written in 1905–6[4] give a carefully detailed if somewhat superficial description of life in Nso' at the turn of the century.

*I am using the concept of hegemony following Raymond Williams, *Marxism and Literature* (Oxford: Oxford University Press, 1977), 110, where he defines it as "a whole body of practices and expectations, over the whole of living: our senses and assignments of energy, our shaping perceptions of ourselves and our world . . . a lived system of meanings and values—constitutive and constituting—which as they are experienced as practices appear as reciprocally confirming . . . [thus constituting] a sense of reality for most people in the society, a sense of absolute because it is experienced reality beyond which it is very difficult for most members of the society to move, in most areas of their lives. . ."

Although technology was rudimentary, the Nso' were sophisticated farmers growing a wide variety of crops for consumption and trade. Maize and sorghum, groundnuts and cassava, several kinds of yam, beans, a wide variety of vegetables, peppers, sugarcane, cotton, and tobacco were cultivated. Stock was plentiful. Fowls, sheep, goats, and a variety of dwarf cattle (now disappeared) belonging exclusively to the *fon* were raised. Kola was grown extensively and was then, as now, an important item in regional and interregional trade. Tobacco, honey, goats, and hoes were important regional trade items, being exchanged against Hausa cloth, imported beads, palm oil, and salt with chiefdoms to the north, east, and south. Elephants were still numerous, and their tusks a royal prerogative. A variety of handicrafts also entered the trading networks: wood carvings, iron tools, pots, narrow-loom cotton cloth and woven mats being the most important.

The German officers were clearly impressed by the neatness and organizational skills of the Nso'. Their reports referring to their first passage in 1902, as well as later reports, describe roomy and neatly built houses, five to six meters high, with floors paved with small pebbles, and "bamboo" (palm rib) storage bins for grains. Reading between the lines we get a glimpse of Nso' government and military organization in the descriptions of warriors' lodges and the meeting and drinking halls with their carved door frames and support posts. The conquest wars of the past century were starkly symbolized in the "900 skulls of Bamoun and Nsungli warriors" hung on the warriors' lodges in Kimbo'. The Nso' are described as a proud people, "confident in their bearing unlike the timid forest people."[5] The Germans were the first Europeans most people in Nso' had seen, and according to one of Chilver and Kaberry's informants, Faay Koŋgir, the Nso' "regarded them as spirit beings" (*a yon ji anyuy*).[6] The official German report gives little attention to the historical origins and the composite nature of Nso', stating that, after the conquest of Ŋkar and Ndzərəm, "the present Bansso kingdom developed as a result of the immigration of great numbers of people native to the neighboring Ndsungle [Nsungli] lands and the conquest of Nko, Djoti and Bebem."[7] It is to an expanded version of that history that we now turn to describe precolonial Nso'.[8] Crucial here are the ways in which the *afon* of Nso', in a relatively short period of time, were able to establish hegemony over a large area, incorporating a number of ethnically and culturally diverse people into a powerful centralized polity.

Legends and Origins

According to most local oral traditions, in the distant past the founders of the dynasty travelled to Nso' from Kimi in the northeast, and succeeded in securing the allegiance of a number of local groups. A colonial speculation, not the locals, suggests that the founders' supposed migration probably began some 300 years ago, and this is often quoted now. Later movements into the region were often initiated by slaving razzias. Population pressure and intragroup feuding also played significant roles.[9] Significantly, the latest and now current version of the charter myth points to a founding ancestress, a princess referred to as Ŋgonso'.[10] Described as the daughter of Fon Kimi of Rifəm, Ŋgonso', accompanied by her husband and servants, left Rifəm following two of her brothers, who subsequently abandoned her. Her brothers went on to found Bamum and Ditam. Ŋgonso' and her party settled at Kovvifəm, some 12 miles to the northwest of Kimbo', among some people Mzeka calls the Visale, (who later became the *mtaar*, or the Nso' "people of the earth"), who "warmly received them."[11] Also telling, it was not Ŋgonso', but rather her son, Jay,[12] who succeeded to the throne of the Visale, uniting the two groups to become the first Fon Nso'.[13] It is widely held that this founding dynasty brought with it "the things of Rifəm," meaning the institutions and the symbols of chieftaincy originating in Rifəm, a sacred site in the chiefdom of Kimi in Tikar country to the northeast, which became as central to Nso' state building as it has to that of Bamum.[14] These claimed to include the most important secret societies in Nso', the regulatory society (*ŋweroŋ*) and the princes' society (*ŋgiri*). The Nso' allegedly later captured *mfu'*, one of the lodges of *manjoŋ*, the warriors' society to which all adult males in Nso' belonged, from Bamum. Also, it was claimed that from the Kimi came the model of seven royal councillors and seven chief palace stewards.[15] Whatever the relation to actual historical events or connections to Tikar institutions this myth embodies, it expresses, in the concrete images of a founding legend, the Nso' view of their political development.

The basic organization of Nso' government can be found outlined in this legend: a model with enough traditional structure to give it stability and yet with an organization flexible enough to incorporate conquered leaders of consequence into its center. Chiefs of large conquered villages like Ŋkar were accorded the title *fon* and left to run things at home, provided they paid tribute (*nshwi*) and acknowledged the Fon Nso' as superior. It has been suggested that the ancestors of some of the *ashuufaay*, the great lineage and clan heads, were at one time considered *afon* by their own people but were "demoted" for political or demographic reasons and incorporated into the palace as important titleholders and advisors to the Fon Nso'.[16]

The consolidation of the Nso' state owes much to frequent, often debilitating, slave raids beginning in the early nineteenth century if not earlier. References are frequently made in Nso' oral traditions to slave raids by

"Baranyam" or "Mbaŋcu" or "Balinyoy," which are described variously as Bali, as Gaza (Hausa, i.e., Muslims), as mounted spearmen, or as mounted bowmen.[17] The nineteenth century was a time of displacements occasioned by the jihad in Adamawa, declared in 1809, and the extension of the predatory slaving frontier. It was a time when various chiefs were raiding each other for slaves both as clients and commodities and in search of empire. The incorporation of diverse peoples into the incipient state of Nso' resulted both from conquest and from smaller polities consenting to tributary status in exchange for protection.

After establishing their capital at Kovvifəm, the Nso' were subjected to a number of raids, two of which were said to be devastating enough to cause first a temporary and then a permanent abandonment of the royal headquarters.[18] Eighteen *afon* are said to be buried at Kovvifəm in 13 graves, some allegedly double ones. One of these, called Fon Saŋgo, according to some, temporarily transferred the capital of Nso' to Taavisa to escape early raids, and is buried there. While at Taavisa, according to one version, the *fon* and all his male children were killed, and for a short time Nso' remained without a *fon*.[19] According to another, the successor returned to Kovvifəm and died there. It is said that after the return to Kovvifəm from Taavisa, Faay Ndzəəndzəv, an important settler from Nsungli, found a prince who had been enslaved in Nsungli country and redeemed him from slavery. He took the young prince to his compound and cared for him and eventually had him enstooled (enthroned) there, since the palace had been destroyed earlier by Banyo raiders.[20] Because of this act of patriotism, Ndzəəndzəv became *ŋga' wiy*, the great one or the great councillor, the first among the seven *vibay* who act as councillors to the Fon Nso', superseding the former primus. He and his lineage, by virtue of his generosity and an affinal link to the Fon Nso', became *duy kikeŋ*, an assimilated distant member of the royal lineage. The founding legend thus justifies Ndzəəndzəv's considerable power vis-à-vis the *fon*. Ndzəəndzəv was not a central member of the royal lineage. Neither is his lineage in a position to provide the mother of the *fon*, a privilege reserved, as we shall see, for the *mtaar*. As head of *yeeŋweroŋ* and in his ability to control access to the *fon*, he became second in command in Nso' providing an important check on the central power of the paramount ruler.

The founding legend also serves as justification for the special position and special privileges accorded the *mtaar*, the "people of the Nso' Earth." In exchange for pledging fealty to the Fon Nso' and removing themselves from direct participation in Nso' palace societies, the *mtaar* were given a variety of concessions. As first settlers, the *mtaar* were left as stewards of the land, which associated them closely with the moral virtues of the ancestors (most of the land north of Kimbo' today is still controlled by *mtaar* lineage heads). Apart from the *fon*, they alone had the right to keep and display the pelts of leopards. More overtly political, the *mtaar* lineage heads had the right to "hold the *fon* to ransom" and to reprove him publicly if he went against their interests. They also had the freedom from the duty to give their sons to the palace as stewards and retainers and their daughters as wives to the *fon*. Yet only *mtaar* were supposed to marry the daughters of the *fon*, and the *fon* had to have a mother of *mtaar* status. When the *fon* wanted a *mtaar* woman as a wife, he had to negotiate with her lineage head. Collectively, the *mtaar* lineage heads represented the father of the *fon*'s mother (*taaryiy ke fon*). He was, in a sense, their son, and had to listen to what they said and take it seriously. The *mtaar*, through these concessions and especially through marriage alliances with the palace, were coopted into the center of traditional politics even while they remained aloof from the machinations of day-to-day governance. The *mtaar*, or commoner titleholders, provided an important check on the power of the *fon* and represented an important force in Nso' traditional government. They spoke of themselves as "scorning to cover their heads" (i.e., with hoods and masks, like the members of *ŋweroŋ*). The *mtaar* "third force" in Nso' government was weakened by colonial and postcolonial rule, and their weekly club meeting with the *fon* (*ŋgwa-kibu'*) became politically less important.[21] Although they continued to control most of the land north of Kimbo' and some in the far south, the *mtaar* power in Nso' traditional government began to be attenuated gradually with the arrival of the Germans, to whom their political roles remained mysterious or even invisible. The demands of the Germans for carriers, labor, and eventually taxes, inevitably strengthened the executive at the expense of the consultative institutions centered on the palace.

The myth of Ŋgonso', who founded a new nation only to have her son accede to the throne, suggests something of the paradoxical relationship between women and power. Women have clearly had significant power in Nso'. They are said to be "like God" (*nyuy*). They have had important political roles in the palace. Women have been recognized as the backbone of the country by virtue of their work in the fields and their role as wives and mothers of the lineage. Their creative power is essential for the reproduction—social as well as biological—of Nso' society, and women figure prominently in most important Nso' rituals of regeneration. Yet women have been excluded from many if not most important decision-making bodies. They have not been allowed to see the inside of the secret society lodges or even the most powerful masks of these societies. They have not had access to the most important ritual knowledge. Women's secret societies have never carried the political or religious clout that men's societies do. While women can and have organized to protest male acts which go against their interests, women's palace societies most often have had male "patrons." Women's political power, while considerable, has been dependent on the recognition of their role as producers and reproducers—the "mothers of the country." Women create society, but society should be ruled by men.

From 1820 to 1906: Consolidating Power and Nso' Hegemony

By the 1820's Fon Sǝm I, Fomukoŋ, a key figure in Nso' state formation, had moved his capital to Kimbo'. By this time the foundation had been laid for a highly centralized chiefdom or incipient state, a foundation supported by the particular interests of those in power. This group in power was able to point to the legitimacy of the Rifǝm founding legend and thus to tradition in order to justify its position. This is what Raymond Williams talks about as an intentionally selective version of a shaping past.[22]

Gramsci makes a distinction between "rule" and "hegemony."[23] Rule is expressed directly in political forms and in times of crisis by direct or effective coercion. The more typical or "normal" situation is hegemony, a complex interlocking of political, social, and cultural forces. Most hierarchic systems combine the two to some degree to legitimate and reproduce the power of the dominant group. Gramsci was writing about the development of the bourgeois state in the West, where "civil" and "political" could be separated as distinct. In a state like precolonial Nso', although there existed competing ritual ideals, civil society and political society were almost coterminous and were supported by religious and ritual ideals. Here hegemony and doxa[24] overlapped significantly. This meant that the fit between the objective and subjective structures which constitute meaning and reality was more immediate, and the world as presented by the dominant group appeared as self-evident. Both were central to the structures of power and must be explained.

Raymond Williams suggests that cultural activity is both tradition and practice: "Hegemony is tradition and practice translated and constituted through cultural activity."[25] What becomes decisive in creating a hegemonic discourse[26] then is not only the conscious system of beliefs and values and ideas, but the whole lived social process as organized by specific practices and dominant meanings and values. An important aspect of hegemony is the ability to absorb, transform, and turn a number of discursive themes into an overarching discourse which supports the dominant group. In Nso', the structures of practice and of meaning have reproduced male status and privilege by assigning them to the realm of doxa, of the self-evident, of that which goes without saying, in which they appear as natural rights, underwritten by strong ritual sanctions and taboos. In precolonial

Nso' these practices and beliefs linked political and cosmological beliefs and supported a hierarchy in which titled men took precedence and controlled the dominant discourse.

Earlier *afon* and their titled men took various steps to reinforce the discursive power of the *fon* and the palace-based associations while undermining the power of the lineage heads.[27] Several of the methods and institutions used to accomplish this goal were particularly effective. *Manjoŋ*, warriors' and hunters' societies, which were open to all males over the age of 18 were brought under the control of the palace and cut horizontally across lineage lines, much like the age grades prevalent in other parts of Africa.[28] Ties of affinity with the palace were widely extended. It has been suggested that the Fon Nso' in the nineteenth century had a great number of wives (some accounts mention over 300 women in the palace), linking him affinally to most of the lineages in Nso' as well as to all the important Grassfields chiefdoms.[29] The *afon* in the nineteenth century instituted a far-reaching system of recruitment of retainers to the palace. While all the major Grassfields chiefdoms had palace retainers and stewards, in Nso' the social category of retainer (*nshiylav*) not only extended to those actually serving in the palace, but also included all men liable for recruitment to the palace service whether or not they were actually called. Finally, and critically, a palace-based title system was instituted, a title system which became a center as well as a source of power and prestige and in which membership became relatively open.[30] Most important lineage titles were hereditary. However, ambitious men could obtain titles and membership in title societies by outstanding feats in warfare or service to the *fon* and by making payments and prestations to the palace. Titles and membership in title societies became important pieces of symbolic capital[31] and objects of accumulation. Titles worked both to incorporate ambitious and powerful men into the central government and to facilitate the personal careers of these men.

It is important to point out here that, in most West African precolonial societies, status and wealth depended on accumulating dependents and followers. The avenue to wealth and power in Nso', as in most of sub-Saharan Africa, was centered on control over people and their productive and reproductive labor rather than on direct ownership of land and the means of production, as was the case in Europe and much of Asia.[32] Therefore, ties of marriage and networks of affinity, of kinship, and of clientage were historically, and remain today, at the center of strategies of accumulation and power. Where such direct control over people and networks is the means to power, it is important that one's right to exercise control be legitimated, displayed, a matter of public record. This focussed the political economy of prestige and power in Nso' on the accumulation of symbolic capital, or symbolic resources, one representation of which was the right to own and display the symbols and practices of title and rank, a right which was, with few exceptions, an exclusively male one. Various tales show the increasing control of the palace over "things" (mostly sacra, such as gongs, specific calabashes, pots, and carved figures, as well as symbolic privileges), the "things of the fathers" becoming *ambuume*, privileges controlled from the center and granted by "the *fon*", that is, the existing palace society. This pattern of accumulation of power, essentially born in the first half of the nineteenth century, still has resonance today.

These methods of incorporation facilitated the establishment of regional hegemony by creating large and diffuse networks of people involved with and loyal to the palace and the Fon Nso'. The dominant group in Nso' was able to take ideas, beliefs, and cultural practices from its various constituencies, absorb some, transform others, and turn all of these into a hegemonic discourse. This process was facilitated and symbolized by the imposition and spread of the Lam Nso' language, which quickly replaced, in most contexts, the diverse languages of conquered and incorporated peoples. Nso' hegemony was reinforced, too, by the religious and ritual connotations of political office.

The Coercive Aspect of Nso' Consolidation

The consolidation of power in Nso' was at times effected through direct conquest or coercion as well as by playing to fears of outside aggression. This last method was not difficult in the nineteenth-century context of ongoing kidnapping and slaving expeditions. The need for constant vigilance against foreign power was represented in the belief that the *fon* and his chief councillors possess superior supernatural powers which make it possible for them to protect Nso' citizens against foreign witchcraft— flying night witches (*arim*) and sorcerers of the night.[33] The *fon* alone has the ability to transform himself into a lion, and he confers the ability to be transformed into a leopard on the most important councillors and men of title. Together the lion and his leopard companions prowl the borders of Nso' in the nighttime vigil of defending the country from evil.[34]

The coercive aspect of Nso' consolidation is commemorated in the stories and legends of subjugated villages. Some villages, such as Ŋkar, were first defeated in battle before becoming tributary to Nso'. Others, either seeking refuge from slaving expeditions or realizing their weak position in the face of Nso' imperialism, "voluntarily" became tributary. All subjugated villages were required to pay tribute (*nshwi*) in various forms to the Fon Nso' and to recognize him as superior. Subjugated villages were required, as part of initial *nshwi* payments, to give boys to the palace as retainers and girls to the Fon Nso' as wives. The imposition of Lam Nso' as the dominant language throughout the chiefdom became a significant sign of the status of subjugated groups as subjects of the paramount *fon*. In German accounts and photographs of the skulls of warriors of defeated villages hung up in front of the Nso' warriors' lodges (*manjoŋ*), we find a more immediate and grim reminder of the coercive aspect of Nso' imperialism.

By the nineteenth century a number of transgressions became designated as treasonous, and thus capital offenses, or else designated as offenses commanding heavy fines requiring payment in persons. These lend some insight into the power held by the *fon* and the palace, a power which became more coercive as Nso' became more centralized and as the political power of the *fon* and the palace societies increasingly took precedence over that of the lineage heads.[35] Centralized power was reinforced by the association of legitimate authority, based on descent (and the ancestors), with the *fon* and his titled men and by the belief in an alternative form of power based on extraordinary talents which are dangerous and must be kept in check. The job of keeping these dangerous talents in check fell primarily on the regulatory society, *ŋweroŋ*. *Ŋweroŋ* functioned as the repressive arm of the palace, carrying out discipline and punishment and overseeing executions. By doing so, the regulatory society distanced the *fon* from the most brutal manifestations of power and thus from the contamination and pollution which were thought to accompany repressive power.[36]

It has been suggested from comparative studies undertaken in the rest of the Grassfields that there were links between a growing involvement in regional and long-distance trade in the second half of the nineteenth century and the social correlates of this trade, the accumulation of wealth and women, and the ambivalence surrounding evil power and wealth on the one hand and socially approved power and wealth on the other.[37] These ambiguities became particularly apparent in the incipient states such as Nso', in which power was becoming more highly centralized and longdistance trade was controlled by, and often a prerogative of, the palace. As noted above, in Nso', as was true of the other Grassfield chiefdoms,[38] there were various ways in which the *fon* was removed from the contaminations of power. He was also restrained from absolute control by a number of checks on the exercise of his power, and was expected to have an "open hand," that is, to redistribute his wealth freely. "The *fon* has everything, the *fon* is a poor man," say the Nso'. The axiom that the maintenance of privilege must include a high degree of redistribution has been an integral part of the Nso' political discourse.

Nevertheless, as Mauss first made clear, gift giving is seldom a disinterested act; it figures inevitably in power relationships.[39] By the end of the nineteenth century, the Fon Nso' had gathered onto himself and the palace societies an increasingly large share of coercive power. In this context an act against the *fon* became synonymous with an abomination committed against the people of Nso'. For example, adultery with the *fon*'s numerous wives was considered to be a capital offense and an abomination. Recall that the Fon Nso' was said by some to have had over 300 wives in the nineteenth century. Most men did not become *fon* until well into their 40s, if not later. Discounting the women who were not of appropriate age for sexual activity, the *fon* was still left with an extremely large number of women for whom he was sexually responsible. Even though sexual activity with men other than the *fon* was seen as an abomination, not to mention an act of treason, it is obvious that illicit sex would have occurred. Some of it, perhaps more than is admitted, was presumably overlooked or undetected. But it was a risky business, and if caught, both the *fon*'s wife and her lover were forced to hang themselves.[40] Obviously, this accusation could be a potent political tool.

Equally ambiguous was the crime of bewitching the *fon*. This was a capital and treasonous offense, which seems to provide easy opportunities for one's enemies to make false accusations, much like the marijuana laws in the United States today. Kaberry and Chilver's fieldnotes are full of stories of men of substance, *asheey* and *afaay*, who were executed for witchcraft against the *fon*. Reading between the lines, we can see that most of these executions—in which the convicted man was "tied" (a rope put around his neck and attached to a tree), forced to pledge loyalty to the *fon*, and then forced to hang himself—were clearly political in nature. Finally, a number of lesser crimes, including having a "strong head" (being obstinate) could result in people, men, and women alike, being sold into slavery.

Consensus and Orthodoxy in Nso' Consolidation

The founding of this large and relatively stable chiefdom could not have been accomplished solely by conquest and coercion and by playing to fears of foreign invasion and witchcraft accusations. It is important, some would argue most important, that hegemony requires consent and consensus about the legitimacy of the dominant discourse. There was wide consensus that the Fon Nso' and his titled men possessed legitimate power. The *fon* was seen to embody the highest religious as well as political values and thus power of the highest order, royal *səm* (*səm vifone*). He embodied these by virtue of his relationship to his ancestors, through whom he gained access to the most powerful (and most moral) authority. Here it becomes crucial to understand the meanings associated with the concept of *səm*, or innate power, in Nso'.

The concept of power in Nso' is morally ambiguous and, as we have seen, can roughly be divided into two categories: legitimate authority based on descent and the ancestors, and power based on extraordinary talents which are dangerous and must be kept in check. *Səm* was seen in the past as inherited in the uterine line; it resides in the stomach and can be used for either good or evil. Much of the ambiguity of power lies in the fact that both the ways in which it is used and the effects it has depend on a person's intentions. *Səm* gives power to its owner, which, if domesticated or socialized, is a positive force used for the good of the individual and the community. All *afon* are believed to possess *səm* and to use it for the good of all Nso'. But if a person who possesses *səm* has hostile intentions, its possession can lead this person to practice evil sorcery and even to kill for personal gain. Thus, *səm* is basically of two kinds, *səm afon*, used for the common good, and *səm arim*, used to do evil. Persons with *səm arim* are said to be possessed by ambition and selfishness, to "eat" or "gnaw" (*kfər*) their relatives. In its undomesticated or unsocialized form, power is always opposed to the moral order.

People in Nso' who are wealthy are seen to attract, rather than seek, wealth objects. Those who attract wealth are felt to be deeply ambiguous in their intentions, for wealth attraction is associated with *səm*. Wealth is believed to attach itself to power and high status. Those who possess *səm* are seen as having the potential of "opposing their bellies" to the *fon*. It is believed that the most powerful and wealthy men must have their power socialized or domesticated, harnessed for the public good. One way of socializing *səm*, beginning in the nineteenth century, has been through induction into *yee ŋweroŋ*, the powerful inner lodge of *ŋweroŋ*. Another has been to bring powerful men into positions of trust in the palace as important councillors to the *fon*.

There is a further notion associated with *səm* which lends insight into the Nso' belief in the ambiguous nature of power. This is the concept of *kibay*.[41] The *kibay* associated with *səm* is also said to reside in the belly, or sometimes in the liver. It, too, is ambiguous, and in its negative form is parasitic, survives death, and may take refuge in a convenient host animal, in particular small snakes, toads, and chameleons. *Kibay* of this kind is associated with both *səm* and *virim*, which is also known as bad *kibay*. The difference between good *səm* and *virim*, or bad *kibay*, is said to be the difference between power used purely for individual advancement and private ambition and power used for publicly approved purposes which involve some amount of redistribution. The idea of *səm* as ambiguous has been reinforced by a widespread belief in witchcraft and sorcery and by the belief that humans, through their actions, can have major effects on the world, including effects on the fate and fortunes of their fellows. It has been believed that the ways in which *səm* is used— for good or for evil—depend to a great extent on the actions and intentions of those who possess it.

These notions of power become important when looking at the various ways in which the *afon* of Nso' consolidated their power both to centralize that power and to achieve hegemony throughout the chiefdom. As noted earlier an important aspect of hegemony is the ability to absorb, transform, and turn a number of discursive themes into a hegemonic discourse with which people will identify. By incorporating leaders of conquered and tributary peoples into positions of power in Nso' central government, the *fon* was able to secure their loyalty and simultaneously to control or domesticate their *səm*.

The maintenance of centralized power, the incorporation of diverse peoples into a common polity, and the spread of Nso' hegemony thus involved a high degree of incorporation by consent. Hegemony was facilitated by coopting people into the center and by successfully spreading Nso' culture in a number of ways. Conquered peoples were assimilated rather than enslaved (as was the custom in the neighboring kingdom of Bamum), and their cultural practices were incorporated into the core culture of Nso'. According the subchiefs the title *fon* and leaving them to manage things at home as long as they pledged fealty and gave tribute to the Fon Nso' as their superior worked to ensure their loyalty to Nso'.[42] As we have seen, the methods by which people were incorporated into the center and the extension of the tendrils of power from the palace outward were various and, in combination, ensured centralized control of the dominant discourse and its dissemination throughout the chiefdom.

It is important to point out that hegemonic power in Nso' did not simply impose itself from a central point downward by suppressing the dominated groups' desire and conscious will. Instead, it worked diffusely, from a number of particular points throughout the society. As we've seen Raymond Williams argue, hegemony is best seen as "a lived system of meanings and values—constitutive and constituting—which as they are experienced as practices appear as reciprocally confirming."[43] This system of meanings and values, as Bourdieu points out, is the product of a double structuring.[44] The first meaning of this double structuring is an objective one. The world is objectively structured by outward appearances, so that properties assigned to particular persons correlate with social position. Nso' titleholders "owned" the privileges and practices associated with the status of their office and had the right to display publicly the symbols which proclaimed that status. They had access to specialized ritual knowledge, knowledge not available to ordinary men (and certainly not to women), knowledge which gave them public authority and power in the chiefdom. Titleholders had more wives than ordinary men. The symbols of their office included elaborate regalia, dress, and caps. They were given the right to control access to land. Forms of greeting and etiquette surrounded the personas of titled men. The right to wear (or remove) particular caps, the right to greet the *fon* publicly (*bun fon*) and drink with him, the right to be called by one's title rather than one's given name, and the acquisition of various forms of ritual knowledge all supported the dominant hierarchy and privileged the position of male titleholders. Some of these privileges were rather arcane, such as the right of the *fon*'s councillors to cork their calabashes of palm wine with a fig leaf. Others, such as keeping one's wives naked, which was the privilege of the *fon* and his councillors, were directly symbolic of control over women. All these practices were gendered in ways which excluded women and reinforced their position as ritually and politically subordinate. Women were (and still are) not allowed to venture inside the clubhouses of the secret societies, much less join them. Women (and ordinary men) were not allowed to see the "things of *ŋweroŋ* or of *ŋgiri*"—the sacra, medicines (*shiv*), musical instruments, gongs, and masks. Most women were forbidden access to all but the most mundane ritual knowledge. Nso' practices objectively structured the social world in ways which made the gendered hierarchic relationships patently and publicly obvious, reproducing them again and again in daily social intercourse.

The second meaning of this double structuring of the world in precolonial Nso' is a subjective one. The world was structured not only by practices, through human action, but also by the schemes of perception about these practices, especially those perceptions inscribed in language itself. The imposition and spread of the Lam Nso' language throughout Nso' created a subjective structuring which expressed the values and categories of a dominant group. Language and experience are not only dialectically related; they are also viewed by some theorists, such as Raymond Williams, as almost coterminous. It is language which allows members of society to grasp social reality and reproduce it. Therefore language, consciousness, and human experience are all mutually constitutive, "an active social presence in the world."[45] Nso' classificatory schemes, including social categories and political institutions, were adopted by the subchiefdoms.[46] As these classificatory schemes were disseminated throughout the chiefdom, the efficacy of Nso' rituals and taboos, the power of titles and of the practices associated with these, were all reinforced by moral appeals to the ancestors and to the earth in which they were thought to reside. The right to make these appeals was owned by the *fon* and titled men, thus reinforcing their place in the formal hierarchy. In combination, the structure of practice and the structure of meaning created and reproduced a unique Nso'

identity, and a reality in which a gendered hierarchy privileged male titleholders at the same time that it assigned to women the task of producing
food and reproducing children.

Thus, through a variety of cultural practices and political strategies,
the titled men of Nso' were markedly successful in establishing a regional
hegemony that exists up to the present day.[47] Consensus could be created
and maintained not only because cultural beliefs and the hierarchy within
which these were embedded remained, if not always within the doxa, at
least firmly orthodox, but also because these were constantly reinforced by
the practices, symbols, and language of everyday life. Within the Nso' political economy of prestige, symbolic capital was the primary object of
accumulation. Emphasis was on turning material wealth into symbolic
capital and using this symbolic capital to gain access to productive and
reproductive labor and thus to more material wealth. Ultimately both symbolic and material capital could be turned into power, including symbolic
power, that is, the power to impose the categories of social reality, a major
dimension of political power. Important here is the ability to determine the
qualities which define male and female as gender categories and to control
the practices associated with these.

Gender, Power, and Hierarchy

The accumulation of symbolic capital in precolonial Nso' was not of
course merely symbolic. It supported complex strategies by which men
gained control over production and reproduction and over regional and
interregional alliances and trade networks. Titled men in Nso' had a number of rights and obligations vis-à-vis their dependents. They had the right
to control access to land. They had the right to demand specific amounts of
labor from both women and young men. They inherited all the wealth of
the lineage and had the responsibility of guarding its patrimony. It is important that they had the right to arrange the marriages of the women of their
respective lineages, and could therefore build up large networks of affinity
and power through their control of women and thus their control of production and reproduction as a basis of power.[48] The *fon*, for instance, had
the right to give away in marriage not only his own daughters and grand-
daughters but also the firstborn among his great-granddaughters and
great-great-granddaughters. Lineage heads controlled, with few exceptions, the marriage of all female dependents and received the bulk of the
services and gifts which husbands were required to give to their affines
during the course of their marriage. It was through control of women's
reproductive and productive labor, and through alliances set up through
affinal arrangements, that men wielded power. Titleholders thus con-

trolled a variety of practices which confirmed and reproduced their power. They were trustees of lineage land and properties, the wife-givers for the groups as a whole, the principal officiants of ancestral cults, and members of title societies in the palace, which in turn confirmed them in office.

The *fon* and the lineage heads also maintained power through their control of access to land. Land was not scarce in precolonial Nso', and supposedly people could have left the social boundaries of Nso' society and moved away to farm, but then they would have been just that: outside the social boundaries and the protection of Nso' society, not an inconsequential and patently undesirable move, given the level of insecurity and slave raiding along those borders not covered by pacts in the nineteenth-century Grassfields. Customary tenure rules reflected the social order. The Fon Nso' had titular rights of ownership, an expression of his political power and his position as a symbol of Nso' unity. Actual management of land was in the hands of a number of lineage heads, the *ataaŋgven* ("the fathers who own the fields"). Their right to control access to land was a symbol of their political and religious position of lineage leadership. It was reinforced by their ritual obligations to the land, by the significance of the Earth as the place of the ancestors and thus the repository of lineage values, and by the related meaning of stewardship of the land as a symbol of political and religious leadership. All Nso' people under customary tenure arrangements were guaranteed access to farmland by right of citizenship as long as they abided by the rules of customary law, meaning the rules of the *fon* and the lineage heads. Although women had guaranteed usufructuary rights to land, men's actual ownership of the land was represented in a number of ways. When a new house was built, the lineage head marked out the foundation with a hoe, symbolizing his right to control access to all Nso' land. When a new bride first went to her farm, her husband first "cut the earth" (*ŋgar nsay*) with a hoe, symbolizing the fact that it is his land, not hers, on which she is farming. Hoes in Nso' symbolize women given in marriage, and a women is supposed to farm with a hoe given to her by her husband.

The division of labor in precolonial Nso' was strictly gendered, allocating women's labor to food farming and men's to hunting, warfare, and trade. Women were not involved in trade; in fact, there was extreme prejudice against women trafficking in the marketplace or handling sums of money, a prejudice that lasted well into the colonial period. Women grew the food crops and were expected to provide the necessities of daily life from their farms. Women's productive labor freed men to participate in trading networks. Female reproductive labor increased the size of the household and thus the status and the labor force of the male head. Any surplus value that women produced over and above what was required for the household and petty barter was in the hands of men, who retained all the profits from its sale. Regional trade was not based substantially on sale of food, although grains were traded and exchanged for palm oil. Instead it consisted mostly of a number of items owned and controlled by men: kola, honey, small livestock, handicrafts and iron hoes, and palm wine. Success in regional trade gave men access to the more lucrative state-controlled, long-distance trade in ivory and slaves. This success depended on the ability of the compound head to organize the labor of his dependents in production and in trading ventures as porters and middlemen. It has been suggested that the highland chiefdoms like Nso' had a trading advantage and were able to grow in power at the expense of the more low-lying palm oil–producing polities. Palm oil requires both male and female labor for processing for trade, whereas in the highlands female labor produced all the necessities plus a surplus, thus freeing male labor for warfare, crafts, and trade.[49]

Men could parlay the profits so gained in regional trade into wealth and status in several ways. They could marry more women and increase the size of their household (and work force). They could join title societies and buy the "*fon*'s market bag" (*kibam ke waay ke fon*), which gave them entry into the trade in slaves and ivory.[50] Lineage heads also owned all tree crops, and thus controlled the extensive kola trade for which Nso' was famous. This long-distance trade provided new kinds of symbolic capital in the form of European goods: cloth, beads, dane guns, and gunpowder. Guns became the royal reward for bravery. A man bringing war captives to the palace might be given a gun or two. Or he might be invited to make payments to the palace to secure membership in a titled society.

Women's productive and reproductive labor thus supported a system of power and wealth controlled by men. Women created a work force and a surplus. That surplus could be invested in regional trade. The profits from both regional and long-distance trade could be invested in increasing the household size, thus both elevating the status of the compound head and increasing the surplus available to him. Ultimately, in combination, symbolic and material capital could be transformed into what Bourdieu has called symbolic power, that is, the power to impose one's view of reality on the social world and become the spokesman for the group.[51]

We cannot ascertain exactly how precolonial Nso' imagined its collective identity or how gender categories came to be constituted in particular ways. We can assume that the construction of gender roles was never unproblematic or anything more than provisional, with meanings attached which reflected struggles between various social actors. Although the hierarchy was clearly gendered, women were not without power either singly or as a group. Women grew all the food and had control over the household food supply in ways which constantly demonstrated men's day-today dependence on their wives' work and good nature and forced them to acknowledge women as the "backbone of the country." Women's political power, although not as consistently public as that of men, was not insignificant. The exchange of women as wives between chiefdoms was an integral feature of nineteenth-century Grassfield diplomacy.[52] Nso' royal women were married into other large chiefdoms such as Kom, Bali, and Bafut, as well as into the related chiefdoms of Oku and Mbiame. The Fon Nso', in addition, received women as royal wives from tributary chiefs. Daughters and sisters of the Fon Nso' married to other Grassfield *afon* acted as important intermediaries and resident ambassadors, even as spies. The *fon*'s representatives in other chiefdoms consisted almost entirely of royal wives, either his sisters or his daughters. A number of women's organizations, such as *coŋ*, gave women a forum and a voice in the public domain. Women could and did assemble to reprove the *fon*.[53] Although we have no records of women's political protests organized in the precolonial era, it seems probable, on the basis of evidence of such protests in the 1950s and 1960s, that women's groups had long possessed the right to protest and made use of that right.

Some women had important political roles in the palace. They organized and ran much of the infrastructure and were the heads (*ayee sum*) of the "houses" (*lavsi*), or ranked social groups, within the palace women's quarters. An inner circle of older wives decided who was going to cook for and sleep with the *fon*, not an insignificant task when the Fon Nso' had many wives. Women were important witnesses in case of adultery, which were, as previously mentioned, an act of treason and a capital offense. Some women, in particular the *yeewoŋ*, a princess, had crucial ritual functions, especially at the death and installation of the *fon*. The queen mother, or *yeefon*, real or surrogate, was important enough to warrant a state funeral when she died. One of the "things of state" of Nso' was the royal hoe, symbolizing the importance of women's productive work.

Wives of the *fon* and of important councillors had important decision-making powers in regard to organizing farmwork on the *fon*'s mensal farm, or *sum fon*. There were a number of women who also had influential positions within the palace, the *yeefon* and *yeewoŋ* being only two among several women in positions of power. Women married to the *fon* brought honor to their families and could expect support from them. Royal wives, or *vikiy nto'* (sing. *wiiy nto'*), forged integral intrachiefdom alliances with most of the lineages and all the subchiefdoms within Nso'. Their sons often assumed political positions and even became important lineage heads in their mother's natal village, where they were frequently sent to live as young children to be protected from harm.

The wives of the *fon* commonly participated in recruiting girls to the palace. If a girl selected was not suitable for marriage to the *fon*, the wife who recruited her could marry her to an *nshiylav*, a page in the palace or in *ŋweroŋ*. The children born of this marriage belonged, not to the father, but to the *wiiy nto'*, or *fon*'s wife who recruited the mother to the palace. Clearly women were critical to both inter- and intrachiefdom alliances, and were far more than pawns in a political game or gift exchanges between men. When the palace was the center of political intrigue, women were important political actors.

The Early Twentieth Century and the Arrival of the Germans

When one of Səm I's successors was extending dominance over the northeastern highlands of the Grassfields, German expeditions were laying claims which would soon challenge and then eclipse that dominance. In 1884, Cameroon became a German protectorate (*Schutzgebiet*). Five years later the first German expedition reached the Grassfields, and by 1902 a German military station had been established at Bamenda. The German expedition reached Nso' in January of 1902 on its way to Adamawa. It was not unexpected. The Nso' had been warned by the Babungo to the south that they would be "well-advised to hide guns, spears and cutlasses and that it would be unwise to fight the Germans."[54]

The Nso' referred to this German expedition as that of the *vijin*, or brides, because it required such extensive, conspicuous, and depleting expenditures. The Germans stayed for two days, and although they were a great curiosity and a subject of ongoing discussion, they clearly did not win the approval or the hearts of the Nso', who later remembered them as "grim and unfriendly people who were difficult to please."[55] The Nso' were struck by the German's hairiness, their long noses, and their apparently soft skin and described them as looking like spirits. Even worse, the Germans looked down on the Nso', who it will be remembered, were renowned warriors, a proud and even haughty people who thought quite a bit of themselves. The Germans did not make presents and therefore were said to have treated the Nso' "like monkeys."[56]

While the Nso' were initially diplomatic and even cordial to the Germans, relations quickly deteriorated, and by 1905 the Nso' were referred to in official German publications as uncooperative. In 1902 a German party en route to Banyo burned down the palace at Kimbo' and claimed to have inflicted casualties. In 1905 the Germans fought the western area of Nso' and in April-June 1906 mounted a full-scale punitive expedition accompanied by Bamum auxiliaries. They killed more than 800 people and took over 1500 prisoners. Much to the anguish and surprise of the Nso', the German forces not only tortured prisoners and arbitrarily killed men, but were also accused of killing women and children, which the Nso' found shocking.

In early June 1906, a group of important *mtaar* (*wir mtaar*) lineage heads confronted Səm II, Fon Nso', in the deep ravine at Dzeng, where he and some his wives were in hiding. By this time Səm was a man in his middle years, rather stout and suffering from gout. It must have been an uncomfortable situation for the *fon*, physically as well as psychologically. Reporting the Nso' casualties—"The seed of men (*ŋgooy wir*) is finishing"—the *wir mtaar* urged the *fon* to surrender to the Germans and restore peace and order in Nso', reminding him that he was "held to be Fon, not to expend people. A Fon exists because of people, if there are no people, there is no Fonship."[57] Səm replied that he had heard. Near the beginning of his reign, he had become dominant in the region by winning a major victory over the powerful Bamum in the 1880s. He had never before had to "give anything with [his] right hand" (he had never surrendered).[58] But he and his people were psychologically and physically defeated. The Germans had machine guns, and were encouraged to be particularly punitive by their comrades-in-arms and Səm's old enemy, the Bamum. On June 5, 1906, Səm surrendered to the Germans. He agreed to pay penalties, supply men for corvée labor on the coast, and provide labor to build roads to the south and west. In return for their aid in defeating Nso', the Germans returned the head of the former *fon*, *Nsa'ŋgu*, to Fon Njoya of Bamum and decorated him. An era had passed.

Themes of the Colonial Era

The colonial era and the national movements which preceded the formation of the modern state of Cameroon have been well described by a number of writers, European and Cameroonian alike.[59] This section is meant to be an epilogue to the precolonial era, a cursory overview of the important historical themes which were reproduced or transformed in the creation of the present relationship between Nso' and the national state.

The Germans were interested in Nso', as in the Grassfields in general, primarily as a source of labor for coastal plantations.[60] Elderly people in Nso' in the late 1970s still recalled that "the Germans took people to carry their boxes and you never saw those people again."[61] Before 1909 at least 2000 Nso' men were conscripted through the *fon* for work in the southwest and on the coast. Palace stewards announced the levy in the marketplace, and *ŋweroŋ* and *manjoŋ* were to round up and assemble the men. Although these obligations did not increase his popularity, corvée labor and colonial taxes collected through the Fon Nso' reinforced his power as long as he acted in accordance with colonial policy. After 1909, it became explicit German doctrine to reinforce the local power of the paramount *fon*. He and his titled men were left in charge of most legal cases. Customary law (or at least the *fon*'s version of it) was administered and protected by German colonial law and administration (the *Schutzbrief*). Although defeated in battle, the regional political and cultural hegemony of the Fon Nso' was supported first by the German policies and then, after 1915, by the policies of the British administration, which, by the 1920s, elaborated its policy of delegated administration into a local version of indirect rule.[62] The colonial administration in its official policies supported the political authority of the Fon Nso' and reinforced male power by ignoring or being blind to the political roles played by women.

Boys, not girls, were educated in the government and mission schools to assume roles first in colonial and later in national political institutions. Wage labor and cash crops were male-dominated prestige activities. The spread of coffee in the 1940s gave men a source of cash income and integrated them into the public sphere of the monetary economy. Women continued to grow all food crops and remained responsible for provisioning the household. They did not engage in substantial trading in the marketplace. It was continued to be viewed as unseemly for women to engage in trade, and many men in the 1950s worried that, if women were to become traders and have access to money, they would become too attracted to the things money could buy and become "harlots." Men assumed responsibility for the purchase of the few goods which required cash. Women's food farming became somewhat analogous to housework in the United States. Clearly the work was necessary, but women's labor was now largely invisible as a prestige social good, and in fact female labor was no longer defined as work. Women's labor now freed men to participate in work in the cash economy. The boundaries between public and private domains, always shifting and contested in precolonial Nso', became more static and rigid within the colonial (and later the national) state. Women became associated with the domestic, private sphere, while men now occupied virtually all public roles and occupations.

While their political role was ignored and their economic role was given a different cast with the introduction of cash crops and wage labor, female institutions which gave women a public voice remained. As more land was taken up with cash crops and the growing herds of the cattle of the Fulani, who shared the region with the Nso', women were forced to begin to farm far away from their compounds. These farms were soon "disturbed" by cattle and goats. Women, angered by this threat to their crops and their livelihood, began to protest. Chilver records a protest in the late 1950s by the women of Din, a small Nso' village.[63] The women of Din, enraged by the crop damage caused by cattle, marched to the compound of the owner of the offending cows and demanded that he leave. When he refused, the women destroyed his compound of five houses and cursed him. When the man, a Fulani grazier, called the police, the women demanded to be taken to the Fon Nso'. They marched into the palace, escorted by the police. Most of the women were bare to the waist, in ragged cloths, covered in leaves, bearing staves, their faces daubed with ash and white clay, which they described as a metaphor of death. Their children were with them. The women demanded, and eventually won from the colonial administration, the removal of cattle-control assistants who had taken bribes from the Fulani.

It is clear that there have existed a number of traditional ways in which women collectively or through representatives can publicly and from a position of inviolability demand redress from men in authority. In the protest of Nso' women we see, not a denigration of men as such, but rather a denigration of the practices in which some men engaged that deprived women of customary control over areas they felt to be rightfully within the female domain of power.[64] But these protests were often unknown to the colonial officers and seldom reported, and although they continued to be attended to by the *fon* and local council in regard to farmer-grazier dissputes, they did not carry much political weight within the political structures of the departing colonial state and even less in the national state.

While the colonial administration supported the political power of the Fon Nso' in the short run, colonial officials instituted policies which undermined his dominant political position in the long run. From the first, the *fon* was forced to share his power with colonial institutions and officials. By encouraging mission education and introducing Native Authority schools as well as new and relatively lucrative occupations for young men, the colonial state set the stage for newly educated elite men to challenge the absolute authority of the Fon Nso' and his traditional government and to demand access to political power. But the new elites did so without questioning Nso' regional hegemony and, as we shall see, sought to appropriate the cultural symbols and practices which supported Nso' hierarchy. Rather than destroying the traditional male hierarchy, these new elites would instead use it to graft new relations of domination onto old hierarchic relationships.

After the Second World War, nationalist ferment in Nigeria spread to the Grassfields. Unsure exactly how to reconstitute their identity as a nation, the new nationalist elites in Nso' nevertheless were sure of two realities. First, they were educated not in the citadels of learning in France, but rather in Great Britain (later in Canada and the United States) or in the neighboring British-run universities of Nigeria and Ghana. This Anglophone identification was and has remained an important political factor in the creation of the modern state in Cameroon. And second, in the hearts and minds of the new elites, the Fon Nso' remained the legitimate ruler, nationalism notwithstanding, while attempts to replace the old structures of indirect rule with local government evoked little enthusiasm among them. Their nationalist identities were constructed in the colonial classrooms; however, the individual identifies of these educated Nso' men were constructed as Lam Nso' speakers, as citizens of Nso' with all the cultural practices this entailed. At no time and in no way did they eschew their primary identity with Nso'.

Pragmatically, the new educated elites needed the *fon* and the *fon* needed them, even within the context of nationalism and independence. The *fon*, not the new elites, controlled the popular vote for national and local office. The new elites were acutely aware of this and of the interdependence it created between them and the *fon*. The alliance between the *fon* and the new elites was often uneasy. Nevertheless, they were united by strong cultural ties as well as by need. The Fon Nso' did not have the education (or the inclination) to become personally involved with the national political process, and instead depended on the new elites to represent his interests.[65]

The Southern Cameroon parties, whose activities eventually led to the separation of the Southern Cameroons from Nigeria and to the ultimate formation of the United Republic of Cameroon, reunifying the Southern Cameroons with the former French Cameroons, were started and led mostly by Western-educated Cameroonians.[66] The new elites, at least a substantial number of them, increasingly realized that any political base in the Grassfields without the support of the *afon* would be impossible. In turn, the *afon* needed the new elites to interpret the new forms and structures of the national movement for the people in culturally acceptable ways, to represent the interests of the traditional rulers, and to carry out their orders within the new national structures.

It can be argued that the Fon Nso' and other *afon* in the Grassfields eventually lost the struggle for political control at the national level to the educated elite, especially after the initial federal structure was dismantled. However, these traditional rulers have remained a potent force in regional politics, and the new national government recognized this very early on. The Grassfield region is one of the most fertile and populous regions in the country, yet it has been ignored and, from the viewpoint of many "Graffi" people (the national term for people from the Grassfields), even marginalized by what they see as a Francophile national government. The infrastructure, started too late and never adequately developed by a British colonial government more interested in developing the coastal area for agriculture than the remoter Grassfields, deteriorated under postindependence governments—first the federal, then, upon unification, the Francophone national center in Yaounde.

Uneasy about potential unrest in the region, President Ahidjo recognized the strength of the traditional rulers and their value in keeping the countryside under control. In the 1960s, he affirmed this in a public speech, asserting that "independently of their [the chiefs'] sentimental value, they still constitute today and surely will tomorrow, by reason of the leadership which they give to the people, an instrument of action which the state cannot afford to do without at present."[67] Peace, security, and stability became the cornerstones of national rhetoric. But those in positions of national power realized from the start that state coercion would be effective only if the national state could locate these goals in regional identifies, and then coopt these identities into a national community.

While the national state was worrying about establishing a state culture and national hegemony, the Fon Nso' was equally interested in maintaining hegemony at home. In 1964 he emphasized the power of traditional legitimacy in a public and well-publicized joint pilgrimage to Kimi with the sultan of Bamum. In the mid-1960s, after independence, aware of the need to keep the new elite loyal to Nso' political institutions, the *fon* began to bestow titles on men who had become important in the national political economy. He then expanded access to titles through what came to amount to outright purchase.[68] Elite men were increasingly awarded titles for achievement in the modern sector, and many of them started to invest in titles and in membership in title societies to validate their local power base. Through adroit manipulation of the title system and by assuming leadership in Nso' traditional political institutions, new elite men were able to graft new relations of domination onto the existing power hierarchy.

Power, Gender, and the Postcolonial State

Within the modern state of Cameroon, legitimacy flows, not from identity with the national center, but rather from sharing in the moral virtues of communal life. When I was first in Nso' in 1979, people often asked me, "Who is your *fon*?" I would answer that we in the United States had a president, not a *fon*. They would reply, "We have a president too, but that is not the important thing. The important thing is your *fon*." I was living in Cambridge, Massachusetts, at the time, so I replied, "Well, I guess Tip O'Neill."

Political legitimacy in Nso' thus flows both from relations with kin and neighbors and from traditional political institutions. A local political base is essential to national power, and in Cameroon, national politics has focussed on regional patronage politics. The result of this has been the institution of "ethnic barons" as power brokers between regional and national political arenas.[69] This has meant that the new elites in Nso' must take the regional hegemony of the Fon Nso' seriously. And they must participate in reproducing it. A local power base is important in securing access to the state, a significant means of accumulation.[70] Access to the state allows important forms of redistribution. The state provides wages and salaries and access to national and international development networks. A direct link to the national bureaucracy facilitates returns on investments such as rental houses, which are most often rented to government officials. It provides access to national land grants, which in turn provide the basis for speculation and surety on loans. In Nso', that access continues to be assured through investment in local networks, and this requires that men have the means to invest in symbolic capital and in the networks which support their power and status.

Women in Nso' have continued to support a male hierarchy within the context of the modern state by providing the labor necessary to reproduce the household. Women's political power, virtually ignored by the colonial state, has become almost nonexistent, except in rhetoric, in the national structures of modern Cameroon, whose slogan is, significantly: Peace, work, and fatherland (Paix-travail-patrie). The ongoing importance of the male title system and the hegemony of male titleholders in Nso' ensure men a privileged position in the local power hierarchy. The intensification of market relations and the separation and solidification of public and private spheres within the modern state, with the public spheres identified as male and the private as female, have created a greater power differential between men and women. Local and national male institutions of power have become mutually constitutive. First within the colonial state and then the national state, precolonial female political power has been attenuated and undermined and women's economic role devalued, and male power has become further entrenched. The next three chapters explore this process further through an examination of the political economy of gender hierarchy.

4

Female Farmers, Male Warriors
Gendering Production and Reproduction

Seated on low bamboo stools in smoky kitchens, women of Nso' gather at
the end of a long hard day of farm work to share gossip and food, and to
swap strategies on how best to circumvent or endure hardships generated
by the current economic crisis. At the center of their talk are allusions to
their menfolk, often the subject of joking derision. Men are frequently
referred to as incompetent, even worthless, unable to care for themselves,
and too irresponsible to take care of their children. Women chuckle, slap
their knees, or ruefully shake their heads and declare, "Men are like children. What good are they? Who feeds the household? Men are useless
somebodies! They only live to drink *mimbo* and converse!" In their words
we can hear the echoes of women's statements to Phyllis Kaberry over four
decades ago when they told her, "Important things are women. Men are
little. The things of women are important. What are the things of men?
Men are indeed worthless. Women are indeed God. Men are nothing. Have
you not seen?"[1]

At the same time, gathered in *mimbo* parlors and off-licenses, men
philosophize about women. "Women," say the men, "should always listen
only to the man." They cannot "reason correctly" because "their hearts get
in the way." This is given as a rationale for keeping women at home, on the
farm, and out of positions of power or public decision making. Listening to
men in Nso' today, one is again struck by the similarity of statements made
40 years ago: "Ruling is for the man. If you catch trouble, will you send for
a man or a women? A woman has farm work. You call her the mother of
the farm."[2]

These conversations provide two very different images of women: on
the one hand, powerful and in control, and on the other, subservient to
men. These may appear as puzzling today as they did to Phyllis Kaberry in
the 1940s, when, perplexed by the contradictions in these differing conversations, she asked the Fon Nso' why, if women were held in such high
esteem, if they were like God and were the "mothers of the farm," did they

not sit on important political councils? The *fon* answered that the women are like God: like God they should stay quiet and let men run the country.[3]

These statements are not as contradictory as they appear on first reading. Control over symbolic, cultural, and material resources is different for men and women, both individually and as a group.[4] The field of power or matrix of power in Nso' is gendered. The "field of possible actions"[5] has changed over time, and relations of power have shifted and taken on new configurations and new meanings. However, as long as men have not threatened women's access to and control over resources considered to be within the female domain, women have been content to subscribe to the legal fiction of male dominance and leave public political power in the hands of men, perfectly secure in the knowledge of their own worth and in the scarcely concealed fact that male power and status have been underwritten by women's productive and reproductive labor. With changing material conditions, however, the boundaries and meanings of relationships, including gender, become newly contested.

The discourse about gender and male-female roles and the division of labor appears much the same today as it was 40 or 50 years ago, and presumably as it was before the colonialists arrived. Farming-food-female continue to be linked as a gender marker while the axiom that "men own the fields, women own the crops" remains central in the gender discourse. Men's identification as warriors and hunters, forged in the distant past when these two occupations were critical to the consolidation and reproduction of Nso' society, remains salient. Men's identification with these two occupations is manifested today in almost universal male membership in *manjoŋ,* the warriors' lodges found in every Nso' village. The image of men as the providers of protection and shelter persists. The male prerogative to the control over land is claimed by virtue of their right to the control and inheritance of real property such as buildings and tree crops, and by their obligations to perform the seasonal rituals for the land. "Men are more important [than women] because they build the house," the Nso' say. The pattern whereby women's productive and reproductive labor forms the basis of male accumulation continues today. Women still have the social obligation of provisioning the household. No longer hunters and warriors, men still control most productive resources and long-distance trading networks, and continue to invest in status and its social correlates, networks of kin and clients.

The context in which men and women live their lives has, however, changed significantly. This changing context is associated with further integration into the world market and can be characterized as one of increasing commodification, including but not limited to privatization of land and labor, and an associated increase in economic stratification.

Within this context, the meanings of gender designations have changed, both in the reality of everyday life and in power relations between men and women. Changes in the political economy over the past several decades have not been advantageous to women as a group. Women work harder today than they did in the past in order to fulfill new demands for a cash income. They assume more of the burden for reproducing the standard of living. The privatization of land, as we will see in the following chapter, has undermined women's formerly guaranteed access to lineage land. At the same time, education and job opportunities have opened up new visions and new opportunities for some women. A gendered discourse of production and reproduction remains central to the structures of power in Nso' today, and the sex/gender dimension and kin-client relationships remain at the center of an understanding of modes of accumulation.

While doubting women's capacity to reason, men continue to acknowledge women's farm labor as the most critical factor of production. Women are believed to be *naturally* endowed with the capacity to do farm work. When questioned about food crops, or indeed about farming in general, men would often say, "You will have to ask the women. It is they who are being the farmers, and it is they who know about farming." Women are moreover seen as physically built for farm work: women's necks and heads are built for carrying the heavy loads necessary for working a successful farm, and they are able to concentrate on "dull work" in ways men cannot. At one point I asked several men if they believed that women then were not intelligent. "Oh, they are intelligent quite all right," I was told. "This has nothing to do with intelligence. It has to do with *reason*." Women are viewed as excellent managers and "responsible somebodies"—masters of the mundane tasks so necessary to the functioning of daily life. But they cannot reason because their hearts get in the way. One young man, when I questioned him about the fact that his mother worked on the farm from dawn to dusk while his father never picked up a hoe, replied, "Well of course. That is her work. If my father went to the farm who would tap his *mimbo*? Who would go to the palace?" Who indeed? While men are busy tapping palm wine and politicking in the palace, women are working in the fields cultivating food crops: over 90 percent of the food is grown by women.

The identification of women as farmers who are responsible for the reproduction of everyday life and the linking of women and indeed "femininity" with farming and food as a gender marker have meant that women have been responsible for the reproduction of the household. Men's primary cultural identification has been as warriors and hunters, although neither occupation has been an empirical realty for most Nso' men alive today. These gender identifications, negotiated in the distant past when warriors were essential to establishing regional hegemomy, have worked to free men from the primary responsibility of provisioning the household. Instead they are able to use their incomes and time to invest in prestige, in entrepreneurial enterprises, and in networks which allow them to accumulate both symbolic and material wealth.

The Context of the Nso' Domestic Economy

Despite the presence of Mercedes trucks and Toyota taxis, of street lights and a modern water system, of green-and-white striped beach umbrellas shading the tables outside Snack, the new snack bar—chicken parlor in the Squares, and the availability of Coca-Cola, Beck's beer, and U.S. country-western music, the domestic economy in Nso' appears strikingly similar to Kaberry's descriptions from almost half a century ago. But appearances can be deceptive. Even relationships which appear to be the same have changed in meaning in the late twentieth century. An increasing tendency to view land as a commodity, the expansion of cash crop production, and the spread of formal education along with new forms of employment have all rechannelled access to resources for both genders, and have influenced ideas of individual responsibility to kin. At the same time, the cultural ideal of measuring wealth in people—the number of kinsmen, followers, and clients who owe one fealty and respect (and favors)—and the social correlates of this ideal, generosity and cooperation among kin and neighbors, have shaped household relations of production as well as investment strategies for both men and women. The accumulation of dependents, so essential to manipulating position within the Nso' status hierarchy, remains an important piece of symbolic capital and is today, as in the past, the basis of many successful economic careers.

This chapter will examine the domestic economy in Nso' today, focussing on continuity and change in the ways in which gender ideology organizes the division of labor, patterns of investment, and access to resources within and between households. But we cannot understand the domestic community in Nso' without understanding the day-to-day context within which people live their lives. Life in Nso' is shaped by daily tasks and a yearly cycle largely determined by the exigencies and needs of an agricultural community. The texture of daily life, the yearly farming cycle, and the ebb and flow of the seasons are essential to an understanding of the lives of people in Nso', who, like agricultural peoples everywhere, interpret much of their existence and identity through the metaphors of the seasons, the crops, and routine tasks.

The Daily Routine

Just before the dawn breaks, a chorus of roosters begins. Their crowing is soon drowned out by blaring radios, mothers shouting directions to their children, and general banter among family members and between people in adjacent compounds. By 6:00 A.M. the fire is lit, food is cooking, and water is heated for washing. Usually enough food is prepared in the morning to last until the women return from the farm to cook the evening meal. By 8:00 A.M. women leave for the farm, carrying hoes and a bowl of leftovers for lunch in their hands and babies on their backs. Preschoolers may accompany their mothers to the farm to stay out of mischief and to help care for the babies, while older children scurry off to school. Once a child is weaned women try to leave all the children in the compound, complaining that children on the farm "bother you over" and "scramble your head"; "it is only when you leave the children in the compound that you get any peace!" By 9:00 A.M. the compound is left to the children and an occasional elderly man or woman.

If men do not have steady employment—and the majority of men in the villages do not—they may leave to tap palm wine, to work on their coffee farms, or to travel to markets in nearby villages to trade. If they have no work to do on any given day, men will sometimes congregate in each other's compound but are more likely to be found in *mimbo* parlors, in off-licenses, in the village square, or at the *fon's* palace and the secret societies. Occasionally in the more rural villages younger children will hang out in off-licenses with the men, where they are passed from lap to lap, teased good-naturedly, and given sips of beer and other treats until the older children return home from school to take care of them.

Men invest a good deal of their productive time in social relationships—in hanging out together, drinking, listening to the radio, and discussing the affairs of the compound and the village, the national soccer team, and news reports from Yaounde and Nigeria. Even men with steady jobs can be found deep in conversation, cup in hand, by midafternoon in public or private drinking establishments, discussing local politics and the fate of the world.

By midafternoon, too, school children return to the compound, scuffling, pushing, shouting, and playing together, often getting into considerable mischief before the adults return. Women arrive home either late in the afternoon or at dusk, depending on the season. Now the children quiet down and are organized to help bring firewood and water, to care for younger siblings, or to run to the corn mill with a tin of corn to be ground for the evening meal. The evening meal is started; the compound is put in order. This is a time for women to sit around the fire and gossip, nurse their babies, and exchange news with visitors or with their husbands if they are around.

Cooking is time consuming, and food preparation, even of the simple local diet, is complex. Corn is usually ground at the corn mill, but it must be sifted. Beans must be soaked and cooked for several hours. If rice is prepared it has be be sifted through for small stones. Vegetable leaves must be picked over and washed, and condiments such as ginger, garlic, and *pepe* must be ground on a wooden or stone slab with a beer bottle. Food is cooked in pots balanced on a three-stone hearth. Since kitchens have only one such hearth, the *fufu* or main starch and the accompanying sauce have to be cooked at different times. The preparation time for the evening meal can be quite lengthy. Only a few wealthy households have ovens. Puff-puffs (fried dough) and eggs are occasionally deep-fried in palm oil. Meat and fish may be smoked and stored for future consumption. Fresh corn roasted directly in the fire is a favorite seasonal delicacy, eaten as a snack or appetizer rather than as the mainstay of a meal.

It is hard to separate women's actual work time from time spent in gossip and visiting during the early evening. Often young male relatives will drop by for an evening meal, and men often bring friends home for dinner. Women are expected to extend the hospitality of the compound at all times, and although a woman's kitchen and storage area are her private domain, she cannot—and would not—fail to entertain her husband's guests. Often, covered pans of cooked food are sent as gifts to neighboring compounds. When there are several adult women living in a household, each will cook separately, although they will take turns feeding the men and will often feed each other's children.

After dinner, children hang around the fire until they are shooed off to bed. Women sometimes join the men in the main house for tea or visit a neighboring compound to sit around the dwindling fire and exchange news. Women rarely venture any farther than an adjacent compound once they return from the farm, and in most rural villages off-licenses close soon after dusk. Most often by 10:00 P.M., if not earlier, the entire household is in bed. Occasionally a dog barking or the drums from a cry-die (funeral) break the stillness of the night, but after dark falls, quiet reigns.

Sundays and "Country Sundays" (ritual days of rest) are exceptions to the daily routine. These are normally women's days of rest from farm work but not from the ongoing routine of household tasks. Country Sundays are most often days when women wash and sew clothes, clean the compound, prepare *gari* (grated and/or fried cassava), or cook puff-puffs to sell in the market. A typical Country Sunday routine for B., the wife in the compound where I lived, started at 5:30 A.M. Before cooking the morning meal, she spent an hour washing up pans left from the night before. Two hours were spent washing clothes before she left for church choir practice at 8:00. Home by midmorning, she grated cassava to fry for *gari* to sell in the market. In the afternoon she went to her nearby vegetable farm to harvest *njama-njama* (a green leafy vegetable) for the evening meal. Returning home at 4:00, she repaired a path which had been washed out by heavy rains and swept the compound before cooking the evening meal. After dinner, B. cleaned the kitchen and bathed the two younger children before leaving for an 8:30 church meeting.

Nso' people who are Christians (over two-thirds of the people in Nso' are either Catholic or Presbyterian) attend church regularly. Women participate actively in the various church organizations, which have replaced traditional women's organizations such as *coŋ* as a focus of female social and political activity. Sunday is a day to socialize. Dressed in their Sunday best, the family members head off to church together. The children return to the compound to play after church, men gather to drink, "discuss life," and attend *njaŋgis* while women visit kin and neighbors and hold their own *njaŋgis*.

The Yearly Farming Cycle

The division of labor in Nso' households is organized around labor-intensive tasks set within an agricultural calendar that is dictated largely by rainfall. The preparation of fields for planting begins in the dry season immediately after the January coffee harvest. Fields are cleared and the soil is tilled over the next two months. Maize, beans, and Irish potatoes are planted as soon as the first regular rains begin in March or April. Fields are often weeded two times, toward the end of April and continuing through July. Beans and potatoes are harvested first (July-August), and the maize harvest follows in the lower regions in late July and continues in higher regions until September. After the harvest is completed the crops are prepared for storage, and the plants remaining in the field are cut down and tilled under for mulch. There is a short respite from daily farming tasks during October and November, but vegetable gardens continue to require ongoing attention.

Farming in Nso' is arduous and labor intensive. There are few technological inputs. Fertilizer and insecticides are used only on cash crops, if at all. These inputs were formerly sold only through the men's coffee cooperatives. Although since the mid-1980s some individual traders have sold fertilizers, often these are not available at the appropriate time. Frequently when fertilizers are available, cash is in short supply. Moreover, fertilizer is believed to have a negative effect on the taste of food.

The only tools used are short-handled hoes, cutlasses, and machetes.

These hoes, while efficient at breaking up the hard soil, are cumbersome and heavy. The steep terrain found throughout Nso' increases the labor of farming. Most farm plots are on land that ranges from a moderate to an almost vertical slope. Contoured horizontal ridges are constructed on hillsides and intercropped with corn and beans. Irish potatoes, usually grown more for sale than for home use, are most often planted separately in small plots. Maize is the most important crop, constituting by far the most significant part of the Nso' diet. Corn *fufu* is the preferred meal and is served at least once daily. Irish potatoes are usually a woman's cash crop, although they are also consumed in the household, along with other tubers, especially during the "hungry season," June and July, when the maize from the previous harvest has been almost depleted and the new crop is not yet ready. Beans, rice, or tubers may replace corn *fufu* as the main meal, but not too often lest the men begin to grumble. Men complain that when you eat rice "you will only catch hunger" before it is time to eat again, that beans are hard on the stomach, and that cocoyams "itch your mouth."

In addition to maize, beans, and potatoes, women grow a variety of vegetables, largely for household consumption. These include a number of leafy green vegetables, the most important of which are *njama-njama*, cowpeas, groundnuts, garden eggs, *pepe*, pumpkins (*egusi*), yams, cocoyams, and sweet potatoes. Tree crops, including avocado pears, plantains, bananas, sugar cane, mangos, and oranges, are also grown, depending on ecological conditions and the availability of land.

Most women in the early 1980s had between two and seven plots under cultivation, and often one or two fallowed plots. This is fewer than the 11 plots per woman reported by Kaberry,[6] but the plot sizes have increased and the distance between them is often substantial. An average farm (the aggregate of plots available to one household for food production) size in 1947 was 1.32 acres; today it is approximately 3 acres (1.22 hectares). Food plots are on average slightly over 2 kilometers from the compound, and many are over 10 kilometers away. Plots farmed by any one woman tend not to be contiguous both because of the pattern of available farmland and because women will try to obtain lots in different ecozones which are most suited to the variety of food they grow. Treks to and from each plot are often arduous, and women complain that they are constantly "ascending and descending" when travelling back and forth between the compound and their farms.

Before describing the household economy in more detail, I will offer a note on the applicability of using the "household" as a unit of analysis. The household in Nso' is not a bounded unit, nor are resources controlled and allocated jointly by men and women. Men and women have different networks which extend outward in specific ways in varying contexts. They operate under different sets of constraints and expectations and usually combine neither their enterprise nor their vision to maximize joint household production. As Guyer has argued, to use "household" as a concept is to designate a complex collectivity as a unit.[7] The units of production and consumption are often not identical, nor is the unit of consumption always coterminous with the group that eats together.[8] The household itself is set within a larger social context, and people move between households depending on season, schooling, and opportunities for access to employment. Children are especially mobile and may within any given year live with several different kin, either because of proximity to schools or, in the case of young girls, to work as "nursebabies" in the household of a relative who needs help with preschool children.

With all these caveats in mind it is nevertheless true that, although there are some labor and food exchanges between households, the primary unit of production and consumption in Nso' can be located in the household, defined as a household head, his wife or wives, and their dependent children. Over 90 percent of food consumed is homegrown, and 85 percent of income is produced within the household economy. The household in Nso' cannot, however, be assumed to be a joint enterprise; it must instead be disaggregated into its individual components, with men and women seen both separately and in relation to each other.[9]

The Nso' Household

Most households in Nso' are located within larger compounds. Residence is ideally patrilocal, although matrilateral and affinal ties may be used to determine residence, depending on the availability of land, on the status of lineage heads, and on temperament and interpersonal relations between kin. The typical compound consists of patrilineally related men and their families—a compound head, his wife or wives, unmarried children, married sons, and often younger married brothers and their wives. Widowed mothers, sisters who have left their husbands to return to their natal lineage, and an assortment of younger siblings, affines, and patrikin sisters separated from their husbands may choose to reside in a given compound, depending on the status and personality of the compound head. Persons living in the compound of a lineage head owe him fealty, respect, and aid as their political and ritual leader. Some compounds of traditional notables extend over several acres and may contain over 100 houses. Within the Nso' political economy of wealth and power, it is important to have dependent kin and clients.[10] The number of dependents living in a lineage head's compound is a measure as well as a symbol of his rank, status, and prestige.

The larger compounds today are thought of more as wards or quarters than as coresidential production units. Increasingly, married men try to establish independent compounds or residences of their own, although the compound of the lineage head or the acknowledged compound head is commonly referred to as the big compound, denoting the status of its head rather than absolute size. Houses are solidly constructed of red mud brick with zinc roofs. The more modern houses have cement floors and glass windows and are plastered and whitewashed inside and out, their living rooms distinctively decorated with overstuffed, red, plastic-upholstered furniture, embroidered doilies, family photos, and religious pictures and statues. A growing number of houses in Kimbo' have electricity; since the introduction of television in the mid-1980s it is not unusual, although still uncommon, to find a television set prominently displayed in the living room of wealthier households. The more traditional compounds (as well as poorer ones) have dirt rather than cement floors and wooden shutters in place of glass windows.

With rare exception men and women routinely share neither bedroom nor breakfast. Husband and wife usually have separate sleeping quarters and seldom eat together. If a man has no male guests he might eat in the kitchen with the women and children, but will usually complain of the smoke and won't linger around to gossip after dinner—except on the cold nights of rainy season, when the smoky warm kitchen is preferable to the cold, dank living quarters. Each adult woman in a household has her own kitchen with a three-stone hearth set in the dirt floor and a granary or storage area in the rafters. Other structures in the compound include additional storage houses and often a *njaŋgi,* or meeting, house.

Mean household size for a sample of 72 Nso' households surveyed in 1981 was 6.8 persons, with the size varying according to the wealth and status of the household head. Between 1981 and 1991 the national economy took a decided downturn. Ten years after the first survey, the household size had increased on average by 1.4 persons, many of whom were young unmarried daughters with babies or sons for whom school fees could not be found or who had returned home from Yaounde, Douala, and Bamenda when it became impossible for them to support themselves in these urban centers.

Men and women are often wary of talking about budgets and income in each other's presence; on several occasions women pulled me aside to tell me that their husbands engaged in some form of semilegal trade, such as trading across the border with Nigeria, and warned me that if their husbands had not reported this they were lying. More often, women asked explicitly that we not reveal what they told us to their husband or other members of the family, although the majority of women interviewed were proud of their ability to earn cash from their farms. Because of this separation of responsibilities and interests, men and women were interviewed separately in each of the 72 households. One-third of the heads of households were polygynously married. When a man had more than one wife, only the senior wife was interviewed, though additional wives were counted in the household census.

Characteristically, wealthy men have many dependents who are not their own children living in a household. Often these are younger kin whom the household head is supporting and sending to school. Fifty-two percent of the total number of persons in the household sample were children under the age of 15.

The age structure of the households, with only 48 percent in the working-age group (ages 15–60), indicates a heavy economic burden for working members. Only 1 percent of the population in the sample was over the age of 60. Thus, in the average seven-person household only three persons fell in the working-age interval. Of these 3, on average 1.7 were men and 1.3 were women. Excluding children under 15 is perhaps somewhat arbitrary and does not reflect an entirely accurate picture of household labor allocation. Children perform a variety of household tasks, including childcare, carrying water, fetching firewood, and running errands. By the time they are seven or eight years old, girls often begin to help their mothers on the farm. However, most children between the ages of 6 and 15 attend school and their labor is available only sporadically for the greater part of the year. The large burden of labor falls to adult women, who are responsible for virtually all food production and household tasks.

In addition to supporting and providing schooling for children of various kin, many wealthier household heads also employ younger kin or provide them with a home near their workplace. The wealthiest man in the sample of 72 households had 21 dependents living with him, only 7 of whom were his own children. The others were younger kin, both agnates and affines, 10 of whom he was sending to school and 4 for whom he had secured employment as drivers or cooperative workers. In return, he and his wife had a rather large "captive" labor force to draw on to perform farming tasks during school vacations and to help with household tasks such as childcare and cooking. Additionally, the older children worked in the wife's provision store. In a society that puts a high premium on a man's ability to attract and keep a large number of kin and clients under his control, these dependents were a significant piece of symbolic capital.

The household head of this particular compound was an astute politician. He viewed the young people living in his compound as clients—educated people he could count on in the future to support him and the programs he advocated for development projects and expanding and strengthening the cooperative in 1981. By 1991 he had become an influential figure in the Social Democratic Front, one of the major opposition parties in Cameroon. It is significant that he was able to rally a lot of support from the younger men who form the more radical element within the SDF. Many of these are young men whose careers he has helped through the years, or young men (and women) who rally to the green and white colors of the SDF and attach themselves as clients to men such as this in hopes of help with future career moves.

Because of his business-political role in the community, people in this man's compound, and in his village, referred to him as Ba or Pa (a term used for elder men with status), denoting this man's position as a political leader and "father" of many. While this is at the high end of the continuum of obligations taken on by wealthy household heads, obligation between kin is a theme that runs through all Nso' life. Virtually all men who earn above an average income give aid and support to a number of kin. Obligations between kinspeople are an integral and institutionalized part of Nso' morality and practice. Helping out less fortunate kin and clients is not merely an altruistic act; it is also an expected gesture. Men who "attract wealth" are seen not only as possessing power, or *səm*, but also as deeply ambiguous because of it. The association of *səm* with wealth is expressed in the term *du kwa' səm* ("go to the farm of sorcery"), used when a person suddenly and unaccountably becomes rich. The ultimate negative stereotype is the evil rich person who makes a compact with the witch world, promising the life of kin in exchange for riches. Such people are said to gnaw (*kfər*) their relatives. There has been a sharp rise in witchcraft accusations within the context of the economic crisis, and urban cults such as *famla'* have become more prevalent. Wealthy men are often the targets of these accusations; as will be discussed in chapter 6, elites living in urban centers complain about the increasing numbers of people from the village who show up at their urban residences seeking favors and loans, a place to stay overnight, or simply a drink or a meal. The more successful a man becomes, the more critical it is that he be viewed as generous.

Supernatural beliefs aside, generosity is an important mechanism by which wealthy men create long-term obligations, gain access to free labor, and solidify and verify social status. At the household level, however, the burden of household support for such kin falls as well to the wife or wives of the household head. As one woman related, explaining the constant demand of kin, "Life is so expensive today. There has to be a lot of sharing back and forth for people just to get by."

Allocation of Labor

The organization of production in Nso' households today, as in the past, allocates women's labor to subsistence crops and domestic tasks. Men's work has varied more through time, depending on their age and status. In precolonial Nso', men were primarily warriors and hunters, a fact they are quick to refer to today when questioned about why they don't participate more in farming activities. Today men's labor is distributed among coffee production and a variety of entrepreneurial activities. Of the 72 women interviewed in the Nso' household sample, only 1, a schoolteacher, declared an occupation other than farming as her first priority. Eighteen, or slightly over 20 percent, of the men held wage or salaried jobs. The remaining men declared themselves as primarily farmers. This is perhaps a bit misleading. Men seldom involve themselves in food crop production, and a man with only a few coffee trees refers to himself as a farmer. Men in Nso' will not use a hoe, which carries symbolic meaning as a woman's possession. In two and a half years in Nso' the one man I saw tilling a field was pointed out to me as a local curiosity: "Wonderful! He is working farm just like a woman!" By the early 1990s in the wake of a long economic crisis within which men were not paid by the government for their coffee for over two years, a number of younger men began farming food crops for cash. Most, however, preferred to go far away from home to farm where they could not be seen. The large forest around Oku, already somewhat depleted by the demand for the bark of trees used for medicinal purposes, for firewood, and for telephone poles, has been further decimated by young men who go into the forest to clear plots to grow corn and beans for the marketplace.

Men who do not have wage occupations are involved in a number of entrepreneurial activities. A few are taxi drivers. Many tap palm and raffia wine and sell a variety of tree crops, including kola nuts, avocado pears, and plantains. They engage in craft production, cut and sell firewood, make bricks, own small shops, and travel around the market circuit selling manufactured goods or acting as middlemen in the food trade. Kaberry's view of Nso' men as resembling nothing so much as Chaucer's Man of Lawe remains descriptively accurate today.[11]

Kaberry's comment on Nso' women also has resonance today. She observed, ". . . women take a pride in their own skill and competence as farmers, in their responsibility for feeding and care of the household, and in their knowledge that they are, in some respects, the backbone of the country."[12] Farming-food-female have remained connected as a gender marker, and there are in Nso' the obvious connections made between food and sex. When a man is going to be married, he says he is "going to eat porridge"; in polygynous households the wife who cooks for her husband is the one with whom he spends the night. Women derive a good deal of status from growing the family food, and women who don't have farms are viewed as lazy, even immoral. Fulani women, who don't farm, were constantly pointed out to me as anomalies among women, with comments such as, "See that woman? She is being Fulani. See how lazy she is looking?"

Forty years ago, women spent 53 percent of their time on the farm and in domestic tasks and 30 percent in leisure, with the remaining time lost to personal illness or caring for sick children. Medical facilities and health have improved, but women today have less time for leisure. Women spend over 200 days annually in food crop production, although the length of the day varies substantially with seasonal labor requirements. Five or six days out of the Nso' eight-day week are spent at the farm, and more time is spent trekking between the compound and farm plots. Women usually work 60 hours per week in farming and domestic tasks, although it is hard to separate domestic tasks from leisure when women sit around the kitchen cooking, nursing babies, gossiping, and overseeing children's tasks. The heaviest farm work season is during planting and harvesting, although women often say they would rather do these tasks than the more tedious and continuous task of weeding their crops. Men's major involvement in food crop production is limited to clearing the land for tilling, which requires less than one week of labor per year and, with the growing tendency for land to be under continuous cultivation, may not even require that. Some men help with the planting. The maize harvest is carried to storage by young men, most often the sons of the household head and their friends, who are given food and beer or palm wine in return for their labor. Usually 10–30 young men participate, rotating from farm to farm. The total household maize harvest can be accomplished in a day or two, because women also form cooperative work groups to work along with the young men at harvest.

Agricultural tasks performed by women include tilling, planting, weeding, and harvesting, which, in combination, are ongoing tasks for much of the year and require almost daily attention. Women often work in cooperative labor groups during peak labor seasons requiring maximum labor input. Groups range from 3 to 20 members, depending upon the task and size of the farm. This is a considerable increase in labor exchange among women from that recorded by Kaberry, who noted that the degree of farm labor exchange in the 1940s and 1950s was quite minimal. At that time, women exchanged labor primarily in times of extreme need, for instance, when a woman was ill or had a sick child. Most women worked alone or with a daughter or mother-in-law.[13] Currently, women's work groups are essential for breaking seasonal bottlenecks, such as making sure that all fields are tilled and ready for planting by the time the first rains begin in late March. The increase in shared labor may be the result of increased farm sizes, including those planted in cash crops that require women's labor. Today over 60 percent of all children attend primary school, so women cannot count on help in the fields from their children during the school year.

Men's agricultural activities and labor time are almost impossible to measure because they vary significantly with age and status and rarely include sustained tasks over a given period of time. As noted above, a small but growing number of young men farm food crops for sale but not for household consumption. However, aside from the initial clearing of land, most men's labor remains little involved in food production, and certainly not in production for the family pot. Men are, in theory, responsible for tree crops, and clearly claim all cash income from these crops. In fact, women most often till the men's coffee farms and, along with young men and children, help with harvesting them.

Very little labor is hired in the average household. An analysis of the average household budget in the 1981 sample of 72 showed that only 2 percent of the expenditures went to hired labor; almost all that labor was hired by men. When labor is hired, it is hired almost exclusively for "men's work"—clearing land and cultivating coffee farms. The few men who grow food crops to market most often hire labor for tilling and weeding their food farms. Men also help each other with pruning and planting coffee trees and may work together in large groups of up to 10 during the coffee harvest season in December and January. The only women who hire labor to help with farm work are those few whose husbands have wage occupations and who are themselves involved in entrepreneurial ventures.

Income and Expenditures and Accumulation

The Nso' say that "it is the man's job to protect the compound and the family," and that "men all the time think only of being big men," whereas women are viewed as "caretakers and providers for food and children." These social values of women as provisioners and caretakers and of men as protectors, status seekers, and authority figures are reflected in patterns of income, expenditure, and investment. Men and women often work in different sectors of the economy and do not necessarily combine or allocate their time and resources to maximize the commodity output of the household as a unit. When questioned about male and female responsibilities to the household, people in Nso' will say that "a woman gets her importance from having food for the family," whereas "men are more important because they build the house," referring to the fact that men own and control property, and women's rights to property are always mediated through a husband, father, or brother.

Individual men and women have kinship responsibilities and obligations that extend outside the boundaries of the household. These obligations are intensified by the current economic crisis because access to cash has diminished for both men and women. Men fulfill these obligations by providing school fees, medical expenses, cash, and often access to jobs for kin and clients. Women make frequent gift exchanges between households, usually but not exclusively between related compounds. Women are expected to give to others according to their ability to secure money. Most exchanges between women are fairly low in value. Those who have access to some cash income make presents of purchased items such as soap, rubbing oil, or palm oil; women who have less expendable income return the favor with gifts of produce, cooked food, or perhaps a few eggs.

Let's look here at V., a woman from Nsə', to gain a better sense of how women organize their work lives, their household budgets, and networks of reciprocity. In the early 1980s, V. had two children, a girl of 4 and an 18-month-old son. Her husband was a schoolteacher. V. was young, 25, as well as bright and energetic. She farmed three plots and was able to sell more than the average amount of corn and beans, which she marketed through her brother-in-law, a local petty trader. In addition to her own farms, she walked several miles to help her aging mother during planting and tilling. She organized a work group among her classificatory sisters-in-law to help facilitate the completion of labor-intensive tasks. Four or five women in addition to V. would pack up a lunch of leftovers. With babies on their backs and young children tagging along to help with the babies on the farm, they would head off to work as soon as the older children were fed and ready for school, usually before 8:00 A.M. V. would often laugh and say, "Let's try to leave the children in the compound today if we can find an old somebody to watch them." By the time her daughter was four, V. would leave the younger child with her daughter in the compound under the watchful eye of an aging neighbor.

In addition to selling corn (and occasionally a bag of beans) V. raised fowls, fried puff-puffs, and engaged in a limited amount of petty trade in soap and other small household necessities. She was reluctant to buy these commodities in large quantities very often, and when she did she tried to sell them quickly or hide them. When questioned about this she replied that if her friends and relations knew she had soap or salt or sugar in the house they would come "beg" it from her. This happened with great regularity, and V. did not refuse to share. According to her, to do so would be impossible; she would be gossiped about as stingy and even greedy. V. was the secretary of the local women's cooperative, which she described as an unthankful task that required a lot of work and brought her a lot of trouble. People were quick to believe that she was using her position in the cooperative for personal gain, and more than once she tried to quit but agreed to stay on when no one with her education and social finesse could be found to replace her. When I "dashed" her some cloth in exchange for some work she did for me, she put it away until after I left, on the premise that if people saw her wearing new cloth they would think she was profitting at their expense. V. was also the treasurer of her local *njaŋgi,* a position of some trust. She is the one who told me, "Life is so expensive today. There has to be a lot of sharing back and forth for people just to get by." She was involved in a wide network of reciprocity, not just in labor exchange but also in the exchange of small commodities. Most often, V. would give salt and sugar in exchange for eggs, *njama-njama,* and small amounts of cooked food. These were not direct or overt exchanges, but instead involved a good deal of visiting and nuance. Sundays and Country Sundays were spent visiting kin and neighbors, and it was during this time that most of these exchanges took place, much like taking a bottle of wine to a dinner party. Not an unexpected or even a disinterested gesture, but hardly an overt business transaction.

V. usually cooked for three or four people each evening in addition to her own family; often the young men from her husband's family would drop in around dinner time, willing to exchange an hour's work carrying water or chopping wood for a good meal and the local gossip. Her day, which started at dawn with the preparation of enough food to feed six to eight people breakfast and lunch, included a two-mile trek to her farm, where she worked for five to eight hours depending on the season, preparation of dinner for family and guests, and ended late in the evening, when more often than not she would sit up with a kerosene light working on the cooperative records or sewing clothes for her children until sleep "caught" her.

Although her husband earned a larger-than-average salary, and she herself a larger-than-average income through her various busines transactions, V. hired no help on her farm. And although her husband had access to a substantial amount of money, V. was responsible for provisioning the household, for either growing or buying all food other than meat, and for her own and often her children's medical expenses. This last obligation ended up in tragedy.

When her younger child was not quite two he developed a fever and flulike symptoms. When it was suggested that he was really sick and needed to have medicine and bed rest, V. said he was only "hotting" and she was giving him nivaquine, the local drug of choice for fever. And besides, he was a "hard-head piken—he no fit agree for lie down" (wouldn't agree to lie quietly in bed). She had neither the money nor the time to seek medical attention for what looked like a common childhood ailment. It wasn't until V. herself became ill and couldn't cope that she agreed to take some money and go to the hospital in Kimbo'. By that time her child, who as it turned out had the mumps and developed respiratory complications from this disease, was dehydrated and gaunt. He did not survive.

During the time V. and her child were in the hospital her husband did not give her money for the expenses, not because he was unaffected by the event, but because he assumed she would take the responsibility for paying the medical expenses involved. Her network of women friends brought her food in the hospital, where family and friends are expected to provide meals for patients. V. had to borrow money from her brother to cover the transportation and medical expenses. This single event really brought home to me what I had known theoretically through conversations with people. Men and women in Nso' have different networks and different responsibilities; they have different expectations and demands made on them. They keep their money and budgets separate because they are in different structural positions with a different set of constraints and responsibilities, both within the household and within networks of kin and neighbors.

Men's and Women's Household Budgets

In the following discussion of household expenditures, yearly income includes off-farm income, the amount received from crops locally marketed, the total value of crops not marketed (food consumed in the household), and income received from members of the family living away from home. Data on expenditures were broken down in two ways: first, women and men, separately, were asked to list all purchases made in a two-week period; second, yearly expenditures were calculated by asking the frequency of purchase of certain items and extrapolating a yearly expense pattern from this information. School fees and medical expenses were included in the latter. Gifts to members of the family living elsewhere were included, but gifts to non-household members and gift exchanges between compounds were not consistently recorded. Consequently, the discussion of these latter exchanges is based upon qualitative impressions rather than on quantitative data. In polygynous households, only one wife was interviewed, but all the wives and children of the household head were included when calculating per capita income or looking at the breakdown of expenses paid by the male head of the household.

In all but three villages surveyed, expenditures exceeded reported annual incomes. There are several explanations for this. First, we did not include payments in cash, kind, or labor for either use of land or basic kinship obligations, which, for landlords and lineage heads, can be considerable. Second, the recall of true yearly income may be somewhat faulty because of the predominance of piecemeal and nonsalaried activities, which vary substantially throughout the year. Recall on a two-week basis or less—the method employed for recalling expenditures—is much more reliable. It is my impression that people were much more willing to disclose expenditures than income—hardly a surprising finding. The three villages where expenditures did not exceed reported incomes included the greatest percentage of people with salaried jobs, who in turn form the majority of households in the sample with high incomes.

Household income for the 72 households in the sample in 1981 was highly variable, with a high of 7 million FCFA (franc communaute financiere africaine) (US $35,000) and a low of 14,500 FCFA (US $72.50).[14] Average household income was 447,270 FCFA (US $2236) with a standard deviation of 427,980 (US $2136), indicating a high level of rural income stratification. Average expenditure for the entire sample in 1981 was 346.183 FCFA per household with a standard deviation of 98.692 FCFA. The income figures were skewed somewhat by the fact that several households were headed by very wealthy men; those households which were headed by men with wage/salaried jobs earned substantially more income than those where male employment was confined to farming. Average per capita income was 27,662 FCFA (US $133). Ten years later, average income had declined to a per capita income of 21,435 FCFA. There was a consistency through the decade in regard to income stratification. Less food was marketed because of Operation Ghost Town, the general strike called by the national opposition parties. Often salaries were not paid for many months, and it was difficult to compute income for this sample on a consistent basis. Many people were operating on a barter system, exchanging services and produce between households. A lot of people were surviving through semilegal ventures—"importing" manufactured goods and petrol from Nigeria, for example.

Male incomes were higher than female incomes. A woman's actual cash income was on the average only one-quarter of a man's cash income. There are several explanations. Food crop prices were calculated on the basis of local market value, and most of the households surveyed were in remote areas where market prices for the staple food crops were low. Few opportunities for employment or income production exist for women outside agriculture. Seventy-five percent of the 72 women, compared with 32 percent of the men, had no income outside the sale of agricultural crops.

Men's primary returns from farming are from coffee and small livestock sales, both highly remunerative compared with sale of food crops.

Men sell their total coffee harvest, whereas women sell only 10–20 percent of their food crops. The rest is consumed within the household. When looking at relative contributions to the household budget, we should bear in mind that homegrown food provides over 90 percent of calories and proteins consumed within the household and almost the total food supply is produced by women.

The largest part of a woman's contribution comes from the market value of her subsistence crops; a man's income is generally evenly distributed between marketed crops and off-farm income. Of the total household income in cash value in 1981, men contributed on average 58.71 percent and women contributed 41.29 percent. A decade later, after six years of hard economic circumstances during which men were often not paid coffee receipts for two years, the household had become more dependent on women's production and income, with women contributing over 50 percent of the household income in cash value. If salaried men are taken out of the sample, the average contribution of women's subsistence crops amounts to over 60 percent of household income. Approximately one-quarter of the families interviewed in 1991 were almost totally dependent on women's production. This trend is probably more representative of the typical rural village household in the context of the current economic crisis.[15]

The structure of male and female contributions to the total household budget today is similar to that recorded by Kaberry in the 1940s. However, at that time women seldom traded at all, and there was a prejudice against women earning or handling large amounts of money. Women who traded regularly handed their earnings over to their husbands. The prejudice against women handling money meant that men assumed responsibility for virtually all cash purchases. Today, women's household obligations have expanded with increased demands on their incomes brought about by changes in the rural standard of living. Women complain that in the past men purchased household necessities such as palm oil and salt, but today they expect women to assume these responsibilities.

Since Kaberry's work in the 1940s, cash demands on both male and female incomes have been increased because of a variety of new expenses now considered essential to the rural standard of living. Manufactured commodities have replaced or supplemented items such as soap, tobacco, rubbing oil, and pots and pans, which in the past were produced within the household economy. Recent additions to the household budget include school fees and medical expenses, building materials, household furniture, radios, ready-made clothing, and, on a more mundane level, kerosene, matches, bush lamps, and "torches" (flashlights).

Average household expenditure for the 1981 sample of 72 households was 346,183 FCFA (US $1826) per year. Seventy-five percent of all household cash expenditures were paid by the male household head, and 25 percent were paid by women, consistent with cash incomes. Men's primary contribution to the food supply has consisted mostly of items not essential to the nutritional level. It is not surprising then that there is no correlation between the level of men's income and the level of nutrition, whereas higher women's income is positively correlated with a high level of nutrition. It is not that men do not care about the nutritional welfare of their families, but rather that they do not see it as their social responsibility.[16]

Men's expenditures have been dominated by larger purchases. They pay most school fees, approximately two-thirds of all medical expenses, and make major household purchases such as zinc roofing, radios, and furniture. Men are more likely than women to buy "luxury" items such as meat, tea, and tinned and powdered milk. Beer and palm wine are major weekly expenditures for men. Most men invest a good deal of money in *njaŋgis* (rotating savings and loan clubs), in men's secret societies, and in giving small gifts of cash to friends and relatives.[17]

Both men and women have contributed to minor household items such as kerosene, soap, and rubbing oil. Women's expenditures are dominated by supplements to the household food supply in the form of condiments, palm oil for cooking, and salt. Additionally, they buy over half of small household items such as rubbing oil, matches, and kerosene. Although the cultural ideal in Nso' is that men pay school fees, and all men interviewed related that they have done so, several headmasters of village schools claimed that women pay at least one-third of the school fees.

Moreover, women constantly complain about husbands not fulfilling the school-fee obligation to their children. Some schoolmasters will put pressure on men to pay school fees by billing them for fees paid by women, and then returning the money to the women if and when the men pay. Men pay their own and often their elderly parents' medical bills, and usually women provide the cash for their own and often their children's medical expenses. Taken together, women's food crops and cash contributions provide for most household necessities. Although most women keep their money separately from their husband's, there are some men and women who combine their incomes. One would expect that those women who give the money they earn to their husband would be the older or certainly more "traditional" women who are following the cultural ideal reported by Kaberry. Yet interestingly, the 20 percent of the women who said they combine their income with their husband's income, usually by giving him the cash and getting money back for household expenses, were the younger, better-educated women married to men with salaried or wage jobs outside the household. We will return to this point in a subsequent chapter, but it is worth noting here that educated men and women are combining their resources and their vision to produce a distinctively modern lifestyle.

While some women told of giving their incomes to their husband, this is clearly not the norm. Most women are careful not to let their husband know how much cash they have lest they be pressured into paying school fees or even paying their husband's taxes. Characteristically, women and men keep their incomes separate and spend their cash on different items, with women spending their cash on household items and children's education and men spending theirs on children's education and items largely outside the household, including gifts to relatives and friends. By assuming responsibility for provisioning the household, women free men's incomes for extrahousehold investment in entrepreneurial ventures, social networks, and status.

The division of labor and responsibilities and men's ownership of land limit women's access to cash income for investment and accumulation. Patterns of access to credit are similarly gendered. In order to cover cash expenses, men and women separately belong to at least one *njaŋgi*, or rotating savings and loan association. Most women belong to small savings *njaŋgis*, sometimes referred to as country meetings, where small amounts of money are saved on a weekly basis, with distributions of total savings taking place once a year, usually around Christmas. Sometimes the money is used to buy wholesale boxes of small household items such as soap to sell to members at below-market cost. The group sometimes buys kola nuts, sells them, and divides up the gains among all members. Members can borrow (with interest), so *njaŋgis* are a source of loans as well as savings. Usually the loan must be paid back within four weeks. Members are charged 5 FCFA for each 100 FCFA borrowed. If the money is not paid back on time, the fine is 100 FCFA per week, plus an additional 5 FCFA per 100 FCFA borrowed. The advantage of these groups is that they are based on ongoing social relationships and trust. Often if a member needs a loan for a real emergency such as medical bills, interest will not be charged if the loan is repaid within what is perceived to be a reasonable time. "Reasonable time" seems to vary in length depending on the borrower's relationship to other members of the group and on their perceptions of her situation. *Njaŋgis* give women access to credit for "crisis" situations and facilitate their ability to pay household expenses. They do not often provide capital for accumulation and growth. It is telling that savings are distributed immediately before Christmas, a time when ready cash is necessary to meet seasonal family expenses.

Most men and a few businesswomen belong to larger credit *njaŋgis* which loan large sums of money. Members put money in a pot on a regular (weekly or monthly) basis. The amounts are often substantial. The men I knew who were petty traders put in from 5000 to 10,000 FCFA per week. Salaried men and large-scale traders often belong to *njaŋgis* where the equivalent of thousands of dollars (US) exchanges hands monthly. The member who is hosting the group, the person who "cooks *njaŋgi*," then "eats" the pot. Each member cooks *njaŋgi* in turn so that a substantial amount of money is available for investment for each member at regular intervals. People will try to time their turn to cook *njaŋgi* in order to have access to cash for particular business or personal expenses; for instance, if a man has to pay secondary school or university fees, he will time his turn to coincide with the payment date. Money can be borrowed from the person whose turn it is to take the pot, but interest rates are high, usually 10 percent per month.

Officially, credit is available to both men and women through formal institutions such as banks and, formerly, the national agricultural development fund (FONADER, the Fonds National pour le Développement Rural), now defunct. In practice, these institutions serve a restricted clientele, namely large-scale farmers and *fonctionnaries*. Small-scale farmers, especially women farmers, are not given credit from these institutions. Women's access to higher levels of credit is especially limited because credit of this kind is channelled through coffee cooperatives and is usually based upon a farmer's level of coffee production. And because women don't own land, they usually cannot use property as surety on loans.

In addition to the *njaŋgi*, credit is available to both men and women through a system of credit unions under a parent organization, the Cameroon Credit Union League (CamCUL). In 1981, there were 112 credit unions operating in the Northwest Province with approximately 18,000 members. Of the 144 people individually interviewed in Nso' households (72 men, 72 women), 33 percent of the men and 18 percent of the women belonged to credit unions. One would think women would be preferred risks, since they have a higher rate of repayment than men and, according to one (male) credit union official, "are more likely to be honest and feel shame than are men." However, since a person can borrow only three times the amount he or she has in the credit union, the amount a woman can borrow is much less than what a man can borrow. Women often view credit unions with distrust, and not without reason. Several village credit unions have gone bankrupt because loans have not been repaid, and women say that "the credit unions only spoil your money." They feel, rightly or wrongly, that if they belong to a credit union, their husbands will pressure them to borrow money for school fees and medical expenses rather than contribute to those expenses themselves.

According to credit union records, as well as the survey and informal discussions with men and women, men borrow money for trade, transport, building supplies, and "family emergencies," school fees or contributions required by kinship obligations such as funeral expenses. When women do borrow money from credit unions, which is seldom, they do so to pay their children's school fees or medical expenses. More often, women turn to a *njaŋgi* to help defray the cost of such expenses.

In sum, the kinds of expenses women spend their money on are most often related to reproducing the household; even those women who are involved in petty trade do not usually have access to enough capital for significant investment and growth. Men more often spend money on expenditures that expand a following, increase individual prestige, and allow for accumulation on a larger scale. The ideal of measuring wealth in one's following of kin and clients, the most important measure of wealth and status in precolonial Nso', has resonance today. This has focussed a good deal of male investment on prestige and symbolic capital. Men make payments to the secret societies and acquire titles in these. The new elites in Nso' have in many ways become the new lineage leaders. They also invest in the social correlates of lineage leadership, generosity, and redistribution to a network of kin and clients. There are frequently contradictions involved in these investments, and men must often make complicated and hard decisions when deciding to invest in these networks. We will return to this issue below. The important point here is to emphasize the fact that women underwrite men's ability to invest in networks of kin and clients outside the household and thus further men's political careers.

Let us return by way of example to our wealthy friend, the cooperative official. As noted earlier, he was supporting 10 younger dependents who were not his own children. These included two brothers' sons and three brothers' daughters for whom he was paying school fees, one sister's daughter and her younger son whom he had employed at the cooperative, and his uncle's son (a classificatory brother), who was employed in his wife's provision store. In addition, he was paying secondary school fees for two boarding students, a sister's daughter, and the son of his wife's brother, and he was sending his brother's son, who was teaching in a nearby village, 200,000 FCFA per year (US $1000). Through these strategies he was able to increase the income of family members, secure employment opportunities for them, and raise the probability that they would be in positions to help less fortunate kin in the future, thus ensuring the well-being of a large network of kin, who would have influence and owe him respect and favors in the future. Because he had access both to a higher-than-average income and to networks of influence, which allowed him to invest a good deal more than the average village man in helping out his relatives, he was expected to help out less well-to-do kin, as other men are who have the means to do so. By doing so, they increase their own status and acquire a group of people who will be obligated to them.

The obligation to redistribute individual wealth to kin often poses a moral dilemma, as in the case of Benjamin, whose older brother had sent him to teacher's college.[18] Benjamin had become the headmaster of a school in Nsə'. By the late 1970s his earnings exceeded those of his brother. Each had several children, and Benjamin was faced with the responsibility of sending both his own and his brother's children to school, a responsibility which would eventually put a severe strain on his income. To complicate matters he was born a prince, a member of the royal lineage in Nsə'. As such, he was expected to give gifts regularly to the Fon Nsə', participate actively in the palace societies, help support his aged mother, and help out his sister and her children. His sister was one of the five daughters of the royal lineage in Nsə' who had been appointed as a *yaa*, or a queen in the palace. Her husband had died and she was spending most of her time in the palace. She had no outside income to help send her children to school and pay for household supplies other than the sale of her produce and gifts from relatives. She produced very little to sell in the market, since she spent a good deal of her time in the palace. Benjamin had already sent his sister's daughter through secondary school.

As a member of the royal lineage with a relatively large income, Benjamin was under many demands from kin. The royal lineage is large, and because of his position as headmaster of one of the few local schools, he had become a frequent spokesman for the *fon* on occasions of state involving visits from outside government officials. He was highly visible in the community. If he were to fail to satisfy obligations to kin, people would say he was only profitting from his position and that he was disrespectful to boot. In fact, people had started gossiping about him, saying that he was using his position as an educated man to get close to the *fon,* to have undue influence on the affairs of the palace, and was in fact angling to become the next Fon Nsə'. Benjamin was caught in a contradiction. If he were to continue to create a following within the royal lineage, he *might* become the next *fon,* but this was a long shot at best and would put severe demands on his finances. Gossip about him had already started. If he were to withdraw aid to his kin, he would clearly be in an untenable position within the royal lineage. If he were to continue to support various members of his kin group, he might end up without enough to live the life of a Nso' elite and make sure his own six children had at least a secondary school education.

Benjamin decided to opt out and leave Nsə'. For him, the move was complicated by the bad feelings between the Fon Nso' and the Fon Nsə'. By opting out, he gave up his networks in Nsə' and became more dependent on the modern bureaucratic structure to ensure himself a position and a career. His name, Fonnsə', identified him immediately in the bureaucracy in Kimbo'—where the spoils of the modern system are distributed and jobs allocated—as a royal member of a rather difficult group. Benjamin decided his options would improve if he were to change his name. He changed his name to Shang, the given name of his real father, the former Fon Nsə'. Shang is a commonly distributed name throughout Nso', and is not immediately recognizable as a Nsə' name. At the same time, people in Nsə' are aware it is the name of Benjamin's father, and therefore it is not perceived locally as a sign of disrespect for him to have changed names. It was important for Benjamin to try to keep his options open in the event he was unable to make a go of it outside Nsə'. By removing himself more or less from the local fields, he was not under such constant pressure from kin as long as he gave up his local political ambitions.

Armed with a new name and relieved of ongoing financial obligations to lineage members, Benjamin secured a position as headmaster first at a small village outside Nsə'; he later moved to Kimbo'. He used old school ties to influence his appointment, which, now that his name no longer attracted attention, was processed without hang-up in the divisional office at Kimbo'. His wife's brother (also an old schoolmate of Benjamin) helped her gain admittance to study for her teacher's certificate; she later became a teacher in a primary school in Kimbo'. When last heard from they were doing well financially, building a large house in Kimbo' while keeping their farm and renting their house in Nsə'. Rumor was that Benjamin and the Fon Nsə' had had a serious falling out and were not speaking, although the details were just that, rumor, and hard to piece together into a coherent story. There were rumors that Benjamin, who had held a rather prominent council position in Kimbo', had "chopped" money, much to the dismay of the Fon Nsə', who saw this as a disgrace to the Nsə' people. Nevertheless the Fon Nsə' and his people—who are, after all, kin to Benjamin—raised the money for his defense lawyer. While Benjamin lost his council position, he kept his job and did not go to jail, and the trial did not deter him from pursuing his ambition to put together a modern lifestyle. Whether the efforts of Benjamin and his wife to make it in the modern economy outside Nsə' proved to be successful is an empirical question. Their choice to attempt to leave Nsə' to do so (in fact, they saw themselves as forced to leave) and the events which led to their decision raise several important issues.

Women's Work and Men's Strategies of Accumulation

Obligations to kin have intensified rather than disappearing within the context of the modern economy. As the woman quoted earlier said, there has to be a lot of sharing today for people just to get by. Elite men with

connections are constantly petitioned for money and favors, and, especially if they have any local or national political ambitions, they cannot
ignore these requests. Nso' men living in Yaounde complain endlessly
about requests from kin who think that these salaried men have more
money and influence than they actually do, and who want them to use their
influence to secure jobs and positions in schools. *Not* to meet at least some
of these demands can leave wealthy men open to accusations of "bad fashion" at best, and may result in allegations of witchcraft.[19] Men living locally find it even more difficult to escape ongoing demands for help. These
demands have increased over the past five years because the economic crisis has grown worse and has decreased the amount of cash in the system,
and because coffee farmers have had to forgo payment for several recent
harvests.

Reciprocal obligations and mutual aid between kin are part of the
very fabric of Nso' society. Obligations between kin form a safety net for
all Nso' people, and one either plays the game or, like Benjamin, tries to opt
out. These obligations are reinforced by ideas about the ambiguity of
wealth and power and the obligation of Nso' leaders to have an "open
hand." As we've seen, the Nso' say, "The *fon* has everything; the *fon* is a
poor man," and this is the model for leadership. The *fon* is supposed to
redistribute constantly through largess at the palace, and when he does not
there is considerable gossip and grumbling. Ŋga' Bi'fon III had a great deal
of difficulty because he was perceived as a businessman first and a *fon*
second, as tightfisted and stingy, with his eye constantly on the bottom line.
During his reign wine and conversation ceased to flow at the palace. People
gossiped that Ŋga' Bifon III was responsible for the death of his predecessor. Even after Ŋga' Bi'fon III's death the gossip continued. It was believed
that Ŋga' Bi'fon had put a curse on the present *fon*, Səm Mbinglo I, render-
ing him sterile. This rumor continued until the birth of Səm Mbinglo II's
first child. Ŋga' Bi'fon III had serious problems with both *ŋweroŋ* and
ŋgiri, and it is he who is blamed for exacerbating, if not in fact creating, the
ongoing feud between these secret societies. All of this is attributed to the
belief that he "loved money too much." In contrast, Səm Mbinglo I, the
current *fon*, extends the hospitality of the palace to all visitors; this has
added to his considerable respect both inside and outside Nso'.

Obligations are highly institutionalized in the whole range of Nso'
relationships between kin, from the *fon* down to the smallest child. As we
have seen, traditional lineage heads are charged with ensuring the welfare
of lineage dependents, and can be destooled if they do not do so. Older
brothers are under obligation to divide up the patrimony of their fathers
equally among younger brothers and can be, and are, taken to court if they
are perceived to be benefitting at their siblings' expense.

Sharing among kin, while institutionalized and expected, is not a disinterested obligation or a purely altruistic gesture, and giving aid and support to less fortunate kin is not a disinterested act. Nor are the relationships set up through these networks of reciprocity relations of symmetry. By helping out younger and less fortunate kin, asymmetrical reciprocal relationships are set up whereby the benefactor is owed allegiance and political support. The children for whom a kinsman is paying school fees are expected to work for him during school vacations, helping on his farm, carrying coffee to the cooperative, caring for younger children, perhaps helping out in a family store or trading venture. These young kin will refer to him as their father and are expected to act towards him with obedience and respect, often putting his requests before those of their own biological parents.

Redistribution of jobs and money sets up asymmetrical relations among kin and clients. Apprenticeships—for tailors, drivers, traders, carpenters, mechanics—are one of the most common patron-client relationships set up outside kin networks. Because it is difficult, if not impossible, to fire a brother or close relative, many men prefer to apprentice an unrelated person rather than risk being stuck with an incompetent relative. Within these pseudofamilies constituted by the new entrepreneurs, people are nevertheless bound by an ethic derived from Nso' tradition which stresses hierarchy and the rights as well as the obligations of a Nso' leader. These obligations are supported by strong moral sanctions regarding the position of leadership in Nso' society.

Take, for example, the relationship between Peter and his motorboy, Stephen. In his early 30s in the early 1980s, Peter started out almost 10 years ago driving for a Nigerian trader, smuggling goods back and forth on the often treacherous mountainous route from Kimbo' to Gembu. While dangerous, the job was lucrative, and after several years Peter was able to buy a rattletrap Land Rover by combining his own savings with some money borrowed from an uncle. He then started driving to local bush markets, plying the more difficult roads to secure passengers that taxis couldn't accommodate. In addition to fares, he was able to conduct an active trade in bush meat—antelope and "cutting grass" (groundhog). Peter's income depended on two things: being able to make several trips a day, and having free time for his trading activities when not driving. He now needed a motorboy to help collect fees, load the vehicle, stash cargo, and help push the Land Rover when it got stuck in the mud, a common occurrence on these roads in rainy season.

Peter hired Stephen, the 20-year-old younger brother of a friend. Stephen was not actually paid a salary; his pay was experience and whatever monies he could pocket for charging passengers for carrying their cargo.

Although he did not move in with Peter, Stephen now called him Ba as a sign of respect for an elder, a common usage for older men but usually not for men as close in age as Peter was to Stephen. When not on the road or in the taxi park, Stephen could usually be found in Peter's compound, chopping wood, working on the Land Rover, building the driveway, or repairing the road in front of Peter's house.

After two years, Peter was able to buy a new vehicle and began to make a more lucrative taxi run. Stephen took over Peter's old route. Stephen continued for a long time as Peter's "client." He continued to help repair Peter's vehicles and spent much of his time doing chores around Peter's compound. He remained as Peter's right-hand man in the taxi park, helping him load his taxi and find passengers. Eventually, Stephen was able to buy out Peter's interest in the old Land Rover and set up in business by himself, but he still remained Peter's client and was available more or less on call to help him out with home repairs on a new house Peter was building and in business ventures.

While women set up networks of their own through labor exchanges and exchanges of small gifts between compounds, they are not able for economic and cultural reasons to set up the kinds of obligations and networks men are able to establish. Women are also an integral part of men being successful in establishing networks. They provide the food for entertaining guests as well as provisioning the household to free men's income for these ventures. In a subsequent chapter we will look at those men and women who do combine their incomes and projects and at the effects this has on rural stratification today.

The typical household in Nso' can be seen as the principal place where commodity and noncommodity relations come together. Women's production is oriented towards production of use value, whereas men's is oriented towards exchange value. Women's income, while less than men's, is reinvested in maintaining the household. Men's income is invested in increasing individual material and symbolic capital.

Increased market involvement and a cash economy, rather than replacing noncommodity relations of production with capitalist relations of production, have reinforced preexisting relations of cooperation and exchange between households and kin in Nso'. The gender discourse linking women with food, farming, and children has worked to facilitate male hegemony by maintaining a gendered hierarchy within which women's labor reproduces a male hierarchy. As primary producers and reproducers, women's labor supports men's activities outside the household. In doing so, women in Nso' produce, reproduce, and support the reproduction of social relations not only within the household but also within society as a whole.

In an agricultural society, land is the most critical factor of production. The social relations of land in Nso' tend to reflect social relations within the larger society. These land tenure arrangements have always been gendered. The reorganization of land tenure reflects the contours of social change. The next chapter will examine the ways in which changes in land tenure arrangements have been shaped by an ideology of ownership within which men own the fields. In a rapidly commodifying world, women's control over food crops becomes weakened and their right to use land becomes attenuated when they are distanced from control over the factors of production so essential to power in a society dependent on agriculture.

Faay Maamo and Faay Faanjaŋ, *ataanto'*, arguing over the distribution of the palm-wine presented by Phyllis Kaberry and her supporters on the occasion of her *kimbunfon* and investiture as *yaa woo kov*, "queen of the forest," 1958. (Photograph by Elizabeth O'Kelly, courtesy of Elizabeth Chilver)

The wives of the *fon* dancing after Phyllis Kaberry's investiture as *yaa woo kov* in the inner palace, 1958. (Photograph by Elizabeth O'Kelly, courtesy of Elizabeth Chilver)

Miriam Goheen with the wives of Fon Nsə' at the "Nseh Cultural Week." (Photograph by Michael Siryi Dzəənblaŋ)

Nso' notables at the Foumban conference "600 Years of Tikari History," Foumban, Ouest Province, Cameroon, December 1994.

Səm Minglo, the Fon Nso', with Miriam Goheen and *won nto'*, the children of the *fon*, at Nto' Nso', December 1994.

Səm Minglo, the Fon Nso', with *nshiylavsi*, at Nto' Nso', December 1994.

Lale, Nto' Nso' women's dance group, at Foumban, December 1994.

Miriam Goheen's installation as *yaa* Nso', in Kimbo', January 1995.

5

Sum and *Nsay**

Access to Resources and the Sex/Gender Hierarchy

Bone weary and dripping wet after a long day of trekking up and down the steep hillsides of Nso' measuring fields in the rain, our research group gathered around a dwindling fire with several people in the compound where I lived. Savoring the warmth seeping into our still damp clothes, we discussed farming in general and issues of land access and use in particular. The conversation droned on, flowing back and forth among men and women. The discussion was initially calm, and centered around the mundane workings of daily farm life: when to plant, expected yields for various crops, why fertilizer makes food "taste" (i.e., taste bad; besides, it is too expensive to use on food crops). Good-natured arguments arose regarding topics as diverse as current market prices and how long it takes beans to boil (it all depends on the type of beans and the size of the fire).

When the conversation turned to land issues, people became more agitated. Even those who had been lulled into a drowsy state by the warmth of the kitchen and the drone of the conversation perked up and began to participate. The head of the compound, a headmaster in one of the local schools and a member of *yee ŋweroŋ*, began to shake his fist and loudly rail against the lineage heads who charged for use of land. "Now they [the "landlords"] are asking for compensation [for use of land]," he complained. "Compensation for what? Do you compensate a man for grass?" "Na true," the women chimed in, and it is "we who suffer." It is the women who are "being the farmers," and it is they who have to "beg" for land to farm food crops. While according to custom, the only payment required for use of farm land is a calabash of palm wine and a fowl, today women are required to give money "dashes" (bribes) to secure use rights. Women explained that today you go to the lineage head to beg for a plot of

---

*Sum is the Lam Nso' word for farm, and *nsay* is the word for earth.

land. An elder in his compound takes your fowl and calabash of wine and tells you to come back again next week with "something else." You go back with another fowl or perhaps some palm oil. He may not "accept" your request. This can go on for several visits, and usually involves a cash dash in addition to gifts of chickens, palm wine, and palm oil. Besides, exclaimed the women, didn't I see that "men suffer their women for here" (require them to work hard)? Did I see the men trekking long distances to farm? No. It is only the women who "go walka" long distances to farm, while men cultivate coffee close to the compound. Wasn't I tired from just one day's trekking about on the steep hills? Women now have to trek long distances almost daily to reach their farms.

In Nso', as in all agricultural societies, land is the most critical factor of production. But it is not only as a factor of production that land becomes a primary focus for viewing gender relationships. Changing material conditions are reflected in changing systems of land tenure. Land tenure rules, systems of tenure, and the relationships these both structure and reproduce emerge as important indicators of power and as prisms which reflect, and sometimes refract, other social relations.[1] While land in Nso' has become scarce in absolute terms only fairly recently,[2] land tenure rules have long been politically important, and conflicts over borders between various Nso' villages appear frequently in the colonial records.[3] It is value, not always attributable to scarcity, which is of concern in trying to discern the meaning of tenure systems and the power relations these set up both between individuals and between categories of people.[4] Land tenure rules "vary not merely with the centrality of land in production relations, but also with its meaning in other spheres of social, cultural and political life. Scarcity has not always been the essential distinguishing feature."[5] Nso' power relations, including the gender hierarchy, are reflected in the rules of customary land tenure.

The power relations which emerge from the structure of land tenure regulations in Nso' are supported by powerful moral underpinnings. Rules of tenure must, then, be interpreted in conjunction with the social philosophy within which they are embedded. Crucial to our understanding of the gendered power relations embodied in Nso' customary land tenure are the gendered ideology regarding inheritance and the distinction made between *sum,* or farm, and *nsay,* or the earth.

According to customary Nso' tenure, only men inherit land. There is an ideology, amounting almost to a taboo: "men own the fields, women own the crops." Customary rules of inheritance or succession define categories of potential heirs to property rather than designating any specific individual as heir.[6] Although women have had secure rights of usufruct, these rights have been mediated through men, and the categories of inheritors have been, under customary law, exclusively male. The rules of transmission of land must guarantee the vital link the Nso' see between the past, the present, and the future, a link talked about in terms of their relationship to *nsay,* or the earth.[7] The *use* of land has been seen as a guaranteed right of citizenship. Land, like water, air, and fire, is viewed as one of the elements of nature, and its use cannot be denied to anyone who needs it. Women can, according to custom, control their crops and are guaranteed rights to use farmland (*sum*). But it is men who control *nsay* on which women farm.

Nsay is also talked about as "the Earth of the dead." It is the home of the important dead, the ancestors, who are responsible for the well-being of the living and of all future generations. The Earth can become "hot" and punish moral transgressions. It can give judgment and is supplicated to do so, especially in regard to disputes over land use. Libations must be poured ceremonially for the Earth, and prayers made to ensure the ancestors' continuing interest in the health and fertility of the living. It is men who are responsible for performing the rituals of the Earth, and it is through this obligation that those who control land under customary tenure justify that control. The lineage ancestors are male, and obligations towards these ancestors are inherited along with the land or the Earth in which they are thought to reside. Through their ritual obligations, male lineage heads control not just access to and use of land but also the labor process. They determine the days when women can and cannot work in the fields and the times when women can plant and harvest their crops. Although these rituals are ultimately governed by practical considerations, they are symbolically important, and people who do not adhere to the customary practices surrounding these prohibitions may have their land reclaimed by the lineage head.

Land rights in Nso', while controlled by men, do not have an absolute character. As in much of the rest of Africa, these rights of control are "subject to certain limitations and modalities that are contained in various principles of social organization, situational contexts, ethical principles, and rules of etiquette."[8] In Nso', political, economic, and cultural structures are continually changing when people become more integrated into national and international markets. Nso' land tenure must be understood today in a shifting context within which the functioning of households, of regional economies, and of national and international systems is interdependent.

Gender and gender relations are central to the hierarchy of land tenure rules in Nso' today. Land tenure is gendered. Since gender relations are largely products of social and cultural processes,[9] changes in material conditions will inflect upon and transform power relations between men and women. Simultaneously, the ways in which changing material conditions have channelled the transformation in the organization of land tenure have been organized by existing gender relations. To understand this dialectical process, we first need to understand the organization of what is considered in Nso' to be "customary land tenure" in popular parlance and thought today.[10]

Customary Land Tenure

In precolonial Nso', wealth consisted mainly of dependents, and power was organized around control over people and their lives rather than ownership of the means of production. Accumulation was centered on marriage strategies and control over marriage alliances, on symbolic resources or capital such as titles and offices, and on the practices associated with these which gave men access both to lucrative trade networks and to control over the fortunes and destinies of their dependents.[11] Land scarcity was not a particularly salient issue, but control over land was a crucial piece of political capital, reinforced by powerful religious and ritual sanctions, so that control over land was a religious as well as a political power. Control over land both reflected and reproduced Nso' hierarchy. This control has been a critical part of regional hegemony and, as we shall see below, acts today as a means of articulating local and national power.

Rights in land in customary tenure arrangements in Nso' have not involved absolute jurisdiction or exclusive individual control, but are instead better viewed as bundles of rights vested both in individuals and in various social categories at different levels of the social order.[12] These rights, both historically and in common belief today, carry obligations. The rights and obligations surrounding land tenure are a reflection both of membership in the group and of power within the social hierarchy of relationships in Nso'.

The basic ownership of land is vested in the whole society, symbolized by the overlordship or titular ownership of the Fon Nso', with established procedures whereby land use rights may be allocated to individuals. The most difficult aspect of discerning customary tenure rules in Nso' lies in clarifying the often subtle relationships between group and individual interests in agricultural land. Analytically we can distinguish four aspects pertaining to rights or interest in land: use, transfer, allocation, and control.[13]

All individuals in Nso' have rights of use in land by virtue of birth and/or marriage. Various rights of administration or control of access, transfer, and allocation are vested in a hierarchy of interests extending from the *fon* downward to individual farmers, depending on gender, status, and kinship relationships. Integral to this hierarchy of interests is the position of the *ataaŋgvən* (the "fathers who own the fields"), the traditional heads of large lineages and the "landlords" of Nso'. Although their position is glossed as landlord, the lineage heads do not own the fields in a literal sense; they are instead the managers or trustees of the land. The office carries moral and ritual as well as legal connotations.

The *ataaŋgvən* are also referred to as the priests of the land, and are required to perform sacrifices and rituals to ensure the fertility of the land and the well-being and fertility of all persons working on the land. These rituals consist of pouring libations of ritual wine onto the ancestral stone or shrine of their fields at least twice a year—before planting and before the maize harvest. Neither planting nor the harvest can begin before these ceremonies are performed. The landlords are also central in settling land disputes. It is believed that when these men pour libations and make oaths regarding ownership of land, the ancestors who dwell in the land encourage the Earth to "speak the truth" about the ownership of the land in question. The ancestors can cause illness, misfortune, and even death for anyone who swears a false oath to the Earth. These oaths are viewed very seriously by Nso' people today. When discussing the rationality behind these beliefs about the ability of the Earth to "give judgment" in land disputes, one Western-educated Nso' man told me, "You know, I don't know how it works, but believe me, it does. People who swear false oaths 'catch misfortune.' "

The *fon* makes annual sacrifices for the productivity and fertility of the land and for the people under his domain. Although he has his own farms (*sum fon*) worked by his wives and other women who owe him labor, he has no particular piece of land to allocate directly to individuals. To do so, he must go through a traditional landlord. This is usually done when the person requesting the land is a stranger who wishes to settle in Nso'. The *fon* sends his "guest" to a landlord through a palace messenger. By this gesture, the landlord is requested to keep the *fon*'s guest, and after a short time he reports on the man's behavior to the *fon*. If the man's conduct is considered proper, the landlord gives the man land for farming and building after the proper gifts have been made. If the man abandons his land to return to his former home, his property (i.e., buildings) becomes the property of the *fon*, and the land reverts to the control of the landlord. There are no mechanisms for non-Nso' women to obtain land in Nso' except through marriage into the community.

It should be reemphasized here that the overlordship or sovereignty of the Fon Nso' over land was historically and is today representative of the territorial aspect of his control over the people of Nso'. Each of the subchiefs who retained control over his territory in return for fealty and the payment of *nshwi,* or tribute, in the nineteenth century was given ultimate rights of control over land in his own village. *Fon*ship is viewed as the external symbol of the unity and authority of the Nso' people, and the *fon*'s titular control of land carries symbolic and political, rather than direct economic, connotations.

The lineage heads' de facto control can be seen as the recognition of their competence as the political and religious leaders of groups of persons. According to Nso' custom, the privileges of each lineage head's de facto control have included calling on his dependents to assist in the cultivation of his mensal farm (*shuu sum*). The product of these mensal farms is not considered to be the exclusive property of the landlords. The food crops cultivated there are regarded as surety for the lineage against hunger in time of scarcity. Along with the gift of a basket of maize due the landlord at harvest by each of the women working on his land, these crops are held in trust for redistribution to his dependents if their crops prove to be insufficient. The existence of such farms is a symbolic aspect of the lineage head's competence as manager of the lineage, as well as representative of his rights of allocation of land. If people working on his land refuse to work on his mensal farm or to present him with a basket of maize at harvest, they can be evicted.

According to tradition, lineage heads also inherit all permanent tree crops planted by lineage members, as well as property such as livestock (goats, sheep, fowls), guns, ornaments, and money. These are by custom considered lineage, not individual, wealth. The landlord's privilege of office has also included substantial obligations to his dependents, the most important of which has been to ensure their physical well-being and to keep the patrimony of the lineage intact for future generations. Inherited property is supposed to be used for the welfare of the lineage as a whole, not as a means to increase the economic wealth of the lineage heads.

The lineage heads cannot, within the traditional Nso' political system, accumulate great amounts of material wealth at the expense of their dependents. The succession of a lineage head is decided by a council of elders within the compound. Most generally the office passes from older to younger half brothers, men with the same father but different mothers. A lineage head's appointment to the office, or stool, has to be confirmed both by the lineage and by the *fon*, and he can be deposed from office if he abuses his privileges.[14] Nso' people emphasize the fact that "a *faay* can claim a lot of power but he cannot profit too much at the expense of his own people." Power through rights in people has remained salient in the dominant political ideology in Nso', and rights imply obligation.

Women in Nso' cannot customarily allocate or control rights in land, but have in practice exercised considerable control over the plots they cultivate. Until fairly recently, women could loan the right to use their farm plots to other women or even transmit such rights to close female kin.[15]

Women have historically farmed on the land of their husband's lineage, and the majority of them continue to do so today. They have, however, had rights of usufruct in land belonging to their mother's lineage or, in some cases, in land of their father's lineage, rights which have been undermined by the monetary value now attached to farmland. According to Nso' tradition, no unmarried person should be allocated personal rights of use to farmland. Land is, according to custom, viewed as a source of subsistence, a means to feed the household, rather than as a means of accumulation or capital growth.

Briefly summarized, the following points are essential to understanding customary rights and interests in land:[16]

1. The lineage head's role in the allocation of land carries moral as well as legal connotations. He is expected to ensure all his dependents enough land for their individual needs. He is obligated to safeguard the patrimony of the lineage and to supplement the harvests of his dependents in times of scarcity. Although he has final say in deciding whether nonmembers of the lineage should be granted plots, he has a moral and social obligation to make such grants only when it does not jeopardize the needs of his own dependents. Since the status of a lineage head depends on the number of clients and dependents who owe him fealty, he must be careful not to alienate lineage members when seeking to increase his following and clients by allocating land to people outside of the lineage.

2. Permanent tree crops, such as raffia and kola, among others, were historically (before the introduction of coffee in the 1940s) regarded as "things of the lineage." If a man planted tree crops he could exploit them while he lived, but the lineage head, rather than the man's own heirs, inherited these at his death. Tree crops could not in any event be planted without the express permission of the lineage head.

3. Once a person is allocated plots by the lineage head, the rights to use these plots are handed down from father to son (or mother to daughter-in-law), so that the use and the inheritance of the use of certain areas of land have tended to become vested in smaller segments of the lineage. Farmland allocated by the landlord can be reclaimed at any time as long as he gives proper notice, but he cannot take back land unnecessarily from his own dependents unless they refuse to recognize his rights of leadership and rights of allocation and management. Such refusal would be marked by their not observing his Country Sundays (each landlord's ritual days of rest, when hoes are not supposed to be used in the fields under his control), by their refusing reasonable requests for aid, by not showing him proper respect, or by gossiping about him or "backbiting" him to others.

4. Land allocated to nonkin, if not reclaimed for use by the lineage within one generation, tends to become permanently alienated, or at least the rights of control over the land become a matter of dispute.
5. Unmarried people, male or female, cannot "beg" plots of land for individual use. Unmarried women farm on their father's land, using a hoe he supplies until they are married, at which time they are given a hoe by their husband and are allocated plots for their personal use by his lineage head. Young men have not traditionally worked food crops, but unmarried men are expected to help clear land for their mothers and other women of their father's lineage, and to help carry the harvest to storage. In addition, unmarried men have in the past been expected to help their fathers and the lineage heads in the kola trade. Before there were vehicles and motorable roads, young men were required to head-load kola long distances into Nigeria.
6. Land, while it can be loaned, should not be sold, pawned, or bartered.

The Political Economy of Customary Tenure

Within customary land tenure rules, the allocation of land has been ultimately controlled directly or indirectly by a group of heads of large lineages, the *ataaŋgvən*, who hold office through the authority of both the *fon* and the lineage. Although the *fon* has no particular piece of land to allocate to individuals, he symbolically holds the ultimate authority over control and access to land. According to local people, no "reasonable" lineage head would refuse the request of the *fon* to allocate land to a "guest" unless the man in question were found to have "bad fashion." Heads of large lineages have been under obligation to allocate farmland to the *fon*'s wives, as well as to other members of the royal lineage. The *fon*'s titular control over land has also included the right to expel rebels and criminals, and to repossess land from any given landlord if the *fon* decides it is in the interests of the Nso' people to do so. He seldom exercised this latter right in the past.[17] However, a number of new development programs and projects have made the *fon*'s role in this regard more explicit. These include the large tea estate in the northeast sector of Nso', rice projects in the Mbo' and Ndop plains, wheat projects in Nsə' and Ŋkar, and government requests for land for schools and official buildings. There is an ongoing and increasingly sensitive need to demarcate new grazing lands continually because of increases in both the human and animal populations. The *fon*'s permission must be obtained from national officials to use land for these purposes, although it is clear that he is ultimately obligated by the national government to give his consent. He "requests" this land from the landlord(s) in question, and hands it over to government officials, usually with great public pomp and ceremony.

The *fon* has the authority to deny the lineage heads' right to give land to outsiders, although he seldom exercises his right in that direction. However, there was a case in Nsə' in the late 1970s when a lineage head lent land to some people from Kimbo'. This occurred at a time when there was a particularly hostile conflict between the Fon Nsə' and the Fon Nso' about rights of allocation over the land in question, and the Fon Nsə' was adamant that no people from Nso' proper be given rights to use land in Nsə'. The Fon Nsə' demanded that the landlord take back the land. When his request was ignored, the Fon Nsə' had the man removed from office and reinstated him only after he agreed to take back the land and pay a fine of 10 goats and 40 calabashes of palm wine, not an insignificant amount of wealth.

Once a landlord allocates land to individuals, the land comes under the control of individual male family heads, whose sons will later inherit the use of the land. The family head—the *taala'*, or "father of the compound"—holds rights of allocation of this family land. At a man's death today, his male heir, usually the eldest son, shares out the rights to use this land to all his younger male siblings. Before the 1940s, all tree crops and valuable property of the dead man reverted to the lineage head as the trustee of lineage wealth. More likely than not, the lineage head reallocated the wealth of the dead man among the man's male heirs, but he was not under obligation to do so, and often the man's property was shared among the man's brothers as well as his sons. The important point here is that, although individuals may inherit and hold secure rights to the use of land, according to Nso' traditional ideology the wealth of the lineage should be kept in perpetual trust by the lineage head, who, from the orthodox view, maintains rights of allocation of all "things of the lineage."

In summary, primary rights of access to and control over land have been held by the *fon*. The *fon*'s ultimate power to make decisions regarding the land and the people working on the land symbolizes the rights to land use by individual members of Nso' society. The *fon*, as the symbol of the unity of Nso', has been under a moral obligation to ensure that all people have enough farm land to feed their households. With the increasing pressure on arable farmland, in the 1970s the Fon Nso' opened up for farming what formerly were royal hunting grounds. The largest such area is around Nkuv, some 15 kilometers southwest of Kimbo'. By the early 1980s there were over 450 families farming in Nkuv.

Primary rights of allocation have been vested in a number of lineage heads, subject to the ultimate, primarily symbolic, authority of the *fon*. A lineage head's rights of allocation carry moral obligations: he is obliged to

ensure his dependents enough land to satisfy their subsistence requirements, to come to their aid in times of scarcity, and to keep the patrimony
of the lineage intact to ensure the well-being of future generations. The
allocation of land to a member of the lineage carries implicit assurance of
permanent rights of usufruct, as long as the recipient complies with kinship
obligations and continues to farm the land, allowing for periods of fallow.
Secondary rights of allocation have been vested in family or compound
heads within the larger lineage, subject to kinship obligations both in terms
of fealty to the lineage head and in terms of ensuring the well-being of all
members of their families. In some cases, individuals have been able to
allocate plots they have farmed and no longer require for use to members
of the lineage, but they have not been allowed to hand their farm plots over
to people outside the lineage, and usually not even to people outside the
compound.

Rights to use of land have been vested in all individuals by virtue of
birth. All Nso' people have had rights to use land as long as they farm on
the land, abide by traditional custom, and comply with the rulings of traditional authorities. While a landlord's primary obligation is to the people of
his lineage, there is also a deep-seated cultural value stressing the belief that
all Nso' people should have access to enough land to fulfill their subsistence needs. If need be, the *fon* can intervene and request a landlord to
allocate land to a given individual if he or she has no other means of access
to land.

Hierarchy of Rights

Interests in or rights of use, transfer, allocation, and control have all been
based on a hierarchy of kinship relations and obligations. The further
down the hierarchy—*fon,* landlords, family heads, individuals—the more
closely these rights are circumscribed by specific kinship ties. This hierarchy reflects patron-client relations within the kin group specifically and
within the Nso' polity in general. The higher up the hierarchy, the broader
the scope an individual man has in exercising various interests and rights in
land, and of increasing the number of people directly indebted to him, thus
enhancing his status and increasing his political power. Women's rights to
land, whether the women are married or single, are always mediated
through men. The rituals which regulate the agricultural cycle and validate
rights of control over land are all controlled by men, although it is women
who farm virtually all food crops.

The hierarchy of rights in land is reflected in the levels of adjudication
of land disputes in customary law. Land disputes, if they are not settled
between the individuals involved, are brought to the compound head. If

the dispute is not resolved within the extended family, the landlord (or landlords) in question is consulted. If these parties fail to reach a resolution, the *fon* is called on to arbitrate the case. The traditional court of final enforcement has been *ŋweroŋ*, the regulatory society. The fact that *ŋweroŋ*, which is associated with the *fon* and the palace, constitutes an important avenue of enforcement is pointed to by Nso' people as evidence that the symbolic control of the *fon* over land is dependent on the Nso' people's recognition of their political allegiance to him. The power of *ŋweroŋ* to be the ultimate enforcer in land disputes has been referred to as *taa nsay* (literally, "father of the earth") which Nso' people say should be interpreted as meaning "the *fon*'s power over the land actually goes back to both *ŋweroŋ* and the *fon*."[18] Although *ŋweroŋ* has publicly supported the *fon*'s decisions, it has maintained the right to dispute these decisions and even to negate his decision-making power. It is also true that it is men, not women, who can take cases to *ŋweroŋ*, whose membership and secret knowledge exclude women from participation. In regard to the hierarchy of adjudication of land disputes, the salient feature of those who have rights to determine the outcome of these disputes is one's relationship to *nsay*, an almost exclusively male prerogative. Women are conspicuously absent from making decisions about land allocation, even though they are the primary farmers.

Several features of the customary tenure system described above need further comment. Customary tenure rules are gendered in a way that privileges adult men, particularly men of title. Within the orthodox version of this tenure system, although the *fon* has had the ultimate symbolic authority, the titled heads of large and powerful lineages have been able to exert a great deal of political control, a control which is reinforced by their ritual obligations to the Earth, or *nsay*. This control has given them access to economic resources, the most important of which is control of the productive and reproductive labor of their dependents. The surplus generated by this labor can be redistributed and invested by the lineage heads to validate their political position. Only men can inherit land and real material wealth, and this inheritance in the past was subject to the control of the lineage heads. Women have had little say over the control or allocation of land but have had secure rights of usufruct in land of various kin, the most important of which is the land of their husband's lineage. Women can transfer their use rights of the land they have "begged" to close female relatives. It has been unthinkable that anyone would be denied rights of land for subsistence farming. Thus rights of usufruct have been part of the doxa, just as belief in the efficacy of the ancestors to ensure the fertility of the land and to sit in judgment of the living is an undisputed part of Nso' cosmological belief.

Contemporary Forces for Change in Customary Land Tenure

The issue of changing practices regarding land in Nso' involves not just new uses for land and population pressures but also types of property different from those in the past. There are today new meanings attached to control of land and different implications of this for various categories of people, including men and women, titled men and commoners, and those with access to the modern state and those without such access. While most land (over 85 percent in the late 1970s) in Nso' has remained under customary tenure,[19] the meaning of this traditional tenure and the actual practices associated with it have changed rather rapidly over the last two decades. In recent years the economic crisis in Cameroon, as in much of Africa, has reinforced people's efforts to diversify their assets and sources of income and has contributed to a proliferation of channels of access to land.[20] New channels of access have created tensions in Nso' when various individuals and categories of individuals claim rights in the same piece of land. These new channels of access have largely worked in favor of men, who have both access to cash and a knowledge of the workings of the state bureaucracy, and against the secure rights of usufruct guaranteed by traditional tenure arrangements. Women have by and large been denied ownership of land, and thus new concepts of property have undermined security of tenure for most women. Recent studies have suggested that women in Africa are forming a new category of the dispossessed. Women's limited access to resources throughout Africa is well documented.[21] Nso' is no exception to the general trend. These are issues which need to be examined in detail, but first it is necessary to describe the context and the processes which have created these problems.

The introduction of cash crops, coffee in particular, and the increasing involvement of the rural sector in the monetary economy have had significant effects on the customary tenure pattern, especially in more densely settled areas. At the same time, the orthodox views that farmland, especially land for cultivation of food crops, is a right of Nso' citizenship and that farmland should not be bought or sold remain dominant in most sectors of the population, even in the face of growing evidence that this is no longer the case.

The greatest forces for change in customary tenure patterns have come primarily from five sources: (1) the introduction and expansion of cash crops, especially coffee, as the primary source of cash income for most Nso' households; (2) the monetary value now attached to land and the growing tendency to view land as a commodity and source of cash income and investment rather than as a means to satisfy subsistence requirements; (3) population growth in general, in particular the growth of an urban or town population, leading to heavy demands and inflated values for land within the more densely populated areas; (4) development projects, funded primarily by international aid and promoted heavily by the national government; and (5) increases in cattle herds, leading to conflicts of interests and competition for land use between farmers and herders. This last point was a gender issue and has become increasingly so with the continual threat to women's food crops and their livelihoods by the growing herds of cattle of both local men and Fulani graziers.

The substantial investment of time and money (magnified by inflation) involved in coffee production has led men to demand that their own heirs inherit their coffee farms. Coffee, along with kola, raffia, and other tree crops under customary tenure, is viewed as a permanent crop which cannot be planted without permission of the landlord. As will be recalled, tree crops have traditionally been considered "things of the lineage" and according to custom are supposed to revert to the lineage head at the death of the man who cultivated them. In most of Nso' today, however, permanent crops, including coffee, are considered individual property and are inherited by individual heirs rather than reverting to the lineage head. Landlords have become extremely reluctant to give out land for any use other than the cultivation of food crops, and even here they will often put a definite limit on the amount of time the land can be used by someone outside the lineage. Permission must be obtained, even by lineage members, before planting tree crops. If a man wants to sell his coffee farm, he must also ask the permission of the landlord before doing so, and should he decide to sell his farm, he is required to give the lineage head the first option to buy.

Pressure on land has its origin in several sources, the most important of which have been the increases in cattle herds and coffee cultivation. Coffee emphasized the individualization of land, whereas cattle grazing activities emphasized the extraction of tribute and fealty by the *fon* and his landlords. Negotiations over use of land for both these activities, as we shall see, have highlighted patron-client relationships and established patterns of authority. Although the influences of these two alternative patterns of land use were divergent, coffee and cattle had one thing in common: they exerted heavy pressure on the available arable land. In this process women have had to bear all the pressure because they either lost their farms to coffee growers or had their crops destroyed by cattle.

In and around villages, land has assumed a real monetary value, and a set price has been established for land suitable for building. Gradually the landlords have come to extend the monetary value of land to farmland, and have begun to ask for cash as well as the traditional prestations (a calabash of palm wine and a fowl) for use of farmland. This is true in smaller villages such as Nsǝ' as well as in Kimbo'. In 1988 land was being sold in Nsǝ' by absentee landlords for 140,000 FCFA for one-quarter hectare. The practice of charging for farmland has enraged many Nso' people, including the compound head whom we met at the beginning of this chapter. Nso' people see access to farmland as a right of citizenship. Whatever the economic benefits might be, this practice has not been an astute political move on the part of traditional lineage heads, whose credibility has been undermined by what is perceived by many as crass, unseemly, and even immoral behavior. Yet many landlords are rapidly selling land tracts. As more people buy land for building and cash crop farming, land is sold rather than given by ordinary traditional procedures for securing usufruct, and women who begged or borrowed land for farming are being dispossessed.

Ŋga' Bi'fon II, in 1972, became so distressed about land issues and the political implications of these for traditional authority that he made a public speech stressing the need for all Nso' people to adhere to the principles of customary tenure. The main points of this speech, reproduced below, underline the inherent conflicts between rights of all individuals to permanency of tenure and the rights of a hierarchy of customary authority to hold and administer land within a context of increasing commodification. His speech emphasizes the religious and moral connotations of stewardship of the land, and denounces what he perceived as a break of faith with the ancestors and the Nso' community on the part of lineage heads who charge for land use.

The text of this speech is of sufficient interest to warrant closer scrutiny. Its central points are:

1. No two persons can represent the *fon* over any one piece of land.
2. Some landlords are collecting yearly rents for land ranging from 500 to 2000 FCFA, and this is contrary to tradition and wrong-headed.
3. There are too many land cases in recent times which have no historical precedents.
4. Landlords should not be represented by others in court because the younger men they send to represent them are not priests of the land, don't know about land matters, and can't perform the traditional sacrifices.
5. Careless handling of land matters is the single most important reason for conflict and lack of unity in Nso' today.
6. All present ill luck stems from the landlords accepting more than the traditional wine and fowl for land.

Although the economic basis of land access and the meaning of property were, by at least the early 1970s, rapidly changing to reflect the growing view of land as a source of income and investment, these were superimposed upon prevailing ideas about land rights and the moral basis for stewardship of land. Practices regarding land had become much more heterodox than the dominant ideology regarding use of land, which remained, if not part of the doxa, at least firmly orthodox. The use of land as a right of citizenship in Nso' remained an important piece of political ideology and local identity. This became clear to me when I first questioned women about prices paid for use of land in the late 1970s. If asked directly, "What did you pay the landlord for your land?" people invariably answered, "A calabash of wine and a fowl, of course." I was puzzled somewhat by this because I had heard so much grumbling about the landlords' practice of asking for under-the-table dashes for land use. Yet everyone seemed to be giving the standard prestations. Finally I began asking, "In addition to a calabash of palm wine and a fowl, what did you give to the landlord for your land?" then I began hearing complaints about demands for cash or gifts in kind (palm oil, zinc, cloth) in addition to the traditional prestations. Payments ranged in value from a few thousand FCFA to more than 40,000 FCFA, depending on the type of use, the location of the land, and the relationship of the person in question to the landlord.

Old rules have come to be explained by the landlords in new ways, making use of what Maine long ago identified as "legal fictions" to bring existing rules or laws into accord with changed social conditions without the letter of the law being changed.[22] The traditional prestations of a fowl and a calabash of wine are the payment for use of land, and the other gifts are simply to allow the payments to be accepted by the landlords. On their part, the landlords defend the practice of asking for at least a small cash payment, declaring that in the old days, land was used only for feeding people, but now people are making a profit from the land, and the landlords feel they are entitled to share in this profit.

The number of disputes has increased dramatically with people using different sets of rules to try to secure access to as much land as possible. Most of these cases are tried in traditional courts, and the landlords see the payments received for use of land as compensation for the adjudication of these land conflicts, which in the past were paid for with gifts of palm wine, small livestock, and palm oil. National bureaucrats ask for and receive bribes for the allocation of national lands. The landlords see this, and feel that they are also entitled to payment for allocating land. Many Nso' people claim that, if the government had not put a price on land, the traditional landlords would not charge the way they do today. We will return to this point in later sections of this chapter.

"Land Reform" and Traditional Control

The commercialization of land and of the products of the land has had important effects on the position of the traditional landlords and on their relationship to their dependents. The institution of national "land reform" statutes in 1974, providing new avenues to land access and instituting individual tenancy as determined by the national government, has created a real market in land. This has undermined both the status of traditional landlords, as alternative avenues of acquiring land are opened up, and the rights of individuals to use land by virtue of birth, as money becomes a requirement for filing for land titles. As will be discussed later, the commercialization of farming, along with new patterns of access and individual ownership instituted by the state, has come into conflict with the traditional ideal of free land and is creating a dual system of land tenure in the rural areas, allowing the new elites to accumulate large amounts of land. The new elites facilitate their ability to acquire land both by acquiring the traditional symbols of leadership by investing in titles and becoming active in Nso' palace politics and by utilizing their knowledge of the national land ordinances to file for allocation of and title to large tracts of national land.

Although most farmland near and around villages has remained at least nominally under customary control, this control is subject to the laws of the state, which temporarily grants rights of allocation to the traditional rulers. In fact, there is a good deal of land in the chiefdom not directly under customary control which the government has claimed as state land to be allocated according to national development programs. It is difficult to find exact figures because, as will be discussed in the second half of this chapter, just what constitutes "traditional or customary control" is open to dispute. Although over 85 percent of Nso' land is officially listed as under traditional control, that control is ultimately subject to the laws of the state, which has, for the time being, allocated some rights of control to the traditional lineage heads.

We will first take a closer look at the traditional lineage heads, and then examine the relationship between population pressure and the commercialization of land, concentrating on the ways in which these, in combination, affect customary land rights on all farmland currently under control of customary landlords. We will then look closely at the national land ordinances, the ways in which these define rights of access to new land, and the ways in which these national laws influence and are influenced by the principles of customary land tenure. In combination all these factors have led to a process of commodification and privatization, a process which has had different effects on various sectors of the Nso' population, especially men in comparison with women. In the final section of this chapter we will look at land issues in terms of gender in the context of increasing rural stratification.

The Landlords of Nsə': Profile of the Traditional Lineage Heads

To understand the traditional landlords more thoroughly, it is useful to look at some of them in closer detail.

All the landlords of Nsə' were interviewed to determine the "typical" rural village land allocation pattern. In the early 1980s there were 16 official landlords in Nsə'. Of these, 7 are *ashuufaay*, 9 are *afaay*, and 1, who said he is "holding the stool until family matters are straightened out," is a *sheey*. With the exception of one *faay*, the Nsə' landlords say their ancestors came to Nsə' travelling together with the Fon Nsə', who then gave them this land to rule in his name. Whether this is historically accurate is not as important as its having become a legal fiction, and the pattern of land tenure in Nsə' mirrors the overall Nso' pattern, with the Fon Nsə' as titular owner of all Nsə' land, and with primary rights of allocation vested in these 16 lineage heads. In Nsə', just as in Nso', they are known as the *ataaŋgvən*, the "fathers who own the fields," or the "fathers" and "priests" of the fields, with obligations to provide for the well-being of their dependents, to offer the necessary rituals to ensure that well-being, and to guard the patrimony of the lineage to ensure continuity between the ancestors, the living, and the unborn generations.

The pattern of succession to office here is typical of Nso' landlords. A council of lineage elders, ranging in number from 6 to 10, picks the lineage head from among those men eligible to succeed. Usually succession passes to a younger half brother. More rarely a son of the previous landlord is chosen to succeed his father, but usually only if there is "no correct somebody" in the former category. Their choice must be validated by the *fon*—in this case, the Fon Nsə'. The *fon* has the right to destool the lineage head if he perceives the man not to be acting in the interests of the family or to be mismanaging the land. the family (lineage) can ask the *fon* to depose a lineage head who is perceived to be acting contrary to their interests.

Interviews took place in the compounds of each of the landlords, who, dressed in traditional embroidered gown, crocheted cap, and ceremonial beads, greeted me with hospitality and elaborate formality. Stools were fetched and palm wine and kola, symbols of hospitality, were offered and consumed. The adult women formally greeted me. The younger children peeked out from behind their mothers, and their older siblings peered out at the proceedings from behind the sides of buildings. A tour of the compound centered on the ceremonial house with its carved gateposts, indicating the landlord's status as head of a large lineage and symbolic of his obligation as its ritual leader to be close to the ancestors and to offer sacrifices. The graves of his predecessors line the courtyard outside the ceremonial house, each marked by a round stone. Here, the skulls of all the former lineage heads are buried, a constant reminder of the ancestors and of the continuity of the lineage leader's duties.

Each landlord was attended by elders of the compound, ranging in number from three to seven. We sat around drinking and talking for several hours while chickens and children wandered in and out of the courtyard. The adult women of the compound, after officially greeting me, initially retreated to their kitchens. Here they gathered in small groups, watching and listening to our conversation, often exchanging rapid comments with a great deal of laughter. Soon it became obvious that, without input from the women, the men could not answer many of my questions about genealogical connections and just who was working what land, so several of the senior women came and joined in our discussion. All in all, the presence of a "European" woman, somewhat of a curiosity in Nsə' in the early 1980s, provided an afternoon of gossip and entertainment.

The landlords of Nsə' appeared splendid and dignified, even opulent, in their official dress; however, their formal status did not denote material wealth. If they were profitting materially from their status and position, they kept it well concealed. Their compounds were larger than the average Nsə' compound, and they had numerous wives and dependents living with them, but many of the niceties of modern village life found in the compounds of men of lower status were absent here. Tattered trousers or *lapas* showed from beneath their embroidered gowns, and their shoes were scuffed and often falling apart. Only 4 of the 16 displayed that widespread modern symbol of success, a wristwatch that works. The compounds of the landlords lacked signs of affluence seen elsewhere—concrete floors and upholstered, overstuffed furniture. The clothes of the women in their compounds were faded and worn. Only three of the Nsə' landlords owned cattle. While all had mensal farms worked by the women who farmed on their land, they were all quick to point out that the produce from these farms was stored to feed their extended families and to entertain guests, and could not be sold as a source of income. Commercialization of land and of the products of the land has, however, had profound effects on the ways in which the traditional landlords think about land and in which they use their power of allocation.

Commercialization and Customary Tenure

The number of "outsiders" (non-lineage members) working on lineage lands has decreased substantially over the past two decades. As commer-

cialization withdraws land from subsistence use, pressure on land for locally consumed food crops grows. An expanding population is now
squeezed onto a shrinking subsistence land base. As might be expected, the
larger the lineage holdings, the more outsiders there are working the land.
Only one landlord interviewed, the most prominent lineage head in Nsə',
had more than 10 women from outside the lineage working on his land. All
the landlords, including this lineage head, claimed that they were no longer
giving out land to people outside the lineage, especially land for coffee
farms and house building. Coffee farms are usually restricted to land
around compounds. Land for building and land for planting coffee are
now viewed as falling into the same category. Both are essentially individual property, which cannot be reclaimed by the landlord without compensation. The landlord's permission must be obtained for planting coffee. If a
man wants to sell his coffee farm, he must consult the landlord, who will
either try to purchase the farm himself or find a buyer from within the
lineage.

All Nsə' landlords agree that they have every right to reclaim
agricultural land, especially from people outside the lineage. Land given
for food crops to women inside the lineage is difficult to reclaim, and
landlords seldom try to take it back. However, all of them claim that they
have a right to do so if the woman working the land (or her husband)
"makes a mistake with me," or if he or she "backbites me to other
people." At least 10 women in Nsə' complained that a landlord had
reclaimed land they were farming, and rumors about this occurring were
numerous. Many women expressed anxiety at leaving land fallow,
fearing the landlord would be bribed into reallocating land not currently
under cultivation.

The amount of uncultivated arable land within trekking distance of
the village has dwindled to the point that only 3 out of 16 landlords say
they still have land to give out, and these 3 say they must do so with cau-
tion. There is no doubt that many people are aware of the impending land
shortage, and are trying to hold on to and acquire as much land as possible
to ensure their sons' access to land.

The pressure on land has undermined women's rights over the land
they are cultivating. While the length of fallow has customarily been left to
individual discretion, the landlords now carefully calculate allocations on
the basis of the total land available. Today the length of time a woman feels
she can let her fields lie fallow before the landlord decides the land is not
being put to proper use and reallocates it has been greatly attenuated. Although Kaberry emphasizes the ways in which women not only had secure
use rights but also had some rights of allocation over the plots they were
cultivating, this is no longer the case.[23] All landlords state emphatically

that it is the women's place to work the fields, not to own or manage them. Nso' men say that women do not have reason, that they know much about farming but not about property or money. Over the past several decades land has come to be viewed as a source of money income and cash investment, even while the idea that all people should have enough land to grow food for the household clearly remains part of the dominant ideology. Women can no longer lend out the plots they are working without express permission from the landlord.

Although most landlords in Nsə' will deny it, there is substantial evidence that they are now demanding a cash payment in addition to the traditional prestations for use of land. The Nsə' landlords all denied doing so, but all also stated that they know the others do so. V., the Nsə' woman whose young son died, complained not only of the money required but also of the time consumed in begging for land today. She said that nowadays, when you go to the landlords' compound it is only the *taa sum*, the elder in his compound responsible for land matters, who greets you. He takes your wine and fowl and tells you to come back again next week. You go back at the appointed time with another fowl, some corn *fufu* or palm oil, and perhaps 500–1000 FCFA. He may give you land to farm or he may ask you to come again in a week's time. If you are a woman of the lineage (a wife of a lineage member), three visits will usually suffice, but others may go several more times with more money or more gifts. Sometimes your husband has to intervene with the landlord for you before the *taa sum* will agree to give you land.

In and around the larger villages this payment can be considerable. The landlords say their people give them things because they "love us too much." *Koŋ*, the word for love in Lam Nso', can be glossed as loyalty and respect for a superior or ruler. Prestations to the landlord, including cash payments, are viewed as a symbolic affirmation of his right to allocate and manage the land of the lineage and a legitimation of his competence as manager of its patrimony. Lineage heads should not, according to tradition, profit too much at the expense of their dependents, and are expected to ensure the welfare of lineage members. While land has tended to become vested in particular lineages and segments of those lineages, under customary tenure it cannot accrue to individuals in large portions as personal property.

Landlords and Dependents

Despite the customary pattern of tenure, the meaning of land and property has changed substantially, with an increasing tendency to view it as a source of cash income and investment, not just as a means to satisfy household subsistence needs. This, coupled with the growing pressure on land, has led to conflicts between lineage heads and their dependents and has created a situation of differential access to lineage land even within the customary tenure pattern. As noted earlier, land has come to be vested in particular lineages, the lineages of the landlords. Cash payments, ranging from a symbolic dash from close lineage relatives to substantial "rent payments" from outsiders, are common. Landlords no longer tend to allocate land to non–lineage members.[24]

The growing land shortage has resulted in a tightening of lineage control over land within the structure of customary tenure. For the average village farmer, customary tenure is the only avenue of access to land. While there is still land available to satisfy subsistence needs, there is little room for increasing the amount of land under cultivation within the customary tenure pattern, and many women travel far to farm. People who belong to lineages whose land has become used up have to beg land from other lineage heads. This is becoming increasingly difficult. While the landlords, as trustees of the land, are under a moral obligation to provide enough land for subsistence to all their dependents, they are not under any obligation to do so for people outside the lineage.

Farmland allocated according to customary land tenure rules cannot be hoarded or used as an investment to obtain capital. Village farmers cannot file for title to the land they have begged from their lineage heads. They possess rights to the use of the land and to the inheritance of the use by their heirs so long as they continue to cultivate the land and abide by the rules of customary authority. When questioned about why they did not file for title to land, many farmers said of course they would not be able to do so, that if they attempted to file, the landlord would take back the land. Furthermore, many people trust the traditional authorities, not the national government. They feel that if they file for title to land, it will become just another means by which the national government can interfere with their lives.

The ambiguous position of the lineage heads' rights over the allocation of land is reflected in the local adjudication of land disputes. According to customary law, the landlords and the *fon*, backed up by *ŋweroŋ*, have a monopoly over rights of allocation of land and have had the final say in determining individuals' rights in any conflict over land use. Today, people say the ultimate power of the traditional authorities over land disputes is being usurped by the land commission, and many express the opinion that land cases, when judged outside customary courts, are decided in favor of the man who is able to argue effectively with the national bureaucracy and "feed" (bribe) the land commission. They say that anyone who goes outside the traditional courts and hires a lawyer is, of course, in the wrong; otherwise why pay money to a lawyer? Many local people express the fear, whether right or wrong, that the national government is going to "push" them out of their land rights.

On the other hand, the traditional landlords still have the right to allocate land within their domains, which include most of the land within and around the villages. Most land conflicts are today still decided by the landlords and the *afon,* with or without consultation with the district officer. The Fon Nso' and two of the landlords in Nso' proper are members of the Bui Division land commission.

Most people in Nso' have retained access to enough land for subsistence needs through customary land tenure. Although a growing number of people are working for wages on other people's farms, this work is seasonal and sporadic, and occurs in addition to, not in place of, the cultivation of their own crops. Women whose access to farmland means trekking long distances to farm say they would rather work for guaranteed wages than try to farm more land far out in the countryside to earn cash. There is not yet a process of rural proletarianization. However, as the population rapidly increases and as cattle herders vie with farmers for land use rights, access to economically and socially viable land (i.e., land within reasonable distance from compounds and markets) is becoming seriously curtailed.[25]

Disputes over Land

Land disputes are exacerbated not only the the commercialization of property and by population growth but also by the growing number of cattle in the region. According to the district officer, the amount of land designated for grazing—59 percent of the available land in the region—was established before the introduction of cash crops and the current commercialization of food crops and when the population was less dense.[26] However, farmer-grazier disputes are now exacerbated both by growth in human and animal populations and by the development of irrigated rice cultivation on the Ndop and Mbo' plains, areas long considered dry-season grazing pasture. The farmer-grazier disputes over land have led to "range wars" and even fatal hostilities. Crop damage by livestock has for several decades been a major source of contention and protest by women in Nso'.[27] It was the major complaint I heard from women farmers when, newly arrived in Nsə' in 1979, I was confronted by 60 women who asked me to intervene with the authorities to help alleviate livestock damage to their crops.

Farmer-grazier disputes constitute the majority of land disputes in Nso'. Basically, these are of two types, the more common being disputes over compensation for destroyed crops. Here goats as well as cattle are prime culprits. Farmers, the vast majority of whom are women, are not allowed to kill animals caught destroying their crops. Instead, they must catch the animal in order to identify the owner. Needless to say, this is often difficult, and ownership of the guilty animal(s) is usually hard to determine. Women claim that the owners of the animals are in a better position to win disputes, which are often costly to bring to court. Although most cattle are owned by Fulani herders, local men owning cattle are much less forthcoming with compensation than are the Fulani, who, if convinced their animals are guilty, will pay up. Conflicts over compensation are often accompanied by counteraccusations on the part of the herders, who claim that women purposely plant crops in grazing areas to gain compensation.

The second, and ultimately more serious, type of farmer-grazier dispute centers around the allocation of farmland from what was formerly considered grazing lands. With the increasing pressure on land, the *fon* and the lineage heads have targeted land under their control which herders have historically considered dry-season grazing land and have reallocated it to local people for farming. This pattern has been intensified by the government rice projects in traditional dry-season grazing areas. These are the cases most likely to result in violent hostilities, and are the most likely land disputes to end up in national channels of adjudication, either in the district officer's office or in magistrate court.

Aside from competition with herders, the most serious constraint on opening up new farmland is lack of adequate infrastructure. Ministry of Agriculture officials in the Northwest Province estimated in the early 1980s that two times the amount of land currently under cultivation could be opened up for farming if adequate roads were built to outlying areas, particularly the Mbo' Plain on the northeast border of Nso', areas such as Nkuv and Lip to the southeast, and some of the valleys around Jottin-Nooni to the west of Kimbo'. Most uncultivated arable land lies in these outlying valleys and plains. Roads to these areas are virtually nonexistent. During the dry season, when four-wheel drive vehicles can reach these areas, transport costs are prohibitively expensive, and most crops are carried out by head-loading. Although there are plans to improve the major transport arteries in the area, there are few funds available for construction of farm-to-market roads.

There are several other reasons why much of the land is not economically viable, most of which are social constraints. People who live in the highlands are loath to move to low-lying, malaria-ridden areas with inadequate medical facilities. The isolation is socially unappealing, especially for young people, but also for the majority of Nso' people for whom kinship networks, membership and participation in various men's fraternal clubs and secret societies, social and church clubs, savings and loan associations, and schools form important and integral parts of social life.

The economic constraints are often insurmountable. Without money to institute a viable development plan and to file for land allocation from the national government, it is virtually impossible to secure large holdings out in the countryside. Labor and transport costs are high. Most of the larger farms in areas like the Mbo' Plain are currently owned by absentee landlords who hire labor or utilize kinship and patronage networks to work their farms. S., a prominent local politician and proprietor of a school in Kimbo', is typical of these new landlords. He maintains a labor force by making the young people from his school do "practical work" on his rice farm in Mbo'. For this work, they may receive a portion of their tuition, but many get only course credits for their labor. Patron-client kin networks are also used as a labor source, with poorer kin managing and working farms out in the countryside in return for a small part of the profit, usually in hopes of future patronage if the owner is rich and powerfully connected.

Lineage Heads and the New Elites

With the increasing pressure on land, lineages in the rural villages have curtailed their lendings and, in terms of land control, have become more exclusive corporate groups. Within the lineage the landlord or lineage head still maintains primary rights of allocation. The traditional lineage heads' authority has, however, in recent years been dependent on support from the new elites within their respective lineages. The economic crisis in Cameroon over the past decade has encouraged people to diversify their assets and sources of income and, as Berry has argued for Africa as a whole, has contributed to the proliferation of channels of access to land as well as other resources.[28] Alternative channels of access to land in Nso' have been opened up by national ordinances regarding allocation and privatization. Because the state now controls these alternative channels of access to land, many individuals and families have come to spend considerable resources establishing patterns of access to the state, notably through education. This provides the rural elite with the knowledge necessary for their admission to the national channels of access to land. However, this is not accomplished at the expense of old loyalties and alliances; rather, these are reinforced. As we shall see, because of the particular way in which national land laws and customary tenure are combined in Nso', this strategy ensures the new elites a diversity of access options.

While the traditional lineage heads depend on support from the new elites, these "nouveaux riches" for their part have started to invest heavily in the symbols of traditional leadership. Just as individual men in precolonial Nso' could advance their status and their access to control of important resources through personal achievement and the adroit use of wealth, so can the new elites today. The most important and public manifestation of this is the acquisition of offices and titles in the secret societies, especially in *ŋweroŋ*. *Ŋweroŋ* has in a variety of ways retained its status and function as the most important traditional decision-making institution. The new elites have in effect assumed leadership of *ŋweroŋ*, which acts as a point of articulation between the traditional and national bureaucrats. By publicly assuming the symbolic trappings of a Nso' leader, the modern big men justify and legitimate their claims of control over the large tracts of land that they beg from the national government. While not every Nso' elite man who joins the secret societies has acquired national lands, many of those who do acquire national land are members of these societies. The exact number of those who have acquired land and the amounts of land they have acquired are hardly state secrets, but neither is the information freely available. Records are kept poorly if at all. While some men brag openly about the land they have acquired, others are more close-mouthed about it.

With the growing predilection to profit from the market for urban land in particular and to use national land grants as surety on loans, the forces stressing customary tenure and those promoting privatization and commercialization have become opposed as aspects of the development process, creating an ambiguous system of land tenure, which is being consolidated by some people's claim to authority over the allocation and disposal of land at the same time that it is being fragmented when others repudiate these claims of authority. There are certain categories of rights of access to land, most notably that of secure rights of use for subsistence, which have been extremely resistant to change. However, the fundamental rules of rights to land have been changed under state intervention in Cameroon. The articulation of the subsistence economy with the national monetary economy and of the traditional Nso' bureaucracy with the national bureaucracy has not only changed ideas about the meaning and value of land; it has also provided avenues for obtaining access to land outside the customary pattern. The control of this access by men reflects existing gender relations in rights to land. In theory, the land ordinances implicitly grant rights of access to women because the national constitution stipulates equality of the genders as a general principle.[29] In fact, by providing for ownership and privatization of land while fusing these with local custom and ideology, without explicit provision for equality of access by gender, these new land ordinances deny rights of access to most women. Male control of access to national lands reflects existing gender relations in customary tenure. But because these new channels provide for new forms of individual control and at the same time by and large preclude women from access to new land, a qualitative shift has occurred in customary tenure patterns.

Fusion of Customary and State Land Authority

In 1974, the Cameroonian government issued *Land Tenure and State Lands: Ordinances Nos. 74–1, 74–2, and 74–3*.[30] These ordinances were viewed as constituting a land reform act, intended to protect the small farmer, to assure him permanence of tenure, and to encourage development in the rural areas. They divide all land into national land, state public land, and state private property; they appoint the state as guardian of all lands; and they guarantee rights of ownership (private property) to "all natural persons and corporate bodies having landed property."[31] All persons legally occupying or holding ordinanced land as of July 6, 1974, were entitled to file directly for a land title certificate. If one had not occupied land before that date, one could not file directly for a land title certificate, but rather had to apply for formal allocation of land through the land commission or land consultation board.

Essentially all land under this ordinance comes under state control or gives the state ultimate control over access to land: land that is private property can at any time be claimed by the state for use "in the national interest." In this event, the state is supposed to reimburse the occupant. However, if the government wants your land and you have no land title, you are not entitled to reimbursement. National land is composed of all lands, "which, at the date on which the present Ordinance enters into effect are not classed into the public or private property of the State . . . or are not covered by private property rights." National lands are divided into two categories: (1) land occupied with houses, farms, and plantations, and (2) lands free of any effective occupation. These latter lands are to be administered by the state "in such a way as to ensure rational use and development thereof."[32]

All developed land within the first category of national lands has a set value attached to it and can be sold for building. However, from the traditional point of view, the cultivation of food crops does not give the cultivator a permanent hold on the land. The perception that farmland is free, coupled with adherence to traditional values and customary law, prohibits not only the small village farmer but also the lineage heads from filing for farmland under their use or management. They do not see the necessity for filing, nor do village farmers feel the lineage heads are entitled to file for title to the land the farmers are cultivating. As one government official put it, "The problem with the traditional land system is that the landlords don't like people to file for land titles." The provincial agricultural delegate put it even more strongly, writing in a report in 1979: "The problem with development is the weak-mindedness of the natives [*sic*] and their hardheaded attitude in holding onto traditional land tenure."[33] For the small village farmer, the traditional land tenure system, which espouses a group morality of allocation of land to individuals for subsistence use, which in turn gives individuals secure rights as well as obligations, ensures a security not inherent in freehold acquisition rights.

National lands not currently exploited can be given out for development purposes by the national government. Initially, this is done on the basis of three- to five-year temporary grants for "right of occupation." An application for these concessional grants must include a plan for development and proof of financial ability to carry out this program. If approved, the land is granted for a period of up to five years, during which time the land must be developed according to the plan submitted. A farmer may ask for an investigation of his progress at any point; in any case, at the end of the five years, if development is substantial, a land title certificate will be granted. Alternately, if development is not complete, an extension may be given; however, if little or no progress has been made, the land can be reclaimed by the government.

Although declaring itself the guardian of all lands, the national government has nevertheless had to take into consideration the position of traditional rulers and traditional law, whose local authority and power it both recognizes and respects. To fuse the national land ordinances with customary rules governing land tenure, the Fon Nso' and two of his traditional councillors or notables must constitute part of the Divisional Consultative Land Board in Bui Division. Other members are the district officer as chairman, the land department representative as secretary, and representatives of divisional offices as appropriate.[34] Although the government technically has declared itself owner of all lands, most farmland is held in trust by the traditional rulers, whose adherence to the custom that "men own the fields" has had, as we shall see, profound effects on the allocation of national land to women.

The land tenure and state land ordinances emerge as fairly ambiguous, both in terms of exactly which kinds of occupancy and/or "ownership" are to be included within categories designated as private property and in terms of the allocation of land to individual farmers. All farmland perceived as being under traditional land tenure at the time of the ordinances (and this includes most arable land within several miles of any village) has remained under customary tenure, with allocation rights still in the hands of traditional landlords. Customary tenure is perceived as secure tenure by most Nso' villagers. They trust the *fon* and the Nso' traditional government, and claim that the national government is out to displace

people from the land, that it allocates land to "big" (rich) people and ignores the needs of most farmers. This belief has informed the response of
people now farming in Nkuv. Fifteen kilometers southeast of the *fon*'s palace at Kimbo', Nkuv was traditionally the *fon*'s hunting ground. As noted
earlier, when land became scarce around Kimbo', the Fon Nso' opened up
land in Nkuv for farming. The people then asked that the *fon* appoint a
landlord for Nkuv to perform the appropriate rituals, to represent them in
the palace, and to arbitrate any disputes that might arise over land in the
area.

Control over Access, Allocation, and Use Rights in Land in Nso' Today

Access to and allocation of land not under customary tenure are controlled
by the national government. Those persons who are aware of the land
ordinances, know the procedures, and have the capital to develop land can
acquire rights of occupancy and land title through government channels as
well as by traditional means. Since the Fon Nso' and two of his landlords
sit on the land commission, an applicant must also be sensitive to traditional politics (i.e., he must have "good fashion" as a true Nso' person) and
often has to be ready to bribe heavily. It can be expensive to go through the
land commission for a land concession. An applicant has to draw up plans,
have a survey made, and prove economic viability to carry out the plan. In
addition, as one Nso' man put it, "You have to 'entertain' the land commission. It cost me over 50,000 FCFA to obtain a certificate of occupancy for
my land." This cost was in addition to the capital required to institute a
development plan.

The national land ordinances have created an ambiguous system of
tenure in Nso'. For the uneducated or uninformed village small farmer (a
category which includes most women) without the knowledge or means to
put together and carry out a development plan, the only access to farmland
remains within the customary land tenure system. Some people have access
to only a small amount of land, especially land within a reasonable distance from their compounds. The average distance to farms throughout
Nso' is over two kilometers. Women living in Kimbo' often travel 15–20
kilometers to farm, thus requiring them to spend a substantial amount of
time away from the village. Land near the villages is seldom left fallow,
and, as we've seen, people farm up to the tops of the steepest hills.

Informed persons with access to the bureaucracy and sufficient capital
to institute a development program can now acquire large tracts of land in
the countryside as well as land in town. By 1980, approximately 100 men
in Nso'—mostly bureaucrats, administrators, cooperative officials, and

large entrepreneurs—had filed for 50-hectare plots, principally on the Mbo' Plain, an area the national government has designated for large-scale agricultural development. Through knowledge of the workings of the national land ordinances, the modern big men, the new elites, can manipulate the ordinances to acquire large amounts of land for themselves. However, although this knowledge is necessary, it is not always sufficient to ensure the validation of their claims to land. They must also be regarded as leaders within the lineage and must secure the approval, or at least not the active disapproval, of their lineage heads and the *fon*. Not to do so would be social, and economic, suicide. Traditional authorities, customary courts, and secret societies have retained power to adjudicate most land disputes, and, while by law the state has ultimate control of land allocation, this allocation is subject to validation by the land commission, which includes members of Nso' traditional government. As noted earlier, the new elites engage actively in traditional politics and often acquire the symbolic trappings of a Nso' leader. The relations of power in the social relations of land tenure have changed dramatically since the introduction of coffee in the 1940s, yet they mask, and so minimize, the extent of social change with practices that affirm the strength of traditional leadership and ultimately the identity of the Nso' as a distinct group.[35]

As noted earlier, land control and management transcend mere economic considerations. In Nso' cosmology, the living are merely trustees of an extended community which includes the dead and the unborn. Local practice is such that local landlords and customary leaders exercise a firm grip on land grants within their areas of jurisdiction. The procedure for individual land acquisition starts at the local level. The local landlord who administers lineage land must be first consulted by the applicant. It is the customary guardian of family land who makes the effective land grant after formal and informal consultations with the elders and other male members of the lineage. Factors taken into consideration are the social and family backgrounds of the applicant in relation to the grantor's lineage, the location of the land, and the purposes for which the land is going to be used.

The typical pattern of investment has somewhat limited the amount of land brought under actual cultivation. Most men will invest in urban land and rental properties, establishing stores or otherwise making investments that assure a steady income. One of the primary interests of the new elites in filing for title to land is to acquire access to bank credit or FONADER[36] loans, using the land as collateral in order to invest further in urban areas and in entrepreneurial pursuits.[37] Although theoretically the government is supposed to inspect and evaluate the progress of development plans, in fact it has insufficient personnel to do so. Most officials will not venture too far out into the bush, and those who do have tended to be low-level officials who are bribed or intimidated into giving a positive report.

Although some men have started to cultivate large farms in outlying areas, they do so only after establishing a secure income from other investments. There are several reasons for this. Urban and entrepreneurial investments bring a faster, more assured return on capital investments. Farming large plots of land in outlying areas requires considerable capital outlay to hire labor and transport, and returns on investment are neither quick nor assured. Farm-to-market roads are poor at best, and many areas are virtually unreachable by vehicles during the rainy season. Produce is difficult to carry out, and transport costs have been estimated as contributing over 60 percent of the difference between farm-gate and final market price, even in areas with better market access.

A crucial question remains about how long the customary land pattern can assure enough land to all households to satisfy even subsistence needs. According to the traditional landlords, there is little land left that has not already been allocated. The average farm size per household is approximately 1.22 hectares, from which the household obtains 80 percent of its income and over 90 percent of the food it consumes. Figures from the 1976 census suggest a natural rate of population increase of 3 percent in the area. The true growth rate is reduced by migration of young people to urban centers outside the area, so we can conservatively estimate that local population increase is about 2 percent. Distribution of farm size is already somewhat skewed, with 26 percent of farms over 1.5 hectares accounting for 57 percent of the land cultivated. Over 60 percent of the households in Nso' grow food for home consumption only. Even with a growth rate of only 2 percent, the pressure on land is likely to increase rapidly over the next decade, especially with an increasing orientation in the direction of growing food for both home consumption and the market and, since national agricultural development projects are encouraging commercial agriculture, often on a large scale. The average size of individual farms has doubled in the past 30 years owing to increased pressure on women to grow for the market as well as for home consumption in order to fulfill their household obligations.

To date, customary land tenure and lineage organization have acted as a form of social security, as a mechanism that assures all households enough food to satisfy consumption needs. The distribution of farm size indicates that, while in theory everyone is equal with respect to access to land, some are more equal than others.

The national government's professed purpose in passing the 1974 land ordinances was twofold: (1) to increase development of commercial agriculture and thus ensure an adequate supply of foodstuffs for the rapidly growing major urban centers, and (2) to keep land profiteering down. The former objective may succeed in the long run if and when an adequate infrastructure is installed and maintained, lowering transport costs and allowing a higher return on investment in agriculture. In regard to the latter objective, as one senior government official told me, "The intention of the government was to protect the small farmers, but the new professional class is taking advantage of their superior knowledge and acquiring more than their share of land. Those who have the money are investing in suburban areas and speculation is becoming scandalous." Farming per se does not lead to great differentiation in wealth; rather, differentiation is a result of access to capital outside the household economy—salaried and wage jobs, urban and entrepreneurial investments, and, perhaps most important, access to the national bureaucracy. The growing rural differentiation in Nso' is reflected in differential access to productive resources: land, labor, income, and credit for capital investments. Access to land is a key to access to the other factors; this access is gendered and, in the context of commodification and a tendency towards freehold tenure, has come to be increasingly biased in favor of men.

Gender, Land, and Social Stratification

Several recent analyses have suggested that women in Africa are forming a new category of the dispossessed; in the context of the modern African state, women's limited access to land and other resources compared with men's has been well documented.[38] It is unsettling and ironic that national economic and agricultural policy favors elite farmers in Cameroon at the expense of small rural producers, the majority of whom are women, since it is women who grow almost all food crops. Women's work in the food sector is a major source of rural family welfare. Furthermore, women's sales of surplus food represent by far the major source of the local, regional, and national commercial food supply.[39] Yet, arguably, the policies of Cameroon's current government can best be understood as an attempt to consolidate political hegemony by meeting the interests of the capitalist, professional, and upper-level bureaucratic and military classes at the expense of rural smallholders in general and women farmers in particular.[40] Agricultural policy, including land allocation and acquisition, is seriously biased in favor of the urban and governmental elite rather than rural smallholders.[41]

The ideology that "men own the fields, women own the crops" in Nso'—an ideology that provided more gender complementarity and made more sense before the commodification of land and food—has affected the ways in which women's access to land has been channelled under the very different material and sociopolitical conditions that exist today. The difference between men's and women's rights to use, allocate, and alienate land becomes clear when we look at the difference between men's permanent rights over land planted with coffee and other tree crops (considered men's property) and the absence of such rights over land used for food crops (considered women's property). Even the fertility of food crop fields depends customarily on rituals performed by men, and women must often wait until the landlord gives his permission before planting and harvesting. Everyone agrees that attempts by women to register land will lead to eviction by the landlord because such an act "threatens family values." Village women do not have a local political base in the national sector and cannot count on the support of either the customary landlords or the local representatives of the national government, such as the district officers or members of the land commission.

Berry has argued that the contemporary agricultural scene in Africa is marked by an increasing complexity of channels of access to land, channels which are shifting and often ambiguous.[42] Access to the state is one such channel. Within this, one of the dominant modes of access today is the "project," controlled both through national channels and by expatriate nongovernment organizations (NGOs).[43] In Nso', the customary attitude towards women owning land limits women's participation in the more lucrative national development programs. The national government, in an attempt to promote increased food production for urban centers and to stem rural-urban migration, has instituted the Young Farmers Resettlement Program. This program is clearly aimed at young adults between the ages of 17 and 25 who have completed a minimum of seven years of school. The applicants must obtain, either through their lineage head or through the government, at least three hectares of land. Once the correct amount of land is secured, the young farmer is provided with a government loan of 360,000 FCFA (in 1980, US $1800), part of which is in direct inputs to the land and part of which is a 160,000 FCFA loan to be paid back.

Although women are the primary farmers in Nso', they are at a clear disadvantage in applying for the program. Neither traditional landlords nor national bureaucrats in Nso' are forthcoming with land which will come permanently under a woman's control. In Kimbo' Subdivision, of 56 Young Farmers Resettlement loans awarded in 1981, only 2 went to women. When questioned about why this was the case, when women are the primary food farmers, the district officer replied, "This program was designed to help young families stay in the rural area, and of course no self-respecting man would want to move to a farm owned by his wife." Whether or not men are reluctant to move to their wives' farms, this ideol-

ogy has effectively worked to protect male ownership of productive resources.

Women in Nso' continue to have access to land by virtue of their status
as wives, mothers, and sisters, access rights which they maintain only for as
long as they meet the family obligations associated with these rights. Virtually all the women interviewed from 1979 to 1981 were farming on lineage
land which they had begged from customary landlords, 90 percent on their
husband's land and the rest on land of their father's or mother's father's
lineage. the juxtaposition of customary tenure and national land ordinances has facilitated male hegemony by denying most women access to
new forms of property. Only 3.3 percent of land certificates (49 out of
1502) issued over a period of 10 years (1976–1985) were issued to
women. The land registered by women represented only 0.1 percent of the
total land mass registered in the Northwest Province. The sizes of the plots
registered, averaging only 9100 square meters, were too small to be of any
commercial agricultural value. Usually attempts by women to register
farmland, as noted earlier, will result in eviction by the customary landlords, since such acts by women are seen as going against Nso' family
values.

Ultimately, the social relations of land tenure are of interest here, not
just because land is the critical factor of production in Nso', but also because relationships of people to land are less important than relationships
of people to each other, which create and determine power. The idea that
women should not exert rights of ownership over land has remained orthodox, while the practices associated with land use have become increasingly
heterodox. The meaning of power in the gendered relations of land tenure
is not part of a mysterious cultural unconscious; rather, the connections
are made consciously and explicitly. One very well-educated and well-
connected government official questioned me about what I meant when I
asserted that women were often discriminated against in national development programs. I pointed out that women had great difficulty getting access to land, and therefore were precluded from participation in the Young
Farmers Resettlement Program or effectively from acquiring national land
allocation grants in general. To this he looked at me in amazement and
said, "Oh well, *land*—of course you cannot be giving women land. It
would destroy our whole social system!" Several men related the concern
that if women could own land they would have no reason to get married, a
point we will return to in a subsequent chapter.

Through their knowledge of both state and traditional politics and
their adroit manipulation of these, new elite men have been able to accumulate new forms of power and intensify the differential power relations
within the existing gender hierarchy. Perhaps most critical within a rapidly

commodifying context, land registration is a reliable economic tool for providing access to capital. And it is men who can manipulate both local and national forms of bureaucracy to ensure their access. Although the final power of attribution of farmland lies with the land consultative board, not with the *fon* and his notables, applicants for land registration grants must pay homage to the palace and give allegiance to ensure a successful application. The applicant is expected to buy drinks and gifts—the current version of the "*fon*'s market bag"—to bring to the palace before the appointed day for land inspection. The point is that all applicants have to follow traditional methods of land allocation before they can apply for registration, and this largely precludes women from applying for any reasonably sized plots.

It is interesting to note, however, that although men have been able to maintain power over land and other resources, that power has not gone uncontested. Elite women have been successful in filing for title to urban properties, and even with the prejudice against women owning land, a few elite women have been able to acquire access to land through development programs. Recently, development projects have explicitly targeted women for agricultural extension programs.[44] During the past decade, women's knowledge of the national bureaucracy has been substantially increased through schooling and participation in women's cooperatives and in credit and seed multiplication programs. At the same time that men have increased their rights to land and other resources vis-à-vis women, women have been able to begin to challenge male hegemony when property becomes commodified[45] and when some women become educated about the workings of the state. Overall, however, the relationship between customary land tenure and the laws of the postcolonial state has reinforced men's control over land in Nso', and although it may not go unchallenged, male hegemony is ultimately strengthened by this relationship.

The link to the acquisition of land, a right that is distributed through customary law, means that significant resources are involved in sustaining tradition. To be viewed as a true son of the Nso' earth, many men spend a substantial amount of their expendable income investing in the traditional title system. The strategy of accumulation of symbolic or cultural capital in this way is multifaceted. Titles so acquired legitimate men's access to land and act as a strategy of accumulation. What is important is that investment in the title system is a way of bringing ethnic and regional clout to bear on the local offices of the national administration and a means of articulating local and national forms of power, a process which further privileges a male hierarchy. This will be explored in detail in the following chapter.

6

The *Fon*'s New Leopards, or Sorcerers of the Night?

The Articulation of Male Hegemony

Newly arrived in Kimbo' in 1979, I spent most of my time trekking around town, greeting people, and trying to familiarize myself with the capital and its inhabitants. One afternoon when I trudged up the steep hill from the marketplace to the Squares, I heard a commotion coming from the direction of the *fon*'s palace, where a group of people had gathered at the top of the hill leading to the palace courtyard. The young man who was accompanying me turned to me and said, "Get down on the ground and cover your head." When I hesitated, he reached over and pushed me to the ground and, when we were both kneeling at the side of the road, said, "The jujus are coming out from the palace." Crouching by the side of the road and peeking sideways, I could see people kneeling with their eyes on the ground. Within a matter of minutes, several costumed figures wearing carved masks ran by, accompanied by hooded men chanting songs and carrying bamboo staves, whips, and cutlasses. After the jujus with their entourage had passed, my friend informed me while we brushed the red dust from our clothes that an important man had died and the jujus from *ŋweroŋ* had come out to "present" and announce his death. This experience gave me my first encounter with the ongoing importance of the Nso' secret societies, particularly of *ŋweroŋ*, the regulatory society. A few weeks later I asked a local bureaucrat, a man of some position and authority in town, "Just who is running the show here—the *fon* or the [national] government?" He quickly replied, "Well, the government, of course. But I will tell you one thing. If the government asked me to do something I did not want to do, I would take them to court, but if *ŋweroŋ* asked me, I would not hesitate, I would do it tomorrow." Much later, when a good friend of mine was initiated into *yee ŋweroŋ*, the inner circle of *ŋweroŋ*, he told me, "This has meant a lot of expenditure and exhaustive planning. Every bit of [my] money has been spent on my *sheey*ship and I am left stranded. However, I do not regret [doing it] for I have received the highest title a man can expect in the *ŋweroŋ*'s compound."

As was noted in chapter 3, when the *afon* of Nso' were consolidating their position in the nineteenth century, they promoted a palace-based title system which soon took precedence in politics over the power of the lineage heads. Ambitious and powerful men were then incorporated into the center of Nso' government through initiation into palace-based title societies, whose membership became relatively open. The most important of these men were those who were thought to possess *səm*, or power, which enabled them to attract wealth and status. These men were viewed as having the potential to "oppose their bellies" to the *fon*, and were often initiated into *yee ŋweroŋ* in order to domesticate or socialize their power. This pattern still has resonance today.

In Nso', and indeed throughout the Grassfield chiefdoms, the men's title societies have retained local efficacy.[1] Titles and membership in these societies have, within the political economy of prestige, remained important forms of symbolic capital and objects of accumulation. Indeed, investment in the title system is partly a result of the importance of ethnic and regional identity in the calculus of national power. When I returned to Cameroon in 1988, after a five-year absence, while scanning the radio dial in my Yaounde hotel room I happened onto "Evening Magazine," a program broadcast by the Cameroon People's Democratic movement. The topic of the broadcast was regulatory societies in the chiefdoms of the Grassfields.[2] During the course of the program, these societies, interchangeably called *ŋweroŋ* and *kwifoyn* by the announcer, were characterized as clubs which "only those with wealth can actually join; small exclusive societies confined to a new ruling class." The announcer went on to explain that members take titles in these organizations and, once initiated, "cease to be true commoners and become aristocrats"; these titled men then constitute "a wealthy minority who have a vested interest in making the *fon* respectable."

Titles and offices in secret societies in Nso' have been central both to the power of Nso' traditional government and to individual strategies of accumulation of wealth, power, and legitimacy. The secret societies have become powerful enough in the local political economy to be taken seriously on the national level. By acquiring titles today, members of the new elite in Nso' are able to graft new relations of control onto old forms of domination and, by doing so, legitimate that control. The Fon Nso', by making these titles available, has been able simultaneously to fill the coffers of traditional government, incorporate the new elite into Nso' traditional government, and ensure their collaboration in furthering local hegemony. By maintaining local hegemony and power at home, the new elites are able to create and maintain a local base which gives them, in the context of national patronage politics, access to the state.

The importance of Nso' secret societies, *ŋweroŋ* in particular, is evident in the ways in which Nso' elites today manipulate genealogies to make themselves eligible for membership. The importance of these title societies as a form of local power and cultural capital is also illustrated by the extent to which the Nso' royals feel distanced from power by the growing importance of *ŋweroŋ*, which has resulted in their attempting to assert the power of *ŋgiri,* the society of the royal lineages. The conflict between these two secret societies was evident in the last enstoolment, when *ŋgiri* backed an educated man as *fon,* thinking he would support their interests. *Ŋweroŋ* wanted a less-educated person whom they thought they could control. *Ŋweroŋ* won the decision, thus illustrating the society's local importance, including its considerable power over the *fon.* We will return to this issue in the following discussion.

Male secret societies have thus remained important political institutions in Nso'. Membership and titles in these have continued to be critical pieces of symbolic capital and an object of investment for ambitious men. Traditional women's societies and titles have not fared as well in the modern political economy. Younger women say the *coŋ* is "only a way for the older women to keep us [the younger women] down," and decline membership in this society. The importance of the women's secret societies has been superseded by associations tied to the institutions of the modern state, such as the women's cooperative and church groups. Women's traditional titles have been tied to the palace and its operation. When the palace declined in relative importance and was no longer the sole center of political decision making and intrigue, women's traditional titles lost their political efficacy. Palace titles today give women a great deal of respect, but little political power. Since the important secret societies are exclusively male (women cannot even enter or see the inside of these organizations, much less join them), their association with the new elites and the resulting articulation between local and national politics work to legitimate and reproduce male hegemony in Nso'.

Legitimation, Power, and Hierarchy

To examine the articulation of the various meanings of legitimacy and authority in Nso' today, a review of the important themes of the precolonial history is necessary here. When the larger Grassfield chiefdoms became increasingly centralized in the nineteenth century, elaborate hierarchies of power came into play—hierarchies which needed to be legitimated when state power began to compete with and supersede lineage power. Several contradictions resulted from the process of centralization. The incorporation of diverse groups into a powerful center required that the legitimacy of moral order and the coercive aspects of power be combined in the same institutions and, indeed, in the same person.[3] This created significant ambiguity, which was partly resolved by the palace-based title societies, most notably by *ŋweroŋ*, which, by assuming responsibility for the more onerous acts of government, functioned to remove the stigma of these acts from the *fon* himself.

A second contradiction lay in resolving the tension between alliance (affinity) and descent. Titles became the means to acquire status and wealth in the state hierarchy and the symbols of having done so. Men of title, with a stock of marriageable wards at their disposal, replenished under a system of deferred exchange marriage, were in a position to build up large affinal networks. In Nso', lineage heads had perhaps more autonomy of control vis-à-vis their dependents than in any of the other Grassfields chiefdoms, but nowhere else in the Grassfields was the appointment of lineage heads controlled so closely by the *fon*, who both ratified lineage appointments and could remove lineage heads from office.[4] For lineage heads who were officers of state and for members of the title societies, loyalty to the state took precedence. Yet unlike in the other large states in the Grassfields, such as Bamum and in the Bamileke chiefdoms, there was a balance achieved between alliance and descent. While the office of the *fon* was sacred and the chiefdom highly centralized, the *fon* was seen as the embodiment of the people, and the language used to describe him was (and is) one of generosity and harmony rather than repression.

The balance reached between alliance and descent can be seen in the position of the *mtaar* in Nso'. As will be recalled from chapter 1, *mtaar* is the name given to the people who were resident when the Nso' arrived and who were given a number of privileges in exchange for fealty to the Fon Nso'. In some situations the *mtaar* see themselves as the *wirmtaar*, "people of the Nso' earth," as opposed to the *wirfon*, or "people of the *fon*." One of the concessions they won was freedom from giving women to the *fon* as wives. Yet the *fon* must have a *mtaar* woman as a mother, so each *fon* must negotiate with *mtaar* lineages for wives. The *mtaar* were a powerful political force in precolonial Nso', partly because of their position as "father-in-law" to the Fon Nso', and partly because of their relationship to the earth and thus to pure or moral legitimacy. They were important in removing pollution and detecting witchcraft. The Nso' believe that the power to detect witchcraft is inherited in the uterine line; since the mother of the *fon* must be a *mtaar* woman, he was, in effect, the *mtaar*'s son-in-law, and they were important in protecting him from the witchcraft of his jealous agnates. The *mtaar* titleholders had the right to reprimand the *fon* if they thought he was not acting in the interests of the country, and they were responsible for important initiation rituals and provided the most trusted diviners to the palace. Through his relationship with the *mtaar*, the *fon* embodied the balance between alliance and descent and combined in his person the legitimacy of the Nso' earth with the more repressive power of the Nso' state. As Rowlands argues for the Bamileke chiefdoms, centralization was possible in Nso' by fusing the ambiguous nature of power with the pure legitimacy of ancestral order in the institution of chieftaincy.[5] This was, however, achieved in Nso' in ways which balanced the principles of alliance and descent in the centralized power of the *fon;* unlike the more repressive Bamileke chiefs, the Fon Nso' was seen as harmonizing, benevolent, and generous.[6]

The Fon Nso' has thus been removed by various means from the contamination of power; various institutions exist which have provided a balance or check on his power, and he has been expected to be at all times generous and to redistribute his wealth. As we've seen, the Nso' say, "The *fon* has everything; the *fon* is a poor man," and he has always been expected to have an "open hand." The *fon* himself is not allowed to see blood or to take part in executions, and he has been, as Chilver argues, "placed at the center of an opposition between the ideal values of an ancestral order, the 'things of the earth,' and those of competitive sorcery, the exercise of will on reality, and committed to an unremitting routine of theurgy."[7] As noted earlier, one of his most important functions has been to protect Nso' from the foreign "sorcerers of the night." The *fon*, using his magical powers, transposes himself into a lion and his most important councillors into leopards. Together they prowl the Nso' countryside, protecting its inhabitants from evil.

In precolonial Nso', as we've seen, men of wealth, who were the marriage guardians of numerous women to be given out, could use this position to build up alliances and networks of power. The *fon* controlled the largest of these networks; not only was he a large-scale polygynist, but also he had control of war captives and retainers, and received from Nso' lineages, from subchiefs, and from other *afon* in the Grassfields both girls who he could marry or give as gifts and boys to act as retainers in the palace. It has been suggested that there were important links between a growing engagement in regional and long-distance trade and an accompanying accumulation of women and wealth on the one hand, and the fluctuating ambivalence surrounding *sɘm*, or power, on the other.[8] *Sɘm* can be either good or evil depending on the intentions of those who possess it. *Sɘm* can become evil or bad under the influence of malice, greed, or unseemly ambition. In its more ethereal images, it has been associated with high winds, travel by night, translocation, clairvoyance, and teleportation. The *fon* possesses *səm* of the highest order, royal *səm,* which is sharply in contrast with *səm arim,* the *səm* of human witches, who possess the capacity to produce evil transforms and to cause the death of kin and rivals.[9] Along with *virim,* or evil power and wealth, foreign *səm (aŋgasəm)*[10] and *səm arim* are opposed to socially approved *səm* and wealth, the most powerful of which is royal *səm.*

The acquisition and possession of wealth alone as the source of political influence and power in Nso' has always been vigorously denied.[11] Wealth has had to be reinvested and redistributed in socially approved ways: it has had be domesticated. This can be accomplished through induction into a title society, whose functions are to contain power, to protect the boundaries of Nso' from hostile foreign power, and to remove pollution. Joining these societies has also required significant payments and ongoing prestations where wealth is redistributed. An individual who uses wealth for purely egoistic goals, one who has a "closed hand," who hoards and accumulates, is apt to be accused of witchcraft. As noted earlier, such a person is said to exchange his relatives for wealth in a compact with the witch world, and is talked of as being consumed with ambition so that he eats or gnaws (*kfər*) his kin in order to further his own personal career.

The palace-based title system has acted both to socialize or domesticate the *səm* of ambitious men and to remove the *fon* from the more repressive and polluting acts of government. These title systems have also become an object of investment and a means of redistribution as well as accumulation. They have both sanctioned accumulation and been a means of accumulation. At the same time, they have given legitimacy to the existing hierarchy by domesticating wealth and power and by transforming these into symbolic social capital. The title system has allowed the *fon* and his notables to invest their wealth in a socially legitimate way and to increase that wealth through privileged access to long-distance trade. The *fon* and his notables have thus been placed at the center of wealth accumulation in the chiefdom as a whole. Yet at the same time, they have been able to remain free from accusations of antisocial behavior through their association with legitimate authority and through ongoing systems of redistribution.

In the structure and practice of traditional government in Nso', then, we find two intertwined themes, that of legitimate authority based on descent and the ancestors, and that of power based on extraordinary talents which are dangerous and must be kept in check.[12] There are numerous ways in which various titleholders[13] have worked in concert with the Fon Nso' to protect the boundaries of the country from witchcraft and hostile foreign sorcerers. There have also existed a number of male secret societies which meet in the palace and are concerned with, among other things:

ensuring that the ancestral libations are poured and the correct rituals for the ancestors properly carried out; protecting the *fon* and the country from witchcraft and hostile *səm;* and removing the *fon* from pollution by performing the more onerous duties of government. The most important of these societies has been *ŋweroŋ*, the regulatory society.[14]

Ŋweroŋ has been the primary executive arm of Nso' government responsible for maintaining law and order. *Ŋweroŋ* is a graded, or ranked, society, and entry into its higher lodges and inner circle, *yee ŋweroŋ*, has involved a potlatchlike distribution of wealth.[15] It was (and is) referred to as the eyes and ears of the *fon*, and people in Nso' say that "*ŋweroŋ* has 800 eyes," referring to the fact that members of *ŋweroŋ* are constantly alert to disturbances in the countryside which might affect the palace and the orderly maintenance of traditional government. It is at times referred to today by some Nso' people as their House of Commons, since members of the royal lineage (with the exception of the *fon*) are excluded from membership, and belong instead to the royal secret society, *ŋgiri*, which has not had significant executive functions in Nso' traditional government. Members of *ŋweroŋ* are drawn in a variety of ways from *duy* (the term used for descendants of the *fon* after the third or fourth generation) and from *nshiylavsi* (retainers who are the palace stewards and the *ŋweroŋ* pages and officers). The *nshiylavsi* provide most of the *ŋweroŋ* staff and constitute the majority of its membership.[16] The *mtaar* have not owed people to the palace or to *ŋweroŋ*, and, again, seeing themselves as *wirmtaar* ("people of the earth") in contrast with the *wirfon* ("people of the *fon*"), with few exceptions they have usually not belonged to the secret societies.

Ŋweroŋ has been responsible for carrying out the *fon*'s orders, which, in precolonial Nso', included overseeing executions. They have been charged with keeping the peace, preventing crimes, mobilizing people for public works, and providing mortuary ceremonies for their members. They have had important ritual and religious obligations and *yeeŋweroŋ* members have played their part in the presentation of a new *fon* to the populace. *Ŋweroŋ* has also provided a check on the power of the *fon*. This society can hold him captive and fine him if he is seen as not acting in the interests of the country. The authority of *ŋweroŋ* and its execution of the *fon*'s orders are impersonal, and its members wear hoods to disguise their identity when they travel out from the palace on official business. Ultimately, the *fon* has been responsible for their actions, not as an individual, but as a collective institution.

Within the colonial and subsequently the modern state, *ŋweroŋ* has lost some of its official functions. It can no longer institute the death penalty, nor can it banish people from Nso' for treason except in unusual circumstances, such as repeated accusations of witchcraft. Yet within the reign of Fon Ŋga' Bi'fon (1910–1947), *ŋweroŋ* wielded an enormous amount of power. The colonial administration, ignorant of the political role played by the *mtaar*, allowed Native Authority jobs to be filled by the *fon*'s nominees, who tended to be overwhelmingly recruited from his favorites, the majority of whom were *nshiylavsi*.[17] Many of these men were former palace pages who were knowledgeable about the workings of intricate and large bureaucracies. With the institution of colonial indirect rule, Fon Ŋga' Bi'fon was the first Fon Nso' to be confronted with the ongoing responsibility of articulating traditional Nso' government with the new requirements of the colonial state. In order to do this, he relied heavily on *ŋweroŋ* to help him make and carry out decisions. *Ŋweroŋ* became so influential and powerful that people in Nso' began to see the Nso' state as ruled jointly by the *fon* and *ŋweroŋ*. According to Mzeka, it was during this period that Nso' people began saying "*woŋ fon win ŋweroŋ,*" which means "the realm of the *fon* and *ŋweroŋ,*" conflating their power into a single source.[18]

Shrouded in secrecy and imbued with mystical power, *ŋweroŋ* has remained a powerful local presence in Nso'. Although the *mtaar* have retained a certain amount of respect and cultural power, their actual political power has been greatly attenuated while, many would argue, that of *ŋweroŋ* has been increased. *Ŋweroŋ* plays a more central role in the choice and installation of the *fon* than it seems to have done in the past, and is clearly more powerful vis-à-vis both the *mtaar* and *ŋgiri*. Aletum and Fisiy, echoing the Nso' man quoted at the beginning of this chapter, write, "Even though the modern state institutions have whittled down the ominous powers of *Ngwerong*, this society still maintains a firm grip on social mores. With just one single announcement, it can render any Nso' element a social outcast . . ."[19] The Fon Nso' in the 1960s began to endow titles on educated Nso' men and to ease requirements so that titles became an object of elite investment. The number of *ŋweroŋ* members grew, and *ŋweroŋ* has become an important political link between traditional government and the new elites and thus between local and national politics.[20]

The Articulation of Legitimacy: Local and National Politics

In Nso' today, the postcolonial state has instituted a new legal code and through this, and through control of virtually all trade and development, has been able to define the overall context of change. However, traditional state and lineage titles, chieftaincy, and men's secret societies continue today as powerful institutions in the local political economy. As noted in previous chapters legitimacy in Nso' is not derived from identity with the national center, but rather from participating in the moral virtues of communal life. In Nso' this legitimacy flows not only from relations with kin and neighbors but also from the institutions of the indigenous chiefdom which surround the *fon* and the palace. As we have seen, pure legitimacy in Nso' is embodied in the moral virtues of the ancestors. Power, or *səm*, is ambiguous, and becomes legitimate only when it is used for social good rather than for individual gain. The *fon* possesses royal *səm*, the highest form of pure legitimacy, exemplified by his role as the most important officiant at seasonal rituals which ensure the reproduction of Nso', and in his relationship to the most powerful ancestors, of whom he is a living expression. Nso' traditional government thus depends on a legitimacy and a source of power which has a religious base and a continuing ambiguity. This concept of legitimacy comes into conflict with the secular legitimacy of the state in a number of contexts, and cannot be understood by a single concept of authority.[21] It is not enough for the new Nso' elites to have access to the state, which has appointed itself as the legitimate legal authority in Cameroon; they must also achieve legitimacy at home.

In Cameroon today the state may not be able to claim as much legitimate local power as it might wish, but it is an important source of wealth and power for individuals. The state is the sole distributor of resources for rural development, and access to development aid is tied to the pursuit of objectives which are consistent with state policies. In order to encourage development—water systems, roads, health centers, schools—and at the same time keep its costs to a minimum, the national state has emphasized a policy known as self-reliant development. This policy encourages local communities to design and implement development projects on their own in order to attract government assistance. This form of development planning has reinforced an emphasis on ethnicity and on local politics, with the rural population, the *fon,* and the new elites working together to attract resources from the state for local development schemes. The *fon*'s approval is necessary to mobilize the local population to implement community development projects, and this has encouraged cooperation between the educated elites who run local development projects and the Nso' traditional government. This is, however, only one aspect of the alliance between the *fon* and the new elites, the modern big men.

In the postcolonial state in Cameroon, individual political-economic careers and access to the state are interconnected and depend largely on local events. The postcolonial state acts as a mediator between rural areas like Nso' and the international economy and defines the overall context of change. Access to the state is the single most important resource and avenue to political and economic success. In Cameroon that access requires a local power base. National patronage politics based on ethnicity or regional identity has reinforced a focus on local identity. In Nso' this power base is acquired through traditionally sanctioned means, including the acquisition of titles and participation in traditional government.

Access to jobs and resources in Nso' thus depends on an individual's ability to manipulate both the traditional and modern worlds. As we saw in chapter 4, one example of this is access to land. While most land for subsistence farming has remained under the control of traditional lineage heads, this land is beginning to be used up for the most part. The national government in 1974 passed several land ordinances to ensure "rational development." Essentially all unoccupied land under this ordinance came under state control or is subject to the state's ultimate authority over access to land. While declaring itself the guardian of all lands, the national government has had to take into consideration the position of traditional rulers and traditional law, "whose authority and potency it both recognizes and respects."[22] The *fon* and two of his councillors constitute part of the divisional land board, which makes decisions regarding large tracts of farmland. Actual access to these "national lands" requires access to the national bureaucracy. In Nso', access to land also requires that one be in the good graces of the *fon* and his notables and have a working knowledge of Nso' traditional government.[23]

Through their participation in Nso' traditional politics, the new elites have become, in effect, the new lineage leaders. In order to legitimate this position and the practices associated with it, the new elites have had to articulate the various meanings of legitimacy and authority in Nso'. They have become the interpreters between customary and national law, and thus the authors of much of the current political discourse. Through their knowledge of both the traditional and the national bureaucracies and their role in these, the new elites have become more powerful than the traditional titled men whose identities they have assumed.

Negotiating Legitimacy: The Changing Meaning of Traditional Titles

The traditional lineage heads, the *afaay* and *ashuufaay,* have retained a high status in Nso'. They are seen as possessing a natural moral legitimacy based on their relationship and ritual obligations to the Earth and the ancestors. However, their political and economic power has been significantly eroded in the context of a monetary economy, and they no longer have dominance over the control of goods and persons. Power and status within the Nso' political economy and the social relations of production are increasingly characterized by control over the ownership and distribution of things rather than direct control over people. Whereas in the past the titled men controlled and inherited all lineage property, today property has become much more individualized, and men's sons rather than the lineage heads inherit their coffee farms and fortunes. The successful entrepreneurs, large-scale coffee farmers, and salaried men, rather than the lineage heads, control jobs and trade and thus control labor. Lineage heads no longer control the marriages of their dependents. Increasingly, marriages are based on individual economic concerns rather than on lineage political strategies.

Most traditional titleholders are not the men of wealth in Nso'. Their compounds may be large, but the buildings more often than not are less modern than those of the typical Nso' household. Their living quarters, often smoky and dark with dirt floors, lack the amenities found in the adjacent buildings of their more affluent dependents. The everyday clothes of many lineage heads, and those of their wives and children, tend to be tattered and worn. Lineage heads continue to inherit the wives of their predecessors, which, in the context of a cash economy, more often impoverishes than enriches them. By the late 1940s, Phyllis Kaberry commented on the plight of polygynous men, especially the lineage heads, noting that many a poor *faay* had to borrow money from his more prosperous dependents to pay taxes and other living expenses.[24] Lineage heads are expected to be generous and entertain on a large scale. They have more wives than the typical Nso' man, and thus have more affines to whom they owe gifts. They have more children for whom they must pay school fees, more women for whom they are obliged to provide cloth, pots, meat, and salt. At times they have to perform sacrifices requiring fowls, goats, and sheep, which they must either supply themselves or coax from their dependents. They are by and large precluded by custom from personally engaging in trade or from working at most cash-earning occupations. Young men who have begun careers in the modern sector are reluctant to become traditional lineage heads, and most claim that they would "run from the office" if they were chosen.[25]

While they are not the wealthy men of the chiefdom as measured by material riches, the titled men nevertheless remain the men of renown. Their title and status ensure them respect and deference, not only from their dependents, but also within the chiefdom as a whole. It is an unwise person who blatantly shuns custom and respect for titled men and gets on the wrong side of the traditional notables. He or she will be gossiped about as having bad fashion, may be fined by *ŋweroŋ*, or, in extreme cases, may be denied access to lineage land. Nso' titleholders remain the embodiment of moral legitimacy. They uphold the moral order and maintain the moral boundaries of the community through various rituals. They talk of their participation in Nso' traditional government as *lim*, or work for their dependents. Lineage elders remain associated with the ancestors and with the

Earth, the repository of lineage values. They are the glue that keeps Nso' society together and maintains moral order in the country.

The titled men of Nso' continue to command the respect and fealty due their status as Nso' leaders. Much of their political authority has been undermined in the context of a cash economy, but they are not without some measure of local economic and political control. They attend the palace regularly, have easy access to the *fon*, and sit on traditional councils. Most farmland is still under their management, and they perform the important rituals viewed as crucial to the fertility of the land and their dependents. Family disputes and disputes over land are most often settled by traditional authorities. The lineage heads interface with the national bureaucracy in making decisions regarding land. The titled men thus play a significant role in shaping local politics. More important, they have retained their position as symbols of morality and political legitimacy, and traditional office and title have remained powerful symbols in the political economy of prestige in Nso'.

The interdependence between traditional rulers and the new Nso' elite established during the nationalist movements prior to independence has continued and is supported by institutional factors. The Fon Nso' is paid a salary and is expected to participate actively in national political life. The Fon Nso' and the Nso' traditional government work closely with the district officer and other local representatives of the national bureaucracy in imposing and enforcing national policies. Bui Division is the second largest division in the Northwest Province, and it essentially follows the boundaries established by Nso' at the turn of the century. National and local governments meet on the divisional level, where the district officer coordinates decisions made by representatives of the national ministries with various traditional councils and personalities. The new elites play a significant role in both bureaucracies. The man one sees in the morning behind a ministry desk wearing a three-piece suit can often be seen late in the afternoon bare-chested, wearing a *lapa* of blue and white traditional cloth, carrying a spear, and swinging a cutlass on his way to attend a meeting of *ŋweroŋ* at the palace.

The new elite men in Nso', whether living locally or in national urban centers, have come to seek titles and membership in secret societies. Aletum and Fisiy (part of the new intelligentsia), point out, "The conferment of the title of *Shu-faay, Faay,* or *Sheey* [all titles of nobility in descending order of importance] by the Fon on any individual who has no hereditary claim to such distinction is an overt mark of recognition and a sure source of power. The quest for such royal decorations and appointments . . . is a veritable source of power and an expression of stately recognition of the individual's contribution to the welfare of the Nso' community, wherever he may be."[26] The majority of these titles are *asheey* in *ŋweroŋ*. The number of *ashuufaay* and *afaay* has increased over time in proportion to a substantial increase in population and a concomitant creation of new lineages over time.[27] Relatively few individuals have been accorded these two titles for personal achievement. There are notable exceptions, such as Bernard Fonlon, Daniel Lantum, Joseph Lafon, and more recently Bonfon Chem-Langhee, but especially the more prestigious title of ashuufaay has been rather closely held by the *fon*. However, as noted earlier, the title *sheey* was explicitly made available around the mid-1960s by the Fon Nso' with the express purpose of incorporating the new educated elite into traditional government. This decision on the part of the *fon* was welcomed by the new intelligentsia, who saw acquisition of titles as an important means of both legitimating power at home and demonstrating their local status outside Nso'. Aletum and Fisiy write, ". . . in order to influence traditional policy, any Nso' . . . in possession of knowledge and/or wealth vies for recognition either by seeking admission into one of the traditional institutions or by vying for a royal decoration."[28]

This move on the *fon*'s part was very clever, and has to be understood as serving various purposes. The first and most obvious was to link the new elite to Nso' traditional government in a way which focussed their loyalty on local events. Second, the payments to the palace and the secret societies served to fill the coffers of traditional government—and of traditional authorities, not least of all those of the *fon* himself. Nso' traditional rulers have lost some of their former sources of income, including tribute payments and control over trade and marriage alliances. The opening up of these titled societies can be seen as a way of allowing the traditional notables to tap into new sources of wealth without becoming involved directly in the marketplace. The *fon* gets the largest cut, but traditional lineage heads receive a portion of the payments from the men they "present" to the *fon* to receive titles. While only the *fon* can create a *shuufaay* or a *faay*, the process by which a *sheey* is created can be initiated by a *faay* or a *shuufaay*, subject to ratification by the *fon* and one of the secret societies. The amount charged varies according to the level or rank attained within the secret society. The initial cost, as reported to me in the early 1980s, was then between 10,000 and 20,000 FCFA.[29] In addition, gifts of goats, fowls, and raffia wine must be presented and redistributed among secret society members. The value of the money and prestations required for entry into a higher lodge of *ŋweroŋ*, particularly into *yee ŋweroŋ*, can well exceed 100,000 FCFA. The initial cost is followed by ongoing requirements to provide food and wine for meetings, yearly gifts of firewood and salt for the palace, and mortuary payments for society members.

A third motive for the *fon*'s move towards active recruitment of the new elite into Nso' traditional government can be read as an attempt to socialize their *səm*. Obviously the new elites must possess *səm* if they are able to attract wealth and achieve status in the modern economy. If left unchecked or undomesticated, these men would have the potential of "opposing their bellies" to the *fon*. The moral order in Nso' is associated with truthful speech as well as with the historical primacy of the ancestors. By declaring themselves adherents of these ancestral values through oaths of office in traditional Nso' institutions, the new elites declare their *səm* and at the same time socialize it. The assessment of whether a successful person has good or malevolent intentions does not depend on abstract moral principles but rather on public evaluation of their actions and their commitment to neighbors and kin and the politics of reciprocity. Coopting ambitious and successful men into secret societies today acts much as it has in the past: to secure their loyalty and socialize their power.

Acquiring a *sheey*ship is today one of the major investments made by Nso' men who have become successful in the modern sector. In order to understand why men seek the title, it is necessary to understand that the respect given to a titled individual is mandatory. It distinguishes him publicly from ordinary untitled men. Once a man becomes a titleholder, his personal name is not used. He is called by his title, and must be greeted through cupped hands.[30] He wears a special cap indicating his status. He is given a special seat or stool even in public beer parlors. If he attends a *njaŋgi* meeting in a compound, he is given a special stool, more wine and food than other people, and first chance to address the gathering. Men who are titled have a chance to voice their opinions on political matters and to acquire political support in ways the average village man cannot.

There are other perks. When a titled man visits a compound, the women must entertain him in a more lavish manner than is required for ordinary visitors. People say that a *sheey* does not have to worry if he travels. He is assured of accommodation and hospitality wherever he goes and can make requests that normal people cannot. If he needs money for transportation, the driver is apt to waive the cost or, more likely, take him on credit. Young men seeking a patron are often willing to carry his coffee beans to the collection depot, carry water or firewood for his compound, or help him smuggle coffee across divisional borders. Titled status confers on the holder an entitlement to ask for favors and to mobilize aid and political support.

The actual material wealth accruing to an individual solely because of his title appears rather negligible, consisting as it does of hospitality, political support, and at times free labor and transport. When questioned about the motives of individual men in acquiring a title, people often replied, "He wants to smooth out his life." Occasionally, and slightly derogatorily, the reply was, "He just wants to be treated like that [with subservience]." For all these men, the practices associated with the title publicly reproduce their status through daily social interaction. The purpose the title serves and what it means to individual men, however, are various. Here it is useful to look briefly at some of the new *asheey*.[31]

Sheey Fonya

Sheey Fonya is a well-educated man who, for reasons of political expediency, left Cameroon during unification and spent 10 years studying in Ghana. Upon his return to Nso' in the early 1970s, most jobs for people with his credentials were controlled by the national government, and he found himself initially unable to secure a salaried job so began farming. Both he and his wife take an active part in local politics. They are members of the Kimbo' Urban Council, and both vigorously promote community development programs. His wife, B., runs a shed in the Kimbo' daily market. B. is better educated than the majority of women who sell in the market. She helps organize collective wholesale buying to cut down on direct costs to the market women and calls for collective protest when the market fees are increased. Sheey Fonya is a trusted palace advisor and a member of *yee ŋweroŋ*. He is also a trading agent for the Ndu Tea Estate, and he travels frequently to Douala and Yaounde, where he keeps up with national news and politics. Sheey Fonya considers himself first and foremost a "progressive farmer." He has tried, unsuccessfully to date, to organize the farmers in his area to put their funds together to buy a Rototiller. He views development from within and self-sufficiency in food production as essential to control over local affairs. When I interviewed him about agricultural development in Nso', he retorted in a voice mixed with defiance and patience for the uninformed, "I know one large agricultural company like those in your country could come in here and use the technology they have to produce more than we can. But then where would we be? What would be our work?"

Sheey Fonya views participation in traditional politics as a means of retaining a sense of pride and identity as well as a means of ensuring local political control. No fan of the national government, he sees *ŋweroŋ* in particular as an institution which ensures local solidarity and decision making outside the realm of national party politics.

Sheey Gham

Sheey Gham is the "CEO" of the local coffee cooperative, which has been one of the most successful cooperatives in the Northwest Province. He attended the most prestigious secondary school in the Grassfields and taught primary school before he became involved with the cooperative movement. He spent a year at a university in the United States in the 1960s. Sheey Gham is one of the wealthiest and most influential men in Nso'. He has 21 dependents (only 7 of whom are his own children) living in his compound. The coffee cooperative is the largest employer in the area. A large number of the cooperative workers come from Sheey Gham's village, and many of them are related to him through both lineage and affinal ties. His wife has been president of the women's cooperative in Nso'. She has also organized a women's cooperative farming venture on land she begged form Sheey Gham's lineage head. Mme. Gham conducts a brisk trade in her convenience store, which she runs with the help of some of the young kinsmen who live in the Gham's compound. People in Sheey Gham's village often address him as Ba or Pa, again, a term of respect usually reserved for much older men.

Sheey Gham, too, sees participation in traditional politics as a means of ensuring local control. He is campaigning in his village and at the palace to increase the political clout of his lineage by influencing the *fon* to create two new sublineage titles and raise the *faay* to a *shuufaay*. Sheey Gham views becoming a *sheey,* not only as a means of access to the traditional power structure, but also as a way of legitimating his personal status as head of a bureaucratic institution not directly controlled by traditional authorities. By participating in traditional politics and adhering to traditional values, Sheey Gham validates and reinforces his position in the modern sector vis-à-vis the local community. His role in traditional politics facilitates the implementation of government development projects channelled through the cooperative system. His position in the palace and in his lineage has enabled him and his wife more easily to beg large tracts of land from traditional lineage heads for experimental farms and livestock programs, some of which are sponsored through the cooperative system.

By becoming a *sheey*, Sheey Gham legitimated his status as a community leader. He furthered his ability to act as a leader in the newly formed opposition political party. He also enhanced his ability to put together development projects in Nso' by increasing his credibility as a Nso' leader with the *fon* and the traditional notables, who must lend both land and their approval to development projects sponsored locally by the national government.

Sheey Tankum

Sheey Tankum is a minister in the national government. As an important national bureaucrat, he spends most of his time in Yaounde, the capital city. His wife is a successful radio announcer in the capital, where, among other things, she runs a radio talk show for women. Sheey Tankum and his wife maintain a large compound in Nso', managed during the year by various relatives and clients. They return to Nso' yearly for vacation, during which time they give a large ceremonial feast and celebration in honor of their wedding anniversary. All Nso' leaders and big men, both traditional notables and modern elites, attend this gala occasion. The compound is alive with masked dancers, men performing sword dances, firing rifles, drumming, and playing a traditional xylophone. Before this event, Sheey Tankum attends the palace to greet the *fon* in traditional fashion and to ask for the royal blessing for the coming year.

Over the course of the year, Sheey Tankum makes several trips to Nso' to conduct local business and to keep in touch with the *fon* and palace politics. Like all citizens of Nso', Sheey Tankum also puts a high value on local control. As a national politician, however, he participates in traditional politics in order to keep his finger on the pulse of local political life and to maintain a network of kin and clients. To maintain his position in national politics it is important for him to establish a local political base. The fact that he is a *sheey* gives him added prestige at home and projects to the outside world an image of Sheey Tankum as a big man in his own locale.

Sheey Wirsey

Sheey Wirsey uses his position as a *sheey* and his rank in *ŋweroŋ* to facilitate his entrepreneurial activities both within and outside Nso'. His father, a former officer in *ŋweroŋ,* was a highly respected and admired member of the Nso' community. On the tenth anniversary of his father's death, Sheey Wirsey gave an elaborate commemorative mortuary feast. Both traditional notables and government officials figured prominently in the ceremony. The mayor, the district officer, and the senior district officer all delivered eulogies to the deceased, praising him for his unselfish service to Nso', his exemplary character, and his good fashion. The celebration lasted all day, and the feast was a magnificent display of largess. Thousands of bottles of beer, uncounted jugs of palm wine, huge platters of meat, and enormous bowls of corn *fufu* were consumed. Dances and drumming exhibitions were interspersed with feasting and eulogies to Sheey Wirsey's father, as well as speeches attesting to Sheey Wirsey's great love and respect for his father and for the traditions of Nso' his father had represented.

During the course of the day I commented to several people on the largess being shown by Sheey Wirsey, speculating that his father must have been a man of some stature for his son to put on this display of filial duty. People replied that, yes, Sheey Wirsey's father was an "important somebody" but no more so than many other Nso' men. A number of people went on to inform me that "Sheey Wirsey is only using this occasion for business reasons." Somewhat mystified by these comments, I pressed for an explanation. Sheey Wirsey is a contractor with business ties to partners and customers in Bamenda, the provincial capital. The anniversary of his father's death provided him with an opportunity to invite leading business-men and politicians from Bamenda and impress upon them the fact that he is a big man in his local community and a worthy business associate.

Sheey Ngee

Sheey Ngee is the headmaster of a local primary school. He is also head of the Catholic Men's Association. He and his wife are active in a number of church groups. They have been instrumental in the organization of innova-tive church-based groups such as peer-conselling birth control, a savings and loan scheme, and a women's consumer cooperative. They have seven children of their own, and are paying school fees for several of Sheey Ngee's relatives.

Sheey Ngee is a close friend of the chief palace advisor, who is also a teacher in his primary school. He is secretary of a local cell of the national party. His initiation into *yee ŋweroŋ* cost him all his available capital, in-cluding loans from relatives. He believes very strongly in maintaining Nso' tradition and custom in the face of what he sees as outside corruption. At the same time, he has a distinctly "modern" outlook and feels that it is essential for the new elites to participate actively in Nso' traditional poli-tics to keep them attuned to events in the modern world. He has a brother who went to the United States to attend a university and who stayed over-seas without communicating with his parents for a long period of time, and Sheey Ngee talks of this with a great deal of anger. His parents, now quite elderly, live in an adjacent compound, and Sheey Ngee helps them out with financial expenses such as medical bills.

Sheey Ngee also is concerned with Nso' retaining as much control as possible over local affairs, and thinks the Anglophone provinces have been given short shrift by the Francophone government. He sees maintaining a strong tradition as one way for Nso' to keep control over local affairs. He also quite clearly sees traditional politics as an arena in which he can realize personal ambitions for prestige by acquiring status within a symbolic sys-tem that he and the people of Nso' recognize as legitimate.

These men are fairly typical of the new *asheey*. Most of them have at least a secondary school education, and many hold fairly high-status salaried jobs. They all became titleholders in their late 30s, the age when men in Nso' are thought to be mature and ready to take on the responsibilities of a family head. All have over five children of their own, and most pay school fees for a number of children of relatives or close friends. Their wives are active in community and church groups, and often are leaders in various women's organizations. The new Nso' men of title have been active in local cells of the national party, sit on community development organizations and village councils, and are often leaders of the new national opposition parties, which are backed by the majority of the Nso' population. They are participating, and often prominent, members of the Catholic or the Presbyterian church. Most of them own large coffee farms and are involved in a variety of entrepreneurial activities. They own taxis, small businesses, and rental properties in Kimbo' and Bamenda. All of them can be characterized as ambitious, and most of them have achieved some degree of local, and in some cases national, political power. There is a wide range in their individual incomes, but all have incomes substantially higher than average for the region as a whole. As a group these men constitute the new Nso' leaders and a new rural elite.

The new elite invests in secret societies and titles, symbolic capital, for a variety of reasons. Titles and membership in palace societies continue to represent achievement and validate status in Nso'. A title confers on its holder a recognition and legitimation of leadership. The practices validated by these symbols have become various, however.

By assuming a title, Nso' men can demonstrate a local power base and legitimate positions of leadership at home and in the institutions of the national bureaucracy. For some men, titles are a business investment. For others, traditional politics provides a local arena to play out a personal quest for public recognition: to be a big frog in a relatively small pond. For all these men it is a means by which they can demonstrate both within and outside Nso' that they are people of substance and consequence: men others will listen to and recognize as leaders.

In the context of everyday life and relations with kin and neighbors, titles and the status they confer are symbols and indices of competence to manage the affairs of the compound, lineage, and neighborhood. Lineage heads look to the modern big men for advice on how best to interact with government agencies and consult with them before deciding cases brought to traditional court. The new elites who work for the state are able to represent a point of view informed by their participation in palace politics, and can look out for the interests of the *fon* in local as well as national offices of the national bureaucracy. In the context of Nso' as a chiefdom, these men demonstrate their loyalty and adherence to customary values and, by extension, to the Nso' people. By investing time and money in the affairs of the chiefdom, these men demonstrate their recognition of the legitimacy of traditional authority, which, while not in direct opposition to new norms and values, is recognized as being in some sense prior, with an innate rather than an imposed legitimacy.

The symbolism and acquisition of titles in Nso' thus have multiple levels of meaning. The title *sheey* has multiple meanings which vary in different contexts and for different individuals. The meaning of titles has been subject to a process of negotiation and to structural changes within which power relations have shifted towards control over commodities and national politics and away from the communal responsibilities of a legitimate Nso' leader. That is, the meaning of titles and power relations have shifted somewhat, but not entirely. The process of negotiation over the meaning of titles is a dialogical one in which the various meanings compete with and condition one another. While cultural systems must be more or less fixed, the repeatable features of culture, such as taking a title, depend on the context in which these are situated. The context then can refract, add to, and even subtract from the amount or kind of meaning these appear to have if we think of them as only part of a systemic manifestation independent of context. From one perspective it could be argued that the meaning of taking a title in Nso' today has more in common with being a Shriner or a Mason (or with the clubs Skull and Bones at Yale or Hasty Pudding at Harvard) than it does with traditional Nso' titled men. But within this process the meaning of legitimate authority and the obligations as well as the privileges which accompany this have maintained an integrity.

The new titled men in Nso' must continue to have an "open hand." They must redistribute the wealth, and they continue to do so. It is still essential that the modern big men redistribute wealth among their kin and clients, for staying in the political limelight depends on the ability to dispense favors and goods, not only at politically expedient times, but always. Redistributing wealth is essential, not only for elites living in Nso', but also for Nso' men who have become urban elites. In various ways, people in Nso' see an opposition between themselves and the foreign power of the national urban centers. Nso' elites living in urban areas have a dual pressure to redistribute. Not only is a local power base essential to success in national political life, but also, to avoid being marked as possessors of foreign *səm*, as individualistic, unsocialized sorcerers, it behooves these new elites to play the role of the generous titled man with an open hand.

There is, however, a significant difference between the structure of redistribution by the new titled men of Nso' and that of their predecessors. Resources which are redistributed are gained primarily through access to the state. New forms of redistribution include access to jobs and higher education. Papers for traders' licenses and applications for buildings and development projects and for access to national lands and national agricultural loans are facilitated through the system. These practices of redistribution all share an important attribute. They allow the new elites to redistribute through mechanisms which do not substantially deplete their own personal wealth but rather draw on their political connections. Unlike traditional lineage heads, the new big men in Nso' can gain clients, support kin, and accumulate a significant amount of personal wealth at the same time. By commodifying specific titles and rank in secret societies, the Fon Nso' created a context in which the new elites gained control in Nso' traditional government and were then able to fuse the power of Nso' tradition, of the pure legitimacy of the ancestors, with the secular legitimacy of the modern state. The new elites are able to legitimate the changing nature of productive relations without negating the overall symbolic validity and meaning of Nso' traditional titles.

As an important local political institution within Nso', where emphasis on local control is a core cultural value, *ŋweroŋ* can, from one vantage point, be seen as a form of what Bayart has called "popular modes of political action."[32] In its possession of a cultural and political style which is distinct from the political life of the national state, *ŋweroŋ* has centered itself within national civil society. But while *ŋweroŋ* is an important political institution stressing local control, it is also, from another vantage point, the repressive arm of the Nso' state. If we examine the complex relationships within *ŋweroŋ* and the networks of the new Nso' elites within and between traditional and national politics, it is clear that the participation of the new elites in traditional politics facilitates and advances their national careers.

By incorporating the new elites into positions of power within Nso' traditional government, the Fon Nso' sought to domesticate or socialize their *səm* within Nso'. But has he succeeded in doing so, in turning the new elites into his new leopards? Or are these new modern big men instead sorcerers of the night, bringing practices into Nso' on the winds of change which will ultimately undermine or even abort the power of the *fon* and his traditional notables? These possibilities may not be mutually exclusive, and arguably, participation in traditional politics and the new elites' national political careers are mutually constitutive.

Traditional Nso' political institutions may have the potential for popular political action against the state by providing an autonomous space of mass expression outside state control. Clearly these institutions are important enough to have attracted the attention of the national government. In a front-page article in the *Cameroon Post* issue of September 13–20, 1990 (No. 42), the headlines read: "FOR ERRING: NSO' FON PAYS PUBLIC FINE." The article goes on to claim that Fon Ŋga' Bi'fon III on August 24, 1990, paid a fine of 50 calabashes of raffia wine, 12 goats, and 12 fowls for "undermining Nso' tradition." Emphasizing *ŋweroŋ*'s supremacy in the palace, one Faay wo Mahmu, acting as spokesman, went on to point out, "It is *ŋweroŋ* who kept the Fon and not the Fon who kept *ŋweroŋ*. No one owns and can claim to control *ŋweroŋ*." The *fon* is quoted as saying, "I am very pleased and at ease to have reconciled with *ŋweroŋ*. If I have been fined by the Kingmakers—*ŋweroŋ*—they are right because traditional laws and customs are subject to the respect of everyone irrespective of his position." This article produced a strong reaction by members of *ŋgiri*, who accused *ŋweroŋ* of doing "much to disrupt the traditional authority of Nso' " and of "trying to usurp unauthorized powers in Nso', when in actual fact they are merely pages of the palace, they are persons only to act on orders of the Fon and his Executive Council." This article was signed by four *ŋgiri afaay* and distributed throughout Nso'. The fight between the two secret societies became so violent and so public that the senior district officer became involved, and the Fon Nso' was warned by the national government that he had better put his house in order or the state would disband the societies. Prominent Nso' men from both *ŋweroŋ* and *ŋgiri* lobbied for settling the dispute, although each side claimed to be in the right. While the argument has not been satisfactorily resolved, things have become somewhat calmer through negotiations between elite men who are members of these societies and representatives of the national government.[33]

When local politics is carried out in this idiom and national and local politics are articulated through the secret societies, women are excluded from participation. The ability of the new elite men to use traditional institutions and the traditional title system to graft new forms of power onto the existing status hierarchy in Nso' articulates local and national male control, and contributes to the dominant discourse of male hegemony. In significant ways the secret societies such as *ŋweroŋ* contribute, rather than pose a counterargument, to the local power of the national elite. But there do exist forms of counterhegemony in Nso'. The next two chapters will explore these.

7
Counterhegemony and Dissent on the Periphery
Chiefs, Subchiefs, and the Modern State

During the course of my stay in Nso', I lived half the time in Nsə', and consequently spent quite a bit of time with Fon Nsə'. I became a regular visitor at his palace and spent many an afternoon drinking palm wine in the courtyard while Fon Nsə', a calm and stately presence, entertained visitors and petitioners for favors, settled disputes, and in general conducted the business of his chiefdom. One afternoon during rainy season when I slid down the muddy path and stood dripping in the entryway to the palace, Fon Nsə', unusually agitated and upset, motioned for me to follow him into a small interior courtyard where a number of the *ataaŋgvən* of Nsə' had gathered. I watched while they filled a ceremonial calabash, or *sho'*, with the *fon*'s palace wine, which is seen to have potent truth-finding power.[1] Swearing an oath to *nsay* and to the ancestors that the ritual they were preparing would seek the truth, each man spit into the *sho'*. The lineage heads then exited en masse, clambered into a waiting Land Rover, raised their umbrellas, and headed out to complete the ritual. Fon Nsə' and I headed back to the relative dryness of the palace.

Soon we were seated sipping palm wine in the interior of the palace in a small private audience room. A dim light seeping in from the narrow, high, latticed windows cast shadows of the figures carved into the *fon*'s throne against the dank walls, evoking images of a Mongo Beti novel. Fon Nsə', still upset but now somewhat calmed by both the wine and the ritual preparation, proceeded to explain the events of the past half hour. It seems his relationship with the Fon Nso' had been strained for some time. The day before, it had been stretched to the breaking point when the Fon Nso' took hoes away from Nsə' women working in fields over which both rulers claimed jurisdiction. (The women had been using hoes on a Nso' Country Sunday, a ritual day set aside by the appropriate ruler and the landlord on the field, a day on which hoes are not to be used as a sign of fealty and respect to the ritual leader and his ancestors.) Not quite knowing how to respond, I took a gulp of palm wine and stared at my cup. Graciously ignoring my lack of response, Fon Nsǝ' continued his story, "We in Nsǝ' are in the right; it is our land. We perform the rituals for the land and the Fon Nso' is a trespasser." The lineage heads were at this moment travelling to the land in question to pour the contents of the ritual calabash on the Earth and swear an oath that this was true. Furthermore, the Fon Nsǝ' went on to inform me that he was not a subject of the Fon Nso'. He emphasized, "I am walking together with the Fon Nso' as an equal, as a brother, using my own power. We helped Nso' fight the Bamum and the Germans, and with the conquest of Din and Jottin. Now he [the Fon Nso'] says he owns us. How can that be when we were moving together as equals? The Fon Nsǝ' was never captured [by Nso']. So the Fon Nso' has a very big head. If you go to meet him now he will not tell you the truth."

All hegemonic processes contain a counterhegemony, a counterhegemony which ultimately has a significant effect on the hegemonic process itself. Nso' is no exception. In both the previous conversations with the Fon Nsǝ' and in the following description of the historical background of the current arguments between these two traditional rulers, we find one discourse of counterhegemony in Nso'. The argument between these two men also shapes the discourse, both by the different versions of history that are recalled and by the present relationship of each of the two rulers to the modern state. As was argued in chapter 3, Nso' is today a state within a state, a complicated place where the multiple strands which constitute its social body are all informed by national politics and the marketplace and are interwoven into a complex multivocal, multiethnic pattern. Categories are fluid; they merge and dissolve into each other only to become distinct and disaggregated when their meaning is negotiated and boundaries shift. What appears as hegemony from one vantage point appears as counterhegemony from another. The orthodox discourse often does not reflect the reality of heterodox practices involved in a particular institution. In the following chapter we will see how this relationship between orthodoxy and heterodoxy is played out in the context of allocation and control over land in the current political economy, and how orthodoxy/hegemony becomes heterodoxy/counterhegemony within the Nso' hegemonic discourse.

As Raymond Williams has argued, most versions of "tradition" can be quickly shown to be radically selective.[2] From the past, which presents multiple meanings and practices with a variety of interpretations in relation to the present, certain meanings and practices are selected to have meaning and efficacy and others are discarded. This selection is then passed off by the dominant group as "the tradition" and "the significant past." Therefore any tradition is an aspect of contemporary power relationships; it is that aspect which is meant to connect with and ratify these in the interest of a dominant group. In the previous chapter we saw how the selective version of a "living tradition" is used to join new relations of domination with old relations of power, and the ways in which the power of the traditional secret societies and titles and offices, which have become a means of accumulation for the new elites, becomes mutually constitutive with the power of the national state to further male hegemony. In this chapter we will look at the paradox created while Nso' asserts one version of history and Nsə' discounts and disclaims it, substituting instead its own selective tradition, and thereby denying Nso' hegemony within the subchiefdoms.

By focusing on the estrangement between these two rulers today, we can see the complexities involved in discerning the multiple layers of reality and meaning, and the internal and external contradictions which are set up while both Nso' and the national government try to establish hegemony in the region. An account of the estrangement between these two men, who, according to the Nsə', "became like David and Jonathan" in the early twentieth century,[3] must, of course, include an understanding of two core symbols in Nso': the significance of the Earth in Nso' cosmology and the related meaning of stewardship of the land as a symbol of political (and religious) leadership. It must also include two relatively recent processes: a growing scarcity of arable land brought about partly by population growth but also by the ambiguous tenure situation created by the contradictions between traditional tenure arrangements and national land ordinances—contradictions which have been exacerbated by a propensity towards commodification and privatization of land and land use. Clearly, the present disaffection between these two men cannot be understood without reference to history. Here there are three aims: first, to locate a form of counterhegemony in the histories put forth today by the Fon Nsə'; second, to see how the structure of relationships both within Nso' and outside Nso' determine the outcome of the dispute; and finally, to understand how the reproduction of particular structures ends up instead as their transformation.[4]

The Changing Meaning of Land in Nso'

As we saw in chapter 5, land shortages are rapidly becoming a serious local issue in Nso'. Old hostilities between Fulani herders and local agriculturalists have worsened, and new tensions between constituencies of the chiefdom have emerged and intensified. The meaning of control over land as symbolic of legitimate political authority has, however, changed less rapidly than the practices associated with the exercise of this control, indeed, less rapidly than the cultural meaning of land itself. Access to land has been viewed as a right of citizenship in Nso'; today that right has been put in jeopardy. As land becomes scarce and begins to have a cash value attached to it, conflicts over the control of rights of access to and allocation of its use have sharpened between the paramount Fon Nso' and his subchiefs. These conflicts have become particularly acute between the Fon Nso' and the Fon Nsə', the chief of a village in the northern reaches of Nso', whom we met at the beginning of this chapter. Both rulers have claimed the right to allocate land lying on the Nsə' side of the Nso'-Nsə' border, each appealing to a different set of rights and a different interpretation of history. Their dispute revolves primarily around rights in people as opposed to rights in territory, focussed here on control of access to land, and around different historical legitimations of these rights.

Struggles over land and over the meaning of its control have accelerated rapidly since the national government passed land ordinances in 1974 encouraging "rational development" through privatization.[5] These land ordinances have enabled an emerging rural elite to acquire large tracts of land under individual title. As noted in chapter 5, these have effectively encouraged not agricultural development, but rather growing land scarcity and conflict. The dispute between these two rulers is just one, albeit an important and public one, among many such disputes, with people invoking various rules of each, and sometimes both, systems of tenure to secure access to land. More important here, this dispute is illustrative of the multiple voices and shifting relationships in Nso' today, and of the need to look at these historically when trying to determine the relationships between various groups.

Nsə': Fealty or Friendship?

As noted in Chapter 2, when Nso' expanded in the second half of the nineteenth century, it achieved its present social dimensions by absorbing or conquering and making tributary a number of smaller chiefdoms. While the Nso' state became increasingly centralized, the *afon* of Nso' incorporated various conquered chiefs and important lineage heads into national political life. The pattern was to endow lesser chiefs with rank, title, and participation in centralized decision making, along with symbolic and economic privileges, in return for political fealty. The chiefs of larger villages, like Nsə', were accorded the title *fon* and allowed to retain their hereditary dynasties and autonomy in the management of local affairs in return for political support and payment of tribute (*nshwi*). Two principles came to be stressed in the system of dues and tribute: local derivation of tribute from the subchiefs and generalized redistribution from the paramount Fon Nso', emphasizing mutual rights and obligations.[6]

Nsə' occupies a special position in relation to Nso'. Nsə' does not have the status of a "younger brother" chiefdom as two of the smaller chiefdoms (Mbiame and Oku) in the division do. Unlike the remaining subchiefs, however, the Fon Nsə' was never conquered, and Nsə' was never invaded or attacked by Nso'. In fact, Nsə' helped Nso' with its military conquest of other small chiefdoms, notably Ŋkor, Lassin, and Din in the late nineteenth century. In addition, Nsə' sent a large contingent to help Nso' defeat the Bamum[7] and fought with Nso' against the Germans in the early twentieth century. In the German war (1906) Nsə' was burned. By that time, Nsə' had joined with Nso' at least as allies, and it would clearly have been in the interests of Nso' to secure its northern border with an alliance with Nsə' after the Banyo Fulani had secured an alliance with Ndu to the north in the 1870s. According to both Nsə' and Nso' people, the Fon Nsə' gave a white fowl, honey, and grain to the Fon Nso' upon the defeat of Nso' by the Germans. These were subsequently given to the German commander as a sign of surrender.[8] But the interpretation of these gifts differs today. The Fon Nsə' insists that he and the Fon Nso' fought together as equals and that he never became a subject of Nso'. The Fon Nso', on the other hand, claims that Nsə' voluntarily became tributary to Nso', that the fowl and honey were symbols of submission, not merely gifts given to an equal to help pay tribute to the Germans. The Fon Nso' complained to me that "the Nsə' people now want their freedom but I cannot give it. They [and people in several other subchiefdoms] no longer love me or want to live in peace with me. They no longer bring food and firewood."[9]

The Fon Nso' marshals several pieces of evidence to prove the claim that the Fon Nsə' voluntarily accepted a tributary relationship with Nso'. He points to the fact that Lam Nso' has replaced Limbum, the original language of Nsə', as the language of everyday discourse (although Nsə' rituals are still performed in Limbum, and older people in Nsə' speak both languages). A white fowl is the traditional gift of surrender, and it was given by Nsə' directly to Nso'. In return, the Fon Nsə' was granted the right to retain all his royal trappings along with autonomy of rule over his territory. Indeed, Nsə' people, while stressing their ties with the Limbum-speaking Nsungli chiefdoms to the north, acknowledge their citizenship in Nso' and, until recent times, the Fon Nsə' provided the Nso' palace with the protective *nzəy* medicine.[10]

Although most Nsə' people agree that in certain contexts they are citizens of Nso', today they stress their differences with and estrangement from the Fon Nso' and assert their independent status. In a pamphlet distributed during Nseh Cultural Week in 1977, a whole page is devoted to the topic "Dissimilarities in the Nseh and Nso Traditions." This publication, put out by a local committee headed by the Fon Nsə', stresses early cooperation and equality between the two rulers. Although it is vague about the origins of the rift between them, it is quite clear about the fact that a rift exists:

> Friendly ties between the Fons of Nseh and Nso increased wonderfully after fighting the Germans. It came to a peak when both Fons agreed to work hand in hand. This cordial relationship continued until the last days of Fon Minglo. . . . Since then these two friends are apart, their dispute whose solution is basically traditional still remains unsolved till today.[11]

By the late 1970s relations between the two rulers had declined to the point that the Fon Nsə' began to assert heatedly and publicly that he was not a subject of the Fon Nso'. In one of my interviews with him, he said angrily, "You [Nso'] never captured me; I was travelling with you, using my own power, and then we were captured in several places, so why should you treat me in such a way? Because he [Fon Nso'] just wants tokens, because the population of Nsə' is so small, that is why he treats us so."

If we look at the time when people say friction between the two rulers began, we can see that it was at a point when two core principles of governance between the center (the Fon Nso' and his government in Kimbo') and the periphery (the village subchiefdoms)—local derivation and generalized redistribution—began to be seriously undermined by changing policies of the colonial system of taxation and tax collection.[12] Until the 1920s the subchiefdoms owed tribute (nshwi), consisting primarily of surplus production and people for service in the palace as wives and pages. The larger part of tribute and prestations given to the Fon Nso' was, however, redistributed either on an ongoing basis through hospitality at the palace or through redistribution in times of food shortage, when the palace storehouses were opened up for distribution to all villages of Nso'. The Nso' have a saying, "The fon takes from Ŋkar and gives to Ŋkar," meaning the Fon Nso' is owed tribute from his subchiefs but is expected to look after the needs of all the people of Nso'.

When taxes were imposed, first by the Germans in 1909 and then by the British administration, they were collected through the Fon Nso' as Sole Native Authority and the commission retained by the fon was viewed locally as a form of tribute. The subchiefs were relieved of the burden of tribute of Fon Ŋga' Bi'fon (the Fon Nso') around 1923 in exchange for their portion of the tax commission. Thus, initially the colonial administration collected all taxes directly through the paramount Fon Nso'. However, beginning in the late 1930s, a new plan was instituted, whereby subchiefs, as collectors, received a commission. Subchiefs then received a percentage of the tax paid directly from the Native Authority Treasury.

The important point here is that the tax commission retained by the Fon Nso' was viewed as a substitute for tribute from the subchiefdoms. When the Native Authority allowed the subchiefs to collect taxes and retain a portion of the revenues, the subchiefs believed that this conferred on them a new status, a far greater degree of politically sanctioned authority than the administration intended to give. As early as the late 1940s the subchiefs, now relieved of tribute payments and receiving a tax commission directly from the Native Authority Treasury, began to question the overlordship of the paramount Fon Nso'.

After the Second World War, the colonial administration began to reorganize the Native Authorities into larger units with a view to basing a system of elective local government upon them, somewhat upon the British model. Nso' was included in a federated body, the South-Eastern Federated Native Authority, which met in Ndop and was itself demoted to a subordinate advisory council. Monies for public works and local development were distributed through this council. The Fon Nso' did not have the same control over the redistribution of taxes that he had over redistribution of tribute. The capital at Kimbo' was developed by the colonial government while village chiefdoms went without roads, medical facilities, and schools. The subchiefs came to believe that the *fon* and people in Kimbo' were profitting unduly at their expense and hence began to campaign vigorously for autonomy.

By collecting taxes through the subchiefs, the colonial administration supported them to an extent not initially intended. Their direct relationship with the administration weakened the authority of the Fon Nso' over his subchiefs. Equally damaging was the fact that taxes, unlike tribute, could not be redistributed through the largess of the Fon Nso'. Local derivation was stressed now in a new context: the redistribution of taxes through implementation of local service and public works. But the Fon Nso' no longer had ultimate control over this generalized redistribution. When proposals from the subchiefs to the Nso' Advisory Council were turned down—actually by colonial administrators but symbolically by the Fon Nso'—the subchiefs thought he was pocketing the tax receipts and developing the capital at Kimbo' without adequately redistributing goods and services to his people in the subchiefdoms.

Colonial tax policies undermined the credibility of the paramount *fon* in his subchiefdoms. But his relationship to the colonial administration had supported and perpetuated his superior position. Upon independence the policies of the West Cameroon government did the same. Even now, local offices of the national bureaucracy work closely with the Fon Nso';

he plays a prominent role on divisional development councils and is a member of the divisional lands commission. According to the national land ordinances instituted in 1974, the Fon Nso' must approve, at least symbolically, allocation of land in the division.

While we can trace the beginnings of conflict between Nso' and Nsə' back several decades, the dispute has sharpened because of pressure on land. The estrangement between the two rulers today is predicated upon a conflict between rights over people and rights over territory, the latter by virtue of ritual responsibility for the land in question. This argument is illustrated by the current dispute over Kuykov (or Kuvluv, as the inhabitants call it), a village on the Nsə' side of the Nsə'-Nso' border. It is this dispute which occasioned the ritual scene with which this chapter opened.

Fealty, Land, and the Ancestors: Arguments over Kuylov[13]

By the 1960s, and perhaps earlier, people from Kimbo' had been moving into Nsə' villages—Ŋgondzən, Mborinyaar, Mbaraŋ, Kuykov. Regardless of whether or not the Fon Nsə' became tributary to the Fon Nso', these villages were in the domain of the Fon Nsə', and he and his lineage heads were responsible for performing the rituals for the land and the people working on the land in these areas. While there were many disputes over extensive crop damage caused by the numerous cattle inhabiting this area, especially around Ŋgondzən,[14] there were, until the 1970s, few disputes about who controlled access to the land in and around these villages. Kuylov constitutes a part of Nsə', and the Fon Nsə' was given rights of local control in his territory. As land became scarce around the capital at Kimbo', people from Nso' proper begged land in outlying areas, including Kuylov. While the Fon Nsə' is not pleased that people from Nso' proper are farming in Kuylov, the dispute is not about the farming of the land as much as it is about control over the symbols of authority over the people farming on the land.[15] The Fon Nso' maintains that he is the supreme *fon* and thus the ultimate overlord of all land in the division. He claims that this position entitles him to control any area where Nso' people have acquired land. Therefore, he insists that people who have settled in Kuylov should observe his Country Sundays and pay taxes directly through him. But since Kuylov is viewed by the Fon Nsə' as part of his territory, he insists that people living there, both Nsə' people and those who have moved there from Kimbo', should pay taxes directly through him and observe the Country Sundays of Nsə'.

Depending on the meaning assigned to various symbols and acts, each argument has an interpretation which gives it customary legitimacy.[16] The Fon Nsə' points to the fact that the Fon Nso' will not perform the traditional wine-drinking ceremony with him to swear the validity of his claim. He presents this as evidence that the Fon Nso' knows the land really belongs to Nsə' and, knowing he is in the wrong, is too cowardly to perform the ritual. The Fon Nso' counters this argument by claiming that he does not fear the ritual, but it is simply beneath his dignity to submit to the request of the Fon Nsə'.

It is important to reemphasize here the significance of the meaning of the Earth (*nsay*) in Nso' cosmology. Legitimate authority is based on descent and the ancestors, and the Earth of the dead is the repository of religious moral values which are given legitimacy by referring to them as ancestral values.[17] The Earth can be called upon to punish offenders. The Earth is viewed as the place where the important dead, the ancestors, reside; they sleep underfoot and can be awakened. If an act occurs which is considered to be a trespass against moral values, the Earth of the dead may get "hot" (angry) and refuse to grow crops and otherwise afflict the area. An act of appeasement is then required so that the Earth is "cooled" and sleeps again. The Fon Nsə' and his lineage heads emphasize the fact that they perform rituals for the land at Kuylov. They view the area as part of Nsə' and claim the fealty of people living there—and invoke their ritual obligations for the land as proof.

Since taxes are seen as a form of tribute, the debate has centered on which ruler people pay taxes through, but the real issue is a conflict between the ideal of control over people as opposed to control over territory as a justification for controlling access to land. With land becoming both scarce and expensive, people on all levels are trying to hold on to as much land as possible. Both sides believe they are in the right, and in a sense both are. They are merely applying different interpretations and resting their arguments on different principles of right and obligation—the Fon Nso' emphasizing the ideal of rights in people, and the Fon Nsə' stressing rights in territory. When asked how the dispute would have been settled in the past, elders in Nsə' claimed that the disputes would not have happened in the past, that the "land was not so difficult [to get] then" and that the land was "blank" (unoccupied). We could add that the presence of a higher court of appeal, the national government, has probably strengthened the resolve of the Fon Nsə' to hold his ground, so to speak, against the more powerful paramount *fon* and the numerically stronger Nso'. Objectively, it is not surprising that the principles of rights in people and rights in territory should come into conflict at this time: historically land was abundant, and direct control over people was the key to power and wealth; today land is becoming scarce, and people more abundant, and no longer do traditional leaders have direct control over their dependents' lives and fortunes. Given the current practice of demanding cash for land and often for the use of land and the government's emphasis on privatization, these values were bound to come into conflict. An unexpected twist in this particular dispute lies in the argument, legitimate from one vantage point, that the claim of the Fon Nsǝ' is the more orthodox. One would expect a claim to rights in territory to be buttressed by more recent or imported values. What is clear here is that, for the Nso', control over land is a central symbol of leadership, both historically and today.

Hierarchy of Dispute Settlement: The Interface between Traditional Authority and National Bureaucracy

Just as the colonial administrations used the existing power structure in Nso' to facilitate their rule, so too does the national government recognize the efficacy of traditional authority and customary law today, and uses them in a kind of indirect rule which is reminiscent of the colonial era. The Fon Nso' is recognized as a civil servant, and is a salaried employee of the national government. The *fon* and the Nso' traditional government work closely with the district officer and other representatives of the national government in imposing and enforcing local law. The subdivision is the level where national and local government interface: the district officer coordinates decisions made by representatives of the national ministries with various village and traditional councils and personalities. The local representatives of the national government who are Nso' men (and the majority of them are) are more often than not also members of *ŋweroŋ* or *ŋgiri*. They are the same actors wearing different hats in varying contexts; however, their identity is as Lam Nso' speakers and Nso' people first, and as citizens of Cameroon only secondarily.

The way in which land disputes are adjudicated reflects the interface between traditional and national authority. Conflicts over land are judged by a hierarchy of institutions and personalities, depending on the seriousness of the case and the people involved. Cases usually begin in the compound with the compound head and then go to the lineage head (who may or may not be the same person); if they are not settled satisfactorily, cases are then taken to the *fon,* the traditional council,[18] the local council or customary court, the district officer as head of the land commission, and ultimately to the magistrate's court.

As was discussed in previous chapters, the Fon Nso' is viewed as the "father" of Nso' and the *fon*ship as the eternal symbol of unity and authority in the chiefdom. The *fon* is titular or symbolic owner of all land within his domain. This titular ownership is, however, a symbol of his political authority, not indicative of ownership in the sense of absolute control or rights of alienability. Actual administration of land, as we saw, is carried out by a number of landlords called *ataŋgvən*.[19] These landlords are heads of large lineages in their respective villages, and are also known as the priests of the land. Each landlord has a sacrificial vessel, calabash called a *sho'*, to be used in land disputes. Several times a year the landlords go to the palace with these vessels, where the *fon* fills them with palace wine. The landlords drink the *fon*'s wine from these vessels as a pledge of just land administration. They then return home and pour some of the wine around the land shrine (*kirə ke nyuy*) in their respective fields. This act is a symbolic representation of the *fon*'s concern for the welfare of all people working the land; it is also representative of the relationship of the *fon* and the landlords. Although the landlords have rights of management over land, these rights are subject to validation and recognition of the landlords' status by the *fon*. This pattern is repeated in the subchiefdoms.

Land conflicts are first brought to the *taala'*, or father of the compound, who will try to settle the dispute. If they are within the lineage, they are brought to the lineage head and his council of elders. If more than one landlord is involved, the dispute was traditionally, and is in some quarters today, settled by a ceremony called *lav-ŋgom*. Here two *sho'*, each containing palace wine, are brought out, and each landlord takes one. They then drink the wine and condemn the alleged trespass on their land. According to local wisdom, the result of this act has always been reconciliation, since no true Nso' landlord will drink the palace wine and swear the oath unless he is convinced by the advice of his elders that he is totally in the right. This ceremony is still widely practiced, although some people claim the elders can be bribed to give erroneous information and even that some landlords can now be bribed to make favorable decisions. It is widely held that if someone drinks the wine in a false oath he will bring bad luck on himself and his family and may even die. A number of landlords will not perform this ceremony even if they believe they are in the right, since the "true," or original, landlord is not always easily traced, and the landlord may not be sure of transactions between his deceased predecessor and the relatives of the man bringing the dispute.

If the dispute is not settled satisfactorily by the landlord(s), in question, the case is presented to the *fon*. If the *fon* cannot, or will not, decide the case on his own, he refers it to the traditional council. If the contestants do not accept this decision, it can be taken then to the local council or customary court, which is composed of one man from each of the quarters under its jurisdiction. To secure a position on the customary court, applications are written to the district officer, who selects the members. If the dispute is still left unsettled it goes to the national administration, first to the district officer. If he doesn't settle it, the case is taken to the land consultative board. The district officer will inevitably call upon the *fon* and the landlords in question to participate in the final decision. In addition, the *fon* and two of his notables are permanent members of the land consultative board.

Only very rarely do cases reach the magistrate's court. Taking a case to the magistrate's court is an expensive enterprise, and only people who can afford both the court and lawyer fees will go this far, and then only if they have a lot to gain or lose. People say that if a case is taken to the magistrate's court then of course the person must be in the wrong; if you were innocent or in the right you wouldn't have to pay all that money to a lawyer. Not only must the person bringing the case to the magistrate's court be able to afford to do so; he or she must also understand the procedures involved in entering a case in court. The only magistrate's court in the division is in Kimbo'. Most people have neither the money, nor the knowledge, nor the inclination to go beyond traditional authority in adjudication of land disputes. One reason for this lies in the fact that *ŋweroŋ*, which many people recognize as the most powerful body of local authority, can be called into action when people disobey the traditional council and can at least theoretically enforce its decisions. Cases seldom go beyond the traditional council when they involve two Nso' people, and even when they do, customary authorities often play a leading role in the decision process. People from the subchiefdoms are even less likely to take land cases for settlement away from the local arena; they often feel, and not without justification, that they will get a better deal at home than in the capital at Kimbo'.[20] The small village farmer more often than not will depend on the wisdom of the *fon* and the traditional court. Traditional authorities will at least try not to leave a person without sufficient land to feed the household. People may lose control over a particular plot of land but will usually be given at least some land to farm, even if it is often less desirable, on the sides of steep hills or far out in the countryside.

When the national administration becomes involved in settling land disputes, the decision almost inevitably involves calling in village elders and traditional authorities both for advice and to put the seal of legitimacy on the decision. First the elders of the compound(s) involved are called in one by one, and their opinion is solicited. If they all agree on the same solution to the conflict, the administration either must accept it or come up with a good reason to overrule their joint decision. If no resolution can be reached, the *fon* is consulted both as the chief authority over land and as a member of the land consultative board.

The chain of decision-making thus runs from the compound head to the lineage head, to the *fon,* to the traditional council, to the local council, to the district officer and the land consultative board; both of the last two consult the *fon* and other traditional authorities before making a ruling. The magistrate's court is the only place where the *fon* is not officially represented and in which decisions do not have to be approved by traditional authority. Once the case goes out of the traditional system, the decision may have to be approved by *representatives* of that system, but no longer is it made strictly according to customary law. Although many of the personalities involved are traditional leaders, and the symbol of traditional legitimacy is sought as a seal of approval, the rules have changed and the traditional authorities must take into account this change in venue.

The Judgment: Between Orthodoxy and Heterodoxy

The inability of the Fon Nso' and the Fon Nsə' to come to a compromise finally led to intervention by the district officer and his staff, men who are seen and who see themselves as part of a new Nso' elite. This was not a "normal" land dispute, nor was it presented as such, but was argued instead on various levels of national government through petitions and personal meetings. Their decision, while not entirely satisfactory to the paramount Fon Nso', favored his position.[21] Attempting, and failing, to emulate the wisdom of Solomon, the judges opted for the status quo, and divided the land between the two rulers. All people farming around Kuylov who were not originally from Nsə' were to pay taxes to the Fon Nso' and observe his Country Sundays, whereas Nsə' people would continue to pay taxes directly through the Fon Nsə' and observe his ritual day of rest. Given his close relationship with the government bureaucracy, it comes as no surprise that the decision favored the Fon Nso'. Yet while the decision favors the paramount *fon*, it does not discount the claims of the Fon Nsə' entirely; to do so not only would increase the hostility but also would go against perceived traditional relationships, even from the view of most Nso' people from outside Nsə'.

If we step back and look at the position of the new elites, it is clear that it would be in their interests neither to cross the Fon Nso' nor to declare publicly an unorthodox position, one which would go against perceived traditional relationships. While the Fon Nso' decries the commodification of land in Nso', he plays a key role in allocating national lands to individuals for development schemes, and is thus a key player in furthering the process of privatization of land. Many of these new elites use their access to the state and their knowledge of the national land ordinances to acquire access to allocation of national lands on an individual basis. Access to the state is necessary but often not sufficient to establish a successful claim to land as private property. The approval of the Fon Nso' and two of his councillors, who sit on the land commission, must also be solicited. The new elites must also be sensitive to traditional politics, and, as we have seen, they often assume prominent roles in traditional politics and acquire titles and offices in secret societies.

By acquiring the symbols and roles of traditional Nso' leaders, the new elites validate the legitimacy of their claims to land and leadership within the chiefdom. In assuming the personas of traditional lineage heads, they reproduce a social, not an individualized, identity,[22] for these are social, not individual, roles with obligations as well as rights attached. Traditional rulers in Nso', once enstooled, are no longer called by their given name but rather by the title of their office. Rights, obligations, and property belong to the title, not the titleholder, so that when a man "takes over the stool" as lineage head, he inherits his predecessor's name, wives, and property. If a lineage head is deposed for not fulfilling the obligations of his office, his cap is removed by a messenger from ŋweroŋ, who then calls him by his given name as a sign that he has become a common man.

The tax dispute between the Fon Nsə' and the Fon Nso' is a symbolic one over the recognition of political allegiance, since actual tax revenue accruing to either *fon* from this area is minimal. It is not surprising that collection of taxes, seen as a sign of fealty and tribute, should become a source of dispute and tension, with the nexus of control over people beginning to change from direct relations of fealty based primarily on kinship to control through ownership and redistribution of resources, including land. The erosion of the credibility of the Fon Nso' in his subchiefdoms when he lost the power to redistribute the surplus, now in the form of tax monies used for development projects, demonstrates the degree to which generosity and redistribution are important political principles and symbols of leadership in Nso' society, both historically and today.

As titleholders and big men in Nso', the new elites must have an "open-hand"—they must distribute the wealth. And they continue to do so. As we saw in the previous chapter, new forms of access to power and control through the modern state have broadened the base of control from an ascribed kin-based form to a more open one which includes an assortment of kin and clients. It is still essential that the modern big men redistribute wealth, for staying in the political limelight depends on the ability to dispense favors and goods, not only at politically expedient times but always.[23]

As noted in chapter 6, there is a significant difference in the structure of redistribution by the new elites. Resources which are redistributed are gained primarily through knowledge of and access to the national bureaucracy. New forms of redistribution include access to jobs and higher education. Papers for trader's licenses, applications for building and development projects, for access to national lands and national agricultural loans are facilitated through the system. In short, redistribution by the new elites more or less openly includes many practices their counterparts in Western countries try to hide (often unsuccessfully) so as not to be accused of graft or nepotism. These practices all share an important attribute. By drawing on political connections rather than on personal wealth, the new elites are able to redistribute without giving up their ability to accumulate. Unlike traditional lineage heads, the new politicos in Nso' can gain clients, support kin, and accumulate a significant amount of personal wealth at the same time.

By taking an active role in traditional government and paying attention to customary law and local opinion when making national decisions, the new elites secure the cooperation of traditional authorities in their leadership and entrepreneurial ventures. They have become the mediators between the local and national arenas, the interpreters as well as the architects of the intersections between customary and national law. What is important is that, by assuming these roles and often acquiring traditional titles, these modern big men assume a legitimate and culturally appropriate social identity.

Although a working decision has been made by the national administration, there are hostilities remaining between the two rulers which neither is willing to resolve in the culturally appropriate way. People in Nso' say the Fon Nsə' can (and should) give a goat to the Fon Nso' to end the problem between them and make peace. They emphasize that the Fon Nso' cannot be the one to give the goat because he is not under the Fon Nsə'. People in Kimbo' point to the fact that the Fon Nso' ended up giving back the hoes to the women farming in Kuylov and therefore made a step towards resolving the animosity between the two rulers. Nso' notables claim that, if a goat is necessary to resolve the issue according to the ancestors, then the Fon Nsə' should provide it; for the Nso' the return of the hoes is already the *kimann*, or resolution, of the affair according to the ancestors. Notables in the palace in Kimbo' claim that if the Fon Nso were to give the goat, it would mean that the land is no longer part of Nso', therefore no goat can be given. Until this issue of the goat is resolved, the death celebration of the late Fon Nso' cannot be celebrated by *ŋweroŋ* in Nsə'. This has meant further estrangement between Nso' and Nsə' and led the Fon Nsə' to emphasize his ties to the national state rather than to the paramount *fon*. This dispute was only somewhat finally resolved in 1993, when both Nsə' and Nso' had enstooled new *afon* who decided that unity was the most expedient course to take given the national political situation. Both *afon* support the opposition party. They jointly decided not to perform the *kimann* ceremony. So while the two leaders are not estranged, the dispute

over Kuylov is not officially finished, but the relationship between Nsə'
and Nso' has been stabilized.

The truth about the tributary nature of the relationship of Nsə' to
Nso' may never be revealed, if indeed there is *a* truth. Clearly the issue cannot be resolved to the satisfaction of all parties concerned. But the dynam-
ics of the contradictions between sets of institutions, as each group recalls a
different history and differentially interprets a set of symbols, and the struggles over meaning and power in asserting rights to control access to land
give us an insight into the discourse of counterhegemony and the ways in
which that counterhegemony in turn shapes the hegemonic discourse.

As Raymond Williams points out, hegemony can never be singular; it
does not exist passively as a form of dominance but has to be renewed, re-
created, defended, and modified continually.[24] Hegemony is also continually denied, limited, altered, and resisted. In the resistance of the Fon Nsə'
to Nso' dominance and in the Nsə' interpretation of history, we can locate
a form of counterhegemony to Nso'. But at another level this counterhegemony is absorbed into the larger hegemonic project of the postcolonial state; ultimately this resolution does not serve to reproduce the dominance of the paramount *fon,* but instead reinforces the power of the state
and the new elite.

8
Conclusion

Gender, Protest, and New Forms of Stratification

Introduction: Arguments over Gender Roles

It is the hot dry season. The winds of the Harmattan have begun to push tired clouds of red dust along the road, washing the landscape with a faded sepia tone reminiscent of pictures in an old-fashioned photo album. Time slows down. By midday most men have gathered in *mimbo* parlors and off-licenses to seek a cool drink and find a diversion in the long hot afternoon. On the walls of the drinking parlors a number of images create a postmodern pastiche: posters advertising Beck's beer, Guinness stout, Fanta, and Coca-Cola compete for space with blinking Christmas lights and pictures of the Pope, the Fon Nso', and the national soccer team. A boom box from the music store across the road blares out "White Christmas" and "Jingle Bells," muffling the afternoon call to prayer that is wafting down the hill from the local mosque.

A number of men sit on bamboo stools and beer crates, drinking palm wine and beer. They argue, gossip, and occasionally call out greetings and exchange news with passersby. A group of young women, several with babies tied securely on their backs with brightly colored cloths, comes into view. The men begin to jest with them, admonishing them to find husbands, get married, and settle down like "normal women." "No be your pa goin' die some day? Wettin then you go do?" admonish the men. The young women begin to banter good naturedly back and forth, but the conversation soon becomes strained and the women defensively retort, "We fit marry for whattee now? If meat and salt e de for our papa he compound, and we get our piken [children] [there too], why we go work for some useless man who no fit 'pay for our head,' who [only wants to] 'worry our life'? Whose side sense de?"

These conversations in the middle of a hot dusty afternoon are not simply isolated incidences, nor are they merely joking relationships to idle away the time. These young women represent a growing trend in which

179

women are choosing to stay single, have children, and live in their parents' compound rather than marry a man for whom they will have to
supply most of the necessities of life with what they perceive to be little
return on their investment. This is not only a regional phenomenon but
also, apparently, a national trend. There are no national statistics available, but on the basis of local-level surveys in Nso' and around Bamenda,
approximately one-third of households contain women who are young
unmarried mothers.[1] If we can believe gossip and hearsay, the numbers
are even higher in many chiefdoms such as Kom and Babanki. Perhaps
most telling here is the way in which this trend has attracted the attention
of the national press.

Male reporters write about this trend with consternation and alarm.
In the *Cameroon Tribune* on Friday, July 29, 1988, a whole page (13) was
devoted to the story "Boys' and Girls' Wrong Approach to Marriage." The
only mention of "boys" (referred to as men within the article) bemoans the
fact that "the bride-price is sky-high in our society [because] so many
young men are more than ready to stretch themselves to pay the high bride-
price," and that "so many bachelors find it difficult to pick the girls they
trust [so that boys] hate to hear any gospel about marriage." In other
words, any "wrong approach to marriage" on the part of young men is the
result of young women's "wrong-headed" behavior. The rest of the article
is a diatribe against women (called girls throughout the article), labelling
them as "love for sale girls," accusing them of "engaging in commercial
flirting," and decrying the fact that women believe "that girls are not born
to suffer" (as though suffering *should* be part of being a woman). The
author goes on to claim that "it seems we have bred a nation of whores
with this sinister generation" largely, perhaps, because "these days, the
girls have stepped into the shoes of men, with the ardent belief that what
men can do, women can equally do. Some of them [women] detest marriage because they want to stay in their homes and achieve everything before thinking of getting married."

Newspaper articles criticizing women for immoral behavior and for
"wanting to behave like men" have become commonplace in national
newspapers; thus, in November of 1990, the *Cameroon Post* ran the three-
part, full-page series "Abortion and Its Effects on National Morals: It Can
Break Marriages [*sic*]," chastising women for using contraceptives as well
as for seeking abortions, and urging parents to teach their girls to remain
chaste. This series included several pages of statistics on the alleged adverse
side effects of abortion. The overall tone of the articles is one of blaming
the victims, focussing on women as being unchaste and bringing their problems on themselves. The trope of the "unnatural" and somehow devious
female is the basis of several popular plays authored by men from Nso';

Succession in Sarkov, by Sankie Maimo, and *Lynda,* by Kenjo Jumban, are two of these works.

A number of articles by women have also begun to appear in reaction both to this public criticism and to the secondary role women play in national political life, in public policy making, and in administration. These articles point to the disadvantages women have in employment and in educational opportunities, even though it is widely recognized that women's labor not only is the backbone of the rural economy but also is crucial to the national welfare.[2] Although these articles sometimes have a self-blaming edge, suggesting that women get jobs in public offices "because our women have indulged in making love without love, to the satisfaction of men," and that women "have allowed themselves to be used [and] abused, relying on their 'bottom power' for success and survival," they are also often quite radical in their content. Several such articles call for equal education and equal job opportunities as well as equal access to agricultural credit for women.

Even more radically, they point to women's role in trade and agriculture, and urge women to "let the men know that the control of economic resources shall not forever remain a male's private domain." These articles call on women to quit supporting men; in the words of one:

> We [women] intend to fight the economic crises whose structure and origin are masculine, by doing our utmost to buy, sell, own and control. In all this we shall always welcome men's advice and assistance, but only when solicited. One area we plan to be careful of, and that is our purses. We plan to keep the menfolk away from them. We may of course assist in paying their taxes to avoid being left in the cold when they are locked up, but we shall strive to let no franc of our sweat be drained into a tumbler of beer. We also do promise to assist in paying children's school fees and hospital bills as we have always done . . .[3]

There is clearly emerging in Cameroon a new group of professional women whose aim is not to abandon the role of being women, but rather to assert the power of being female. In January of 1993 the Cameroon Association of Female Jurists held a panel discussion in Yaounde at the Goethe Institute. The stated purpose of this organization is to fight discrimination and to disseminate information regarding women's legal rights, primarily to draw attention to increased violence against women. They have established two chapters in Yaounde and Douala to give free advice. Although this organization cuts across ethnic boundaries, women from the Northwest Province are in high profile in the organization. The women on the panel argued for affirmative action, for an end to job discrimination, and for better child care and scholarships for women at the national university.

They claim that women have been primary contributors to the democratic process, pointing to both of the major opposition parties, which have women who start and lead major rallies and declarations. They argue that women are "natural democrats"; "women work for all people and not just for themselves." Although women have been prime movers in national politics and in the democratic process in Cameroon, there is only one female minister in the current regime—the minister of social affairs, who is actually a vice minister. Increasingly, this role of women as second-class citizens is protested in the alternative press and in declarations of the major opposition parties. This form of protest and public stance is rather new and is clearly a departure from earlier women's publications sponsored by the women's wing of the national party, the Women's Cameroon National Union (WCNU), which emphasizes women's obligations to family and stresses the need for women to be subservient to men socially. Thus, one woman wrote in 1982 in an article on the integration of women into the state, ". . . there is no question of comparing oneself with men. Men and women are fundamentally different . . ."[4] Women protesting gender inequality today do not agree in principle with this statement; their interpretation of the meaning of gender differences is very different from the one pushed by the state. Women today are determined to claim power they feel is their due by virtue of being female and are acting to assert a complementarity of gendered power.

Arguments over gender roles have entered the public arena on both the local and the national levels. These arguments and negotiations lie at the very heart of political discourse. This is hardly surprising, since gender is, as Donham has pointed out, a category which crosscuts *every* other axis of inequality in society.[5] Gender has been the basis of inequality and hierarchy in Nso' for as long as people can remember. Today, the construction of gender and of gender inequalities has become an increasingly politicized issue in Cameroon, both locally and nationally. Until fairly recently the WCNU functioned primarily to rubber stamp male decisions and to satisfy the social ambitions of elite women. The Social Democratic Front and other newly formed opposition parties have included women's issues in their platforms, which go far beyond the typical national political party agendas, calling for reforms that would give women equal access to education, to agricultural credit, and to professional-level jobs.[6]

There is evidence too that gender roles have become a politicized issue throughout Africa, enough of an issue to enter the international press. An example of this is found in two articles published in the *New York Times* in February and March of 1991. These two articles, although at times displaying an appalling lack of understanding of indigenous gender roles, point out two ends of the spectrum of gender relations in Africa today. In an

article on women in Uganda, the reporter argues that there is a feminization of poverty, with rural women not only assuming the bulk of the economic burden but being victimized by their husbands. Many of these
women, the article argues, stay with their abusive husbands because they
have no choice "under the traditional system." Although a growing number of poor women are choosing to remain unmarried, they are worried
about becoming even more impoverished without the small amount of
money income a husband would provide. The second article, entitled
"Elite Kenyan Women Avoid a Rite: Marriage," points to a growing tendency for elite women in that country to remain unmarried.[7] These successful women, mostly lawyers and academicians, choose to have children
without getting married by the time they are 35. Both of these articles deal
harshly with African men, calling them chauvinistic, drunkards, and wom-
anizers, without any real contextual analysis and certainly no systemic or
cultural analysis. They see such trends with a Western bias and are relatively uninformed about African life, particularly so about the history and
meaning of gender relations. But they do point to a reality which is also
manifested in the lives of women in Nso', in Cameroon, and throughout
Africa. Poor and elite women alike see no real advantage to marriage,
which they frequently view as a drain on their resources and often as an
unacceptable constraint on their lives. Within the context of the growing
economic crisis women have assumed an expanding burden, a burden
which they have come to see as imposed on them by men, and one which
they are increasingly unwilling to shoulder.

Gender both constructs relations and is representative of them. It is
thus constitutive of the very shape of society. Consequently, the current
negotiations over the meaning of gender and gender roles within African
societies are likely to have a transforming effect on the structure of power
relations within the modern African state. As we have seen in previous
chapters, several discourses of counterhegemony have emerged in Nso'.
But there is a question of whether or not these discourses are transformative, substantially opposed to the dominant discourse—emergent in the
strict sense—or merely novel and even supportive of the power of the dominant group. The inverse of a hegemonic discourse does not constitute a
counterhegemonic discourse. Women's resistance to marriage, or rather to
a particular structure of marriage, may be complicitous with a new form of
hegemony which depends on the creation of a new national elite, an elite
whose focus is ultimately more individual than communal, more accumulative than redistributive. As noted earlier, capitalist relationships promoted
by the state have become an arena of contestation, for capitalism brings
cultural as well as material change. In Nso' two multifaceted, multilayered
forms of hegemony interpenetrate and compete with each other for control

of the dominant discourse. Both of these contain within them forms of counterhegemony.

Gender is at the very center of this struggle as women attempt to redefine their relationship to work, to men, and to the factors of production. Local and individual resistance has thus become a larger strategy within a larger arena, and local individual action taken out of local logic has repercussions in the larger system. This book has argued that most of the counterhegemonies are mutually constitutive of the local-national power of male elites but that there is one area that *is* transformative, and that is negotiations over the meaning of gender and gender roles. It is here that we will be able to locate both the formation of a new elite class, and also a form of resistance and a counterdiscourse which will challenge the composition of gender categories, the structure of gender relations, and the hegemony of male power. This is, however, an ongoing process. The reluctance of women to marry men whom they must ultimately support and who share neither their domestic responsibilities nor their vision of modern marriage may be seen from one vantage point as resistance or counterhegemonic; however, at another level or from another vantage point it can be seen as supporting the hegemonic project of the state by encouraging the formation of a national elite where class has the potential of transcending regional identity.

Continuity and Change in the Meaning of Gender Roles

The dominant symbolic framework in Nso' has been one which has privileged titled men through their association with good *səm*, their identification with the ancestors and the Earth (*nsay*), and their obligation to provide a moral balance in society. But this symbolic framework is also one which has assumed a complementarity of gender roles and a balance of power between men and women. It has been argued in previous chapters that women's role as producers and reproducers, as the "backbone of Nso' society," provided the basis for male accumulative strategies. This in turn gave women substantial economic and political power in precolonial Nso'. For women as a group, this feminine power has gradually been eroded with changing material conditions and a shifting political and cultural reality.

As we saw in chapter 3, although gender was embedded in a male-dominated hierarchic system, women in precolonial Nso' were important if not equal political actors. The inequalities based on gender were exacerbated under colonial rule and increased after independence. While women retained certain political rights, many of their political prerogatives came to be attenuated, first by the colonial and then the national state. The boundaries between public and private, always shifting and contested in precolonial Nso', became much more rigid, with men associated with the former and women with the latter domain. Within the context of the modern state, the national state has combined with the traditional precolonial pattern of privileging male titleholders to create a gender system in which women are subordinate to men. Men control large parts of women's lives, yet take little or no economic responsibility for them.

Women in Nso' today must meet the increased demands of underwriting male participation in a new context, one in which land and labor have become commodified and men's obligations to accumulate symbolic capital have become, if anything, more expensive and complex. The emphasis Nso' men put on bigmanship and its social correlates, generosity and redistribution to kin and clients, has put a cap on the ability of most men to accumulate large amounts of money capital or to reinvest their earnings in the household. Nor do most men see provisioning the familial group as part of their social responsibility, choosing instead to invest their earnings in networks and enterprises outside the domestic unit. Consequently the provisioning, as well as the reproduction, of the household is almost entirely dependent on women's labor.

In many ways "traditional" views of gender persist in present-day Nso'. Farming-food-female continue to be linked as a gender marker while the axiom, amounting almost to a taboo, that "men own the fields, women own the crops," remains central. The pattern whereby women's productive and reproductive labor forms the basis of male accumulation continues. Women still have the social obligation of provisioning the household, and men still control most productive resources and long-distance trade networks. However, while from one vantage point women have lost much of the complementarity of power inherent in precolonial gender roles, from another at least some of them have gained access to new forms of symbolic capital embodied in education and jobs and in the ability to make decisions about their lives, which has put negotiations over the meaning of gender and gender roles at the heart of a discourse of counterhegemony.

Gender as Counterdiscourse

Women in Nso' work longer and harder today than they did in the past in order to fulfill new demands for a cash income. They assume more of the burden for reproducing the standard of living. The privatization of land has undermined their formerly guaranteed access to lineage land. Yet at the same time, education and jobs as well as new forms of media communication, such as television, foreign magazines, and a recently expanding and relatively free press, have opened up new visions, new opportunities, and new ideas of what it is to be female. These new perceptions of gender have been contested, revised, and, like all new ideas put to new uses. The negotiated meanings have had and will increasingly have different effects for and on different social groups. The changing perceptions and visions women in Nso' have today about their role have begun to transform not only the meaning of gender but also the structure of Nso' society.

Women in Nso' are quite willing to talk about these matters.[8] For instance a growing number of young women who have been educated beyond primary school and who have access to further education and training or to employment other than farming are choosing to stay single. They say they want "to have something of their own" before they make a decision about marriage; they rhetorically ask, "Why should we get married and just work farm?" They will also tell you in a rather exasperated way, as though it should be obvious to you if you've been around for a while, that once you get married and set your foot in your husband's compound, "that's all for you," meaning your life will be circumscribed by childbearing, cooking, and farm work. Once a woman is married there are limits on the amount of time left free for her to work to accumulate enough social and economic capital to be released from the ongoing round of farm labor and drudgery. Most of these single women have children, for having children remains the mark of adult status for both men and women. But they do not want to marry men who will not combine incomes and visions to create a lifestyle in which men and women contribute equally to the welfare of the household. In other words, women are no longer willing to underwrite men's accumulative strategies without a more substantial reward than the lip service given to them as the backbone of the country. The choices young women make today regarding marriage on the one hand demarcate a distinctive social space for the creation of a new elite, and on the other open up a discourse that may prove to be substantially alternative,[9] that is, constituting a new hegemonic phase rather than being merely novel.

Gender and the Making of a New Elite

Bourdieu points out that groups, such as social classes, are *to be made*.[10] They are not given in "social reality." People are constantly engaged in the negotiation of their own identity; new meanings and values, new practices, new relationships and kinds of relationships are constantly being created. The same act, in this case making a decision about marriage, both portrays a unity of meaning and expresses a plenitude of meanings, some of which are intended and some of which the participants or actors are unconscious of. By looking briefly at the lives of several young Nso' women and the meaning of the practices surrounding marriage in Nso' today, we can better understand these dual roles and multiple meanings.

Gladys[11] is a daughter of the royal lineage in one of the subchiefdoms. We are trekking up a steep narrow path to her mother's farm, she striding confidently while I, slipping and sliding, am trying both to keep up with her and to avoid falling down the mountainside. Gladys combines toughness and good humor with a quiet shyness. She has just finished secondary school, where she studied home economics. She started out last year working in Kimbo' for room and board at one of the missions and has just been offered a job at the hospital as a nurse's aide. Glancing at me out of the corner of her eye she says, rather shyly, that she will maybe someday want to get married, but not now, not until she has established herself in a job and "has something of her own." She helps her mother farm on the days she is free from her hospital work, and commutes weekly to and from Kimbo', where she lives with a relative during the week.

Mary is a small, round, compact woman with an air of competence and intelligence. Her rather deliberate movements scarcely contain her energy and ambition. She is often tired from her several roles as a full-time hospital worker, a mother, and the oldest responsible female in her father's compound. Mary is a nurse's aide in one of the hospitals in Kimbo', a job at which she excels and which she has had for over 10 years. She is trying to save enough money for advanced training, enough both to take the courses and to bribe someone into letting her take the exams. Now in her 30s, Mary has a four-year-old son, John, whose father is, according to local gossip, a former Nso' pastor. She doesn't talk directly about his identity (referring to him as John's father), but she does claim that she will not marry him as a second wife, and in fact he cannot, given his religious position, marry her without divorcing his wife. Mary does not receive child support from her son's father because she worries that he could then claim the child as his own and take him to live in his compound in the town where he is now working.

Mary lives with her father and two younger siblings in Kimbo', works long hours at the hospital, and is a primary source of income for the family. She is determined in her decision not to marry in the traditional manner; that is, she does not want to marry, either polygynously or monogamously, and become subservient to the man of the household. Arriving home from work, she sinks into an overstuffed chair in the living room of her father's compound, rubs her feet, and calls for her young son to fetch us a Fanta. With a quiet intensity she defends her decision not to be married. She has a sister married to a local man who is a university student in the United States. Mary says if she were able to make a marriage like her sister's she would consider marrying, but until then she will just stay as she is and raise her son in her father's family. By the time I leave she is sitting in the kitchen, beginning preparations for the evening meal and sharing the daily gossip with her younger sisters.

Helene is in her early 20s. Her father is a schoolteacher in a Catholic secondary school outside Kimbo'. After talking with Helene for a while it is obvious that many of her ideas about modern life have come from French fashion magazines, which she pores over with intense interest. She often asks for explanations of various advertisements and is convinced of the skin-softening virtues of Lancôme and Dior, products she has never seen and which are unavailable outside the major urban centers, and are available there only at a prohibitive price. She has a three-year-old son whose father was a classmate of hers in school. She declined to marry him—he was too young and had no prospects—and finished a secretarial course while living at home with her parents. She lived at home until she met the man to whom she is currently married. Her son remained with her mother in Kimbo' while she and her husband, a successful trader, moved to a nearby village and established a store. A striking young woman, Helene often comes home to visit, dressed in the Western skirts and low-cut, puff-sleeved, satiny blouses that are the hallmark of fancy modern dress for young women. She has had a second child, another son, and she and her husband are working hard to expand their store and add an off-license and a small eating place. They are, as a couple, very ambitious, and Helene is determined not to become a farmer like her mother, who, it should be noted, has had to assume the burden of rearing Helene's first child, who is of almost identical age with the mother's own last child.

Maggie is barely 20. Her father is the headmaster of a school in Kimbo'. Extremely bright and competent, she is seen by her father as the most intelligent of his children and the one who will make a mark for herself (and for him) in the world. When she became pregnant in the last year of secondary school, Maggie declined to marry the father of her son. When questioned about his identity she just smiles and shakes her head; her father claims that the father of Maggie's son was "just a schoolboy—they were only playing" and asks rather rhetorically, "What does he know about having a family? The child is my responsibility."

This is just fine with Maggie, who has passed the university entry exams and plans to go to Yaounde. She will leave her son with her mother while at the university and come home on holidays and in the summer. Sitting in the kitchen preparing corn for grinding, Maggie's movements are efficient and as determined as her voice when she talks about a career in law or some related subject. Her aspirations are relatively vague, but she is determined not to stay in the village and farm, or to marry someone who doesn't share her vision of a modern lifestyle.

Ida is a vibrant, outgoing, energetic woman in her mid-20s whose hearty laugh sometimes masks a quick intelligence. Her father is a success- ful Nso' businessman. Ida has just had her second child. After finishing secondary school she first worked in the coffee cooperative for two years and then became one of the assistants in the office of community develop- ment. Bright, competent, and well-connected, she has become active in local women's politics. Ida jokes about the competencies of men, or rather the lack thereof, and treats them in the same warm, offhanded, friendly but firm manner that she treats her older son, who is now four years old. She doesn't talk much about the father(s) of her children, and while she clearly enjoys the company of men, she doesn't seem intent on marrying in the near future. Her wealthy father has married several women, and she lives, as does her mother, in her maternal grandfather's large and bustling com- pound near the palace.

Presca is a schoolteacher in one of the small villages outside Kimbo'. Now in her late 20s, she has a four-year-old daughter. She lives in the compound of and with the family of the headmaster of the school, to whom she is related. Her father visits often. She goes home to her natal compound in a nearby village during weekends and school vacations, and helps her mother farm, in return for which she receives enough food not to have to worry about purchasing staples in the market. She has never re- ceived support from the father of her child, and when questioned about this explains that she did not want him to have a claim on her daughter. She has a steady man friend, an agricultural extension agent who appears regu- larly (and loudly) on his motorcycle, from Kimbo'. They may end up marry- ing, but unlike Helene she is not willing to marry a man who will not also accept her daughter as part of his family, and it is unclear whether her current leather-jacket admirer is willing to do so. She may marry someday but is independent enough and has an income which will allow her to remain so until the right person comes along.

These young mothers are not atypical of a growing number of similar young women who have children without the benefit of marriage rather than marry a man who they feel is unable or unwilling to combine interests and resources to reproduce what they perceive to be a desirable standard of living. While that standard of living may have various interpretations, there is a shared vision among these young women of what it means to be modern, including the ability to consume and display a variety of Western commodities and the inclination and ability for husband and wife to com- bine resources at critical moments to produce this distinctive lifestyle.

A further shared attribute of the young women described here is that they all come from relatively elite or middle-class households. Their nonelite sisters who are mothers without husbands have a less enviable lifestyle. With few employment prospects outside of subsistence agriculture, and no family money to provide for their education or support, these young women are often referred to as "secondhand." Nonelite single mothers often have few or less desirable marriage prospects. There is reason to believe that a "feminization of poverty" is growing in the countryside as well as in the cities in Cameroon.[12] Nonetheless, although the decision not to marry will have different consequences for different women, a growing number of women, both elite and non elite, are choosing to remain single and raise their children in their natal compounds. The resulting economic configuration clearly has important implications for elite class formation.

Just as marriage was a male strategy of accumulation in precolonial Nso', so it continues as a strategy of accumulation today. Women's production and reproduction continue to support male investment and status. The current context, however, has shifted the focus of these strategies, and has in fact opened up new visions and new opportunities for some women. Marriage has become a strategy of accumulation for women as well as for men, particularly for those from middle-class or elite households. Elites in this context include salaried workers and large-scale coffee farmers and medium–to–large-scale entrepreneurs, perhaps 15–25 percent of the population, and their wives and children, most of whom have completed school through grade seven and many of whom have completed secondary school and often have at least some postsecondary school education.

In elite households women continue to assume primary responsibility for provisioning the household, but unlike their nonelite sisters, they have access to resources which allow them to contribute directly in cash to total household accumulation. At critical points in their marital careers elite men and women tend to combine resources in order to realize a shared vision of a distinctive middle-class lifestyle.[13] Thus elite men are apt to invest in their wives' careers and enterprises, either paying education or training expenses or lending them money for business ventures. Men and women in elite marriages are also apt to combine incomes for major purchases, such as a television set or a set of modern living room furniture, or to pay school fees to ensure all their children a postprimary school education. In doing so these couples are able to carve out a distinctive social space which operates symbolically to signify their elite status in contrast with those who do not have the vision or the opportunity to be middle class. Through these practices they create not just a distinctive set of objective relationships but also a new set of subjective schemes of perception which legitimate and reproduce these new relationships.

It is important and crucial that educated and successful men and women are marrying each other, and bridewealth has, like dowry, come to match "like with like"; that is, people of equivalent social and economic status marry each other. This trend tends to separate middle-class or elite groups into a distinctive social space rather than integrating and homogenizing various statuses, as bridewealth has done in the past. It has encouraged a movement towards what Goody calls diverging devolution, the combining of male and female property to be passed on lineally to the couple's children, a type of inheritance which is at the very basis of elite class formation.[14]

To illustrate this trend it is useful to look at a typical middle-class marriage of a rural elite couple, and then at the elite marriage ceremony of two successful professionals from Nso' (now resident in Yaounde) who came home to Kimbo' to be married.[15]

Elites at Home . . .

Matilda, who once told me that for most women "when you get married that's all for you" and that "men suffer their women for here" (require them to work hard), clearly made a decision not to conform to the stereotypes she was so fond of quoting. Matilda has a definite idea of just what constitutes an appropriate husband. A suitable spouse must not only build a substantial house and pay school fees, but in addition should talk over his plans with his wife and hear her point of view. Matilda's husband, Benjamin, slightly arrogant and clearly not as bright as his wife, depends on her advice and help. By combining resources at critical moments in their married career, they have been able to finance a fairly successful middle-class lifestyle.

Benjamin is the headmaster of a village primary school. When they were married Matilda was only 19. She was a "school-leaver" (had finished through class seven) but was not qualified as a teacher. She subsequently had two children, became the secretary of the women's cooperative in the village where she lived, engaged in petty trading of foodstuffs, and worked a farm slightly larger than average size. After the birth of her third child at age 26, she decided to return to school to get a teacher's certificate. Her husband was instrumental in her return to school, providing encouragement and some financing. She took the younger children and went to Bamenda to live with her brother and attend teacher's college. The oldest child was by this time in primary school, and stayed with his father in the village.

When Matilda finished college, she and her husband both found employment teaching in Kimbo', where they began to build a large, modern, cement-block house, and had four more children—two sets of twins. The house has not yet been completed; because of the current economic crisis most teachers are owed back salaries often exceeding six months. Yet the building is quite ambitious, with large glass windows, wrought iron fences, electric lights, and tiled bathrooms. The kitchen is not yet finished, and Matilda cooks out back in a dirt-floor kitchen with the three-stone hearth typical of Nso' traditional cooking. The living room, which is finished, is furnished in typical Nso' nouveau-elite style, with over-stuffed red vinyl and faux velvet furniture, heavy plastic-topped coffee and end tables with velvet inserts, crocheted doilies adorning the couch and armchairs, and a large cupboard with sliding glass doors in which china plates, glasses, and cutlery are displayed. A color television set, newly acquired, is prominently displayed in the living room and, when reception is clear and broadcasts available, has begun to dominate a good deal of the family's social time.

With the help of her oldest daughter, now a secondary school student, and some relatives in the village, whom she pays in small amounts of cash and with a percentage of the harvest, Matilda continues to farm in the rural village where her husband was born, using land begged from his lineage head. She spends school vacations, summers, and occasional weekends during the year on her farm. Using some of the money from her salary, she has become quite successful as a petty trader, buying produce from women in the small bush market in the village where she farms, and selling it in the larger market in Kimbo'. She and her husband plan to send all their children to secondary school and hope that at least some of them will be able to go to college or even the university. Benjamin would like to study abroad, but is aware that he actually has neither the background nor the resources to do so, and in reality at the age of 47 he is too old to begin a foreign course of study. He is constantly on the lookout for correspondence courses that might help him advance his career.

While Matilda and Benjamin have separate earnings and keep separate accounts, they combine their resources at critical times in order to pursue a shared idea of an elite lifestyle, symbolized by their ability to consume and display a variety of Western-manufactured goods. By joining her earning potential with her husband's at crucial points in their joint economic career, this couple—she in her mid-30s, he in his late 40s—has been able to put together a distinctively elite lifestyle, denoted by the clothes they wear, their house and furnishings, an emphasis on cleanliness and neatness in their and their children's presentation of self and on formal education and "development," and especially by a combined vision of the *meaning* of a modern lifestyle and the willingness to join incomes and projects to achieve this.

. . . And in the City

George and Mary's choice to marry each other pleased both of their families—and with good reason. Both are from large prestigious Nso' families influentially linked to the palace and to the Catholic church. George, a physician, and Mary, a nurse, are both government employees in the national capital in Yaounde. Their wedding was one of the social highlights of the season in Kimbo', and indeed throughout Nso'. It gathered together Nso' elites from all over the country—Bamenda, Douala, Yaounde, and Limbe, as well as from all the important villages of Nso'. Women's organizations in Nso' (in which members of both their families play leading roles) spent a week cooking in preparation for the affair. The large guest list included ministers of state, prominent doctors, lawyers, and businessmen, as well as a number of important traditional notables.

The event lasted from midmorning until far into the night, moving from the bride's compound to the church to the community hall. The wedding guests' attire ran the entire spectrum one finds at elite formal occasions in Nso' and seemed a kaleidoscope of contrasting images: black tuxedos and form-fitting satin and velvet dresses worn with spiked heels, juxtaposed to the brightly colored, embroidered gowns of traditional titled men and the sedate head ties and matching *lapas* of various women's church and lineage associations.

Seated with the guests of honor on a raised dais, the young couple was regaled with speeches praising their accomplishments and their families, and showered with gifts formally presented and displayed over the course of the evening. Pots and pans and radios, carved stools and jugs of palm wine, fathoms of cloth and china dinnerware, offerings of cooked food and live chickens, of corn flour and woven baskets, of money and tins of potatoes poured onto the dais, accompanied by speech making and singing. By the time the newlyweds departed for Yaounde at the end of the holiday season, they had accumulated more than enough goods to establish themselves in style in the capital city.

George and Mary's elite status is symbolized rather than created by this surfeit of wedding gifts. Their government jobs—with perquisites like subsidized housing and petrol, travel, and telephone allowances—ensure them a lifestyle out of the reach of most village residents. This couple is unusual but not unique in their ability to combine family resources, education, and a vision of success into a distinctively elite lifestyle. Elite couples like George and Mary—or Matilda and Benjamin, for that matter—combine consumption and behavior patterns and values stressing education and a Westernized (but not a Western) lifestyle in a cultural logic which, in Bourdieu's terms, has created a unique social space, a social space we can identify as an elite social class.[16]

Gender and the State: Gender as Counterhegemony

The basis of male accumulation in Nso' has depended on women's productive and reproductive labor for as long as people can remember. The dominant symbolic framework in precolonial Nso' linked female with farming and food as a gender marker and espoused a gender-power balance and a complementarity of gender roles. The prevailing ideology has continued to link female-farming-food with the accompanying caveat that women have power by virtue of their role, and responsibility, as producers of food and reproducers of people. Like all ideologies this one has contained an element of truth. Women have both formed the basis of male accumulation and been accorded a significant amount of power precisely because of their gender role. This ideology, like ideologies everywhere, is powerful precisely because it fails to take into account changing contexts and changing circumstances.[17] The dominant discourse linking female with farming and food as a gender marker and the responsibilities and roles associated with production and reproduction have not served women well within the colonial and the postcolonial state. While women's role in production and reproduction remains the linchpin of Nso' domestic society, commodities have undercut their control of necessary resources.

In the colonial and subsequently the postcolonial state, the meaning of the dominant symbolic framework has shifted to erode the complementarity of gender roles and to foster new forms of male hegemony. This shift can be attributed both to the commodification of productive resources and to a superstructure which has reproduced productive inequalities.

Productive relations remain gender identified. These are carried out and reproduced today in a national state whose laws and practices have both rigidified the boundaries between public and private and encouraged an articulation between the local discourses of male dominance and the male-controlled national hegemonic project. An emphasis on ethnicity within the national *recherche hégémonique* has further promoted male hegemony through the creation of "ethnic barons"[18] as power brokers for the national state.

Thus it can be argued that local male political institutions such as the secret societies, even when these protest national policy and stress local control, support rather than threaten national hegemony of the state. The various interpretations of history and the resulting conflicts over power and meaning between the paramount Fon Nso' and his subchief, the Fon Nsə', are illustrative of the conflictual nature of Nso' regional hegemony and the various negotiations over Nso' regional dominance. These conflicts are not substantially alternative or opposed to the dominant hegemonic discourse but are instead, like the male secret societies, a means of articulating the power of local elite men with the power of the national state: they are mutually constitutive of male hegemonic power.

The marginalization of female power has not gone unnoticed by women, who have never abandoned their right to protest the abuse of power by men.[19] Unlike most Western feminist movements, protests by women in Nso' are not designed to appropriate or negate male power in order to create a nongendered category of power. Instead, women are asserting, or reasserting, female power in the interest of constructing a gender complementarity aimed at nullifying the public-private distinction. This is not necessarily an essentialist standpoint but one that addresses the meaning of the complementarity of male-female power within a culturally specific context.

In the national response to women's marital choices and sexual practices, we can locate one form of what Bayart has called the over-politicization (*surpolitisation*) of daily life in Cameroon, where seemingly nonpolitical acts acquire a political impact.[20] Thus women's protests in all their multiple forms can be seen as "popular modes of political action," asserting pressure on the state from below.

Examining the contours of Nso' history gives us an insight into the position of the region as central to the formation of new political parties and as the center of opposition to the current national government. The evidence suggests that women in Nso' have always been part of the political process. It is significant that women in this region have become active in opposition politics, insisting on the addition of women's rights to party platforms and often calling for the most radical changes in national law and practice.

Several works have argued that state formation most often generates systematic gender hierarchy defined as an association of social power with maleness or masculine attributes. Alternatively, it has been argued that hierarchic societies may tend towards gender equality, since status within them is often based on distinctions other than gender, so that each case must be considered within the historical and cultural specificity of its context.[21] There is a cogent argument to be made that an alliance between precolonial patriarchic patterns and the postcolonial state in Africa has worked to marginalize women's power.[22] Thus, Bayart attributes Ahidjo's success in uniting the large number of diverse ethnic groups in postindependence Cameroon to an alliance (*alliance hégémonique*) between local elite men and the *recherche hégémonique* of the postcolonial state.[23] The silence of women's voices in these analyses is deafening.

I have argued that men's status and power in Nso', as in much of Africa, have derived substantially from their control over women's productive and reproductive labor.[24] Inequalities based on gender have been exacerbated within the postcolonial state. The ideology linking female-farming-food as a gender marker has both accorded women a degree of power and worked to undermine that power within the current political economy. In a number of ways and from a variety of standpoints women have protested the erosion of female power.

Women's protests have multiple voices and various forms. Women have called for equal access to jobs, to land, and to credit within national party platforms. They have demonstrated against male appropriation of farmland and the destruction of their farms by cattle on the village level. They have published protests in national magazines and newspapers against what they perceive to be men's inability or unwillingness to contribute to the household, and have labelled the economic crisis, rightly or wrongly, a direct result of men's mismanagement of the economy. In the refusal to marry men whom they see as more of an economic drain than an asset, we can locate a discourse which is likely to become a counter-hegemony with the potential to restructure power and gender relations within Nso' and indeed within the postcolonial state.

The resistance of young women to marriage—if we can call it resistance for a moment—is one example of a conflict over power occurring in locations which have previously been labelled private or cultural. This raises an important question regarding just what weight can be attached to power struggles that occur in locations of everyday life. I have argued that these struggles must be understood not only as multilayered and multifaceted but also within their historical and material contexts. Ultimately these cultural negotiations and actions not only reproduce but also alter the structure of power and hierarchy. The political and potentially transformative aspect of the struggles over the cultural meaning of gender cannot be ignored. To call these a popular mode of political action[25] may be accurate but misses, I believe, the transformative potential of this process. Relations of kinship and affinity are becoming radically altered, relations which are not merely symbolic or social systems that neutrally order people's lives but which are central to Nso' hierarchy, power, and culture. The outcome of this process is, of course, not obvious. Like Bakhtin's concept of language,[26] culture too is stratified at any given moment into multifaceted, multilevelled perspectives. As is true of many forms of counterhegemony, this trend may be assimilated into the dominant hegemonic process and could ultimately support the *recherche hégémonique* of the state by facilitating the formation of a new state elite. It is not only gender which will affect and be affected by this process but also a variety of socioideological subcultures based on age, residence, status, and class—all those attributes which structure the relationship between the dominants and the dominated within the modern state.[27] But the political power of gender cannot be ignored. It is clear that the postcolonial state in Cameroon has had far-reaching effects on the gender hierarchy. It is just as clear that gender has had equally transformative effects on class formation and the state and that these effects will increase in the days to come.

Notes
Bibliography
Index

Notes

Chapter 1. Introduction

1. Jean Comaroff, *Body of Power, Spirit of Resistance: The Culture and History of a South African People* (Chicago: University of Chicago Press, 1985), p. 2. See also Aiden Foster-Carter, "The Mode of Production Controversy," *New Left Review* 107 (1978): 47–77.

2. The term "*recherche Hégémonique*" is from Jean-François Bayart, *L'État au Cameroun* (Paris: Presses de la Fondation nationale des sciences politiques, 1979). It has become part of the common vocabulary among scholars writing about the postcolonial state in Cameroon.

3. For an analytic discussion focussed on resistance as a category, see Jeffrey W. Rubin, "The Ambiguity of Resistance," unpublished paper, 1993.

4. Phyllis Kaberry left her Cameroon fieldnotes and papers to the British Library of Political and Economic Science, London School of Economics, to which I am grateful for permission to make use of Elizabeth Chilver's transcriptions, generously made available to me.

5. See Comaroff, *Body of Power,* for rituals of the Zionist church in South Africa; James C. Scott, *Weapons of the Weak* (New Haven, Conn.: Yale University Press, 1985); Aihwa Ong, *Spirits of Resistance and Capitalist Discipline* (Albany: State University of New York Press, 1987).

6. For an extended discussion of the structure and meaning of various patterns of marriage transactions and alliance in West Africa, see Richard Fardon, "Sisters, Wives, Wards and Daughters: A Transformational Analysis of the Political Organisation of the Tiv and Their Neighbours," in *Africa* 54, no. 4 (1984): 2–21.

7. Antonio Gramsci, *Selections from the Prison Notebooks,* trans. and ed. Quintin Hoare and Geoffrey N. Smith (New York: International Publishers, 1971); Raymond Williams, *Marxism and Literature* (Oxford: Oxford University Press, 1977); Pierre Bourdieu, *Outline of a Theory of Practice* (Cambridge: Cambridge University Press, 1977); Pierre Bourdieu, "Social Space and Symbolic Power," *Sociological Theory* 7, no. 1 (1989): 14–25; Bayart, *L'état au Cameroun;* Jean-François Bayart, *L'état en Afrique: La politique du ventre* (Paris: Librairie Arthème Fayard, 1989), Peter Geschiere, *Village Communities and the State: Changing Relations among the Maka of Southeastern Cameroon* (London: Kegan Paul Interna-

tional, 1982); Peter Geschiere, "Hegemonic Regimes and Popular Protest: Bayart, Gramsci and the State in Cameroon," in Wim van Binsbergen, F. Reyntjens, and G. Hesseling, eds., *State and Local Community in Africa* (Brussels: Centre d'Etude et de Documentation Africaines, 1986); Jane Guyer, "Food, Cocoa and the Division of Labor by Sex in Two West African Societies," *Comparative Studies in Society and History* 22, no. 3 (1980): 355–73; Jane Guyer, "Household and Community in African Studies," *African Studies Review* 24. no. 2/3 (1981): 87–138; and Jane Guyer, *Family and Farm in Southern Cameroon* (Boston: Boston University African Studies Center, 1984). Donald Donham's work on Marxist theory contains one of the clearest and most elegant statements I have found which outlines the basic premises I have tried to address in this book. Donald Donham, *History, Power, Ideology: Central Issues in Marxism and Anthropology* (Cambridge: Cambridge University Press, 1990).

8. See in particular Bayart, *L'état au Cameroun;* Bayart, *L'état en Afrique;* Geschiere, *Village Communities;* Geschiere, "Hegemonic Regimes"; and Achille Mbembe, "Provisional Notes on the Postcolony," *Africa* 62, no. 1 (1992): 3–37.

9. Almost a decade ago, Sherry Ortner noted this relationship as one of the significant trends in anthropology since the 1960s. S. Ortner, "Theory in Anthropology since the Sixties," *Comparative Studies in Society and History* 26, no. 1 (1984): 126–66.

10. Bayart, *L'état au Cameroun;* Bayart, *L'état en Afrique;* Comaroff, *Body of Power;* John Comaroff, "Dialectical Systems, History and Anthropology: Units of Study and Questions of Theory," *Journal of Southern African Studies* 8, no. 2 (1982): 143–72; Donham, *History, Power, Ideology;* Sally Falk Moore, *Social Facts and Fabrications: "Customary" Law on Kilimanjaro 1880–1980* (Cambridge: Cambridge University Press, 1986); Guyer, "Food, Cocoa, and the Division of Labor"; Geschiere, *Village Communities;* and Geschiere, "Hegemonic Regimes." This focus on the relationship between history and anthropology has not been confined to either Africanists or anthropologists. See also Benedict Anderson, *Imagined Communities: Reflections on the Origin and Spread of Nationalism* (London: Verso, 1983) Nicholas Dirks, *The Hollow Crown: Ethnohistory of an Indian Kingdom* (Cambridge: Cambridge University Press, 1987); *American Ethnologist* 16, no. 4 (November 1989).

11. Donham, *History, Power, Ideology*, 7, 11, and 196.

12. Bourdieu, "Social Space and Symbolic Power."

13. For an extended discussion of the relationship of hegemony to ideology, see Terry Eagleton, *Ideology* (London: Verso, 1991).

14. See Bourdieu, *Outline of a Theory of Practice*, chapter 1 and passim.

15. Eagleton, *Ideology*, 156.

16. Eagleton, *Ideology*, 156.

17. Pierre Bourdieu, *Questions de sociologie*, quoted in Eagleton, *Ideology*, 157.

18. Bourdieu, *Outline of a Theory of Practice*, 192.

19. See Deborah Reed-Danahay, "The Kabyle and the French: Occidentalism in Pierre Bourdieu's Theory of Practice," in James G. Carrier, ed., *Occidentalism,*

21–42 (Cambridge: Cambridge University Press, forthcoming). Reed-Danahay convincingly argues here that Bourdieu has essentialized the practices of kin-based societies in his studies of the Kabyle; he stresses practices he views as timeless, unchanging, and taken for granted, and completely ignores the role of the state in Kabyle life.

20. Hans Heinrich Gerth and C. Wright Mills, eds., *From Max Weber* (New York: Routledge and Kegan Paul, 1948).

21. Ghoran Hyden, *No Shortcuts to Progress: African Development Management in Perspective* (Berkeley: University of California Press, 1983); and Ghoran Hyden, *Beyond Ujamaa in Tanzania: Underdevelopment and an Uncaptured Peasantry* (Berkeley: University of California Press, 1980).

22. See Philip Corrigan and Derek Sayer, *The Great Arch: English State Formation as Cultural Revolution* (New York: Basil Blackwell, 1985).

23. Émile Durkheim, *Professional Ethics and Civic Morals,* trans. Cornelia Brookfield (London: Routledge and Kegan Paul, 1957; originally published in French in 1904).

24. Bayart argues that the state in Cameroon is an arena for the promotion of individual and group interests. Access to the state is actively competed for through what he calls local popular modes of political action (*modes populaires d'action politique*). These modes of action are often diffuse and difficult to define, and may not be overtly political. While these may provide a check on the totalizing power of the state they have not provided many Cameroonians with access to elite status. Bayart quotes P. F. Ngayap (*Cameroun, qui governes? De Ahidjo a Biya: L'Heritage et l'enjeu* [Paris: Harmattan, 1983] when pointing out that, of 7 million people, only 950 are designated as ruling class. J-F. Bayart, "Civil Society in Africa," in Patrick Chabal, ed., *Political Domination in Africa: Reflections on the Limits of Power,* 109–25 (Cambridge: Cambridge University Press, 1986).

25. Nantang Jua, "Power, Ethnicity and Counterdiscourse in Post-colonial Cameroon, 1982–1990," paper presented at the Black Studies Seminar Series, Amherst College, April 29, 1991.

26. Michael Rowlands and Jean-Pierre Warnier, "Sorcery, Power, and the Modern State in Cameroon," *Man* 23, no. 1 (1988): 118–32.

27. Bayart, *L'état au Cameroun.*

28. Geschiere, "Hegemonic Regimes," 321.

29. Geschiere, "Hegemonic Regimes."

30. Williams, *Marxism and Literature,* 110.

31. Bourdieu, "Social Space and Symbolic Power."

32. Ortner and Whitehead and the contributors to their edited volume argued this point over a decade ago, as did Carol MacCormack and Marilyn Strathern. Since then it has become a central piece of anthropological understanding. S. Ortner and H. Whitehead, "Introduction: Accounting for Sexual Meanings," in Sherry B. Ortner and Harriet Whitehead, eds., *Sexual Meanings: The Cultural Construction of Gender and Sexuality,* 1–27 (Cambridge: Cambridge University Press, 1981); and Carol MacCormack and Marilyn Strathern, *Nature, Culture and Gender: A Critique* (Cambridge: Cambridge University Press, 1980).

33. Claire Robertson and Iris Berger, eds., *Women and Class in Africa* (New York: Holmes and Meier, 1986); Sharon Stichter and Jane Parpart, eds., *Patriarchy and Class: African Women in the Home and the Workforce* (Boulder: Westview Press, 1988); Christine Gailey, *Kinship to Kingship: Gender Hierarchy and State Formation in the Tongan Islands* (Austin: University of Texas Press, 1987); Kathleen Staudt, "Women's Politics, the State, and Capitalist Transformation in Africa," in Irving Markovitz, ed., *Studies in Power and Class in Africa*, 193–208. (Oxford: Oxford University Press, 1987).

34. Gayle Rubin, "The Traffic in Women: Notes on the 'Political Economy' of Sex," in R. Reiter, ed., *Toward an Anthropology of Women*, 157–210 (New York: Monthly Review Press, 1975); Claude Meillassoux, " 'The Economy' in Agricultural Self-sustaining Societies: A Preliminary Analysis," in David Seddon, ed., *Relations of Production: Marxist Approaches to Economic Anthropology* (London: Frank Cass, 1978; originally published in 1960), 127–57; Claude Meillasoux, *Maidens, Meal and Money: Capitalism and the Domestic Community* (Cambridge: Cambridge University Press, 1981; originally published in 1975); Pierre-Philippe Rey, *Les alliances de classes* (Paris: Maspero, 1973); Pierre-Philippe Rey, "The Lineage Mode of Production," *Critique of Anthropology* 3, no. 11 (1975): 27–79.

35. Robert Brain, *Bangwa Kinship and Marriage* (Cambridge: Cambridge University Press, 1972); Claude Meillassoux, *The Development of Indigenous Trade and Markets in West Africa* (London: Oxford University Press, 1971); Michael Rowlands, "Local and Long Distance Trade and Incipient State Formation on the Bamenda Plateau in the late 19th Century," *Paideuma* 25 (1979): 1–20; Jack Goody, *Production and Reproduction: A Comparative Study of the Domestic Domain* (Cambridge: Cambridge University Press, 1976); and Jack Goody, *Technology, Tradition and the State in Africa*. (Cambridge: Cambridge University Press, 1979).

36. This is a common pattern in Africa and indeed throughout the colonized world. The argument has been made in so many ways in so many places that it has become commonplace. See especially M. Etienne and E. Leacock, eds., "Introduction," in *Women and Colonization: Anthropological Perspectives* (New York: Praeger, 1980), 1–24; Gailey, *Kinship to Kingship;* Robertson and Berger, *Women and Class;* and Stichter and Parpart eds., *Patriarchy and Class.*

37. Ronald Cohen and John Middleton eds., *From Tribe to Nation in Africa: Studies in Incorporation Processes* (Scranton, Pa.: Chandler Publishing Company, 1970).

38. Bayart, *L'état au Cameroun.* Bayart argues that in Africa class formation seems to be dominated by the process of state formation itself, and he emphasizes the insufficiency of the concept of class to analyze the complex relations between "dominators" (*dominants*) and the "dominated" (*dominés*) in the Cameroonian context.

39. The marketing study resulted in two publications: John Van Deusan Lewis, ed., *Agricultural Marketing in the Northwest Province, United Republic of Cameroon* (Yaounde: USDA/USAID, 1980); and William Scott and Miriam Mahaf-

fey (Goheen), *Executive Summary: Agricultural Marketing in the Northwest Province, United Republic Cameroon* (Yaounde: USAID, 1980).

40. See Edgar Ariza-Nina et al., *Consumption Effects of Agricultural Policies: Cameroon and Senegal* (Ann Arbor: University of Michigan Center for Research on Economic Deveopment, 1982).

Chapter 2. Nso' Geography and Social Setting: A Background

1. E. Chilver, "Thaumaturgy in Contemporary Traditional Religion: The Case of Nso in Mid-century," *Journal of Religion in Africa* 20, no. 3 (1990): 226–47.

2. The following information is based on two and a half years of fieldwork in 1979–81 and 1988. During that time I alternated living arrangements between Kimbo', and capital of Nso', and Nsə', a subchiefdom on the northwestern border of Bui and Donga-Mantung divisions. I did this in order to get a perspective from the periphery as well as the center of the chiefdom and to look for an alternate view of Nso' hegemony in social location as well as gender.

3. *"Fon"* is a title of chiefs in the Grassfields, generalized in the British colonial period to include all Grassfield chiefs.

4. In much of the literature the "Cameroon Grassfields" refers to the highlands of the Northwest and Ouest provinces. The area lies directly north of the tropical forest zone and ranges in altitude between 2000 and 6000 feet above sea level. The Bamenda highlands lie within the northwestern part of the area and are defined by a series of escarpments which lead down into the lowland forest zone of the upper Cross River valley to the southwest and the Mentchum and Kumbi valleys to the north. "Grassfields" as used hereafter refers to the former Bamenda Province of Southern Cameroon and does not include Bamum or Foumban or the Bamileke region.

5. It is telling that one of the most important political alliances in Cameroon today is between the Anglophone (mostly the Grassfields) region and the Bamileke of the eastern Grassfields, whose precolonial history and structure is very similar to that of Nso' and the other large Grassfield chiefdoms but who ended up on the French side of the colonial border. This alliance, referred to as the Anglo-Bamileke or Anglo-Bami alliance, is the strongest political opposition in the country.

6. Mark DeLancey, *Cameroon: Dependence and Independence* (Boulder: Westview Press, 1989).

7. See H-J. Koloss, "Kwifon and Fon in Oku," in Erna Beumers and H-J. Koloss, eds., *Kings of Africa,* 33–42 (Maastricht: Foundation Kings of Africa, 1992).

8. Elizabeth Chilver, "Nineteenth Century Trade in the Bamenda Grassfields, Southern Cameroon," *Afrika and Übersee* 45 (1961): 233–58.

9. P. Nkwi and J-P. Warnier, (*Elements for a History of the Western Grassfields* [Yaounde: University of Yaounde, 1982], 29) speculate that the Grassfields were a forest zone and were occupied some six to nine millennia in the past by small bands of hunting and gathering peoples who were probably ancestors of some of the contemporary Grassfield peoples (see also J-P. Warnier, "Histoire du

peuplement et genèse des paysagee dans l'ouest camerounais," *Journal of African History* 24, no. 4 [1984]: 395–410). The historical and geographic information in this background section has been taken from a number of sources. Much of the information has entered the realm of general knowledge. If I were to footnote each and every fact, this introductory setting would be difficult to read. With the exception of direct quotes or single source information I will not cite a source for each factual statement in this chapter. Given the paucity of documentary materials, much historical reconstruction has relied on linguistic evidence, oral tradition, and, more recently, archaeological materials. I have depended primarily on E. Chilver and P. Kaberry, *Traditional Bamenda: The Precolonial History and Ethnography of the Bamenda Grassfields* (Buea: Ministry of Primary Education and Social Welfare, 1967); P. Kaberry, *Women of the Grassfields: A Study of the Economic Position of Women in Bamenda, British Cameroons* (London, Her Majesty's Stationery Office, 1952); Nkwi and Warnier, *Elements for a History of the Western Grassfields*, M. J. Rowlands "Local and Long Distance Trade and Incipient State Formation on the Bamenda Plateau in the Late 19th Century," *Paideuma* 25 (1979): 1–20; B. Chem-Langhee, V. G. Fanso, and E. M. Chilver, "Nto' Nso' and Its Occupants: Privileged Access and Internal Organisation in the Old and New Palaces," *Paideuma* 31 (1985): and 151–81; and P. Mzeka, *The Core Culture of Nso* (Agawam: Paul Radin, 1980). For basic ecological information I have used W. Scott and M. Mahaffey (Goheen), *Executive Summary: Agricultural Marketing in the Northwest Province, United Republic of Cameroon* (Yaounde: USAID, 1980); and J. Champaud, *Commentaire des cartes: Atlas regional, Ouest II* Yaounde: ORSTROM, 1973). Any misinterpretations are of course my own.

10. An exception to this within Nso' is the Nooni subchiefdoms, which were conquered in the late nineteenth century. Most of these have the curious institution of dual chieftaincy and, along with the subchiefdom of Nsə', which was Limbum-speaking before being incorporated into Nso', have bridewealth marriage, whereas Nso' proper has a marriage system built on brideservice and an institutionalized system of prestations owed during the life course by the husband to the lineages of both his wife's father and mother. The Nooni subchiefdoms still speak languages of the totally distinct Misaje subgroup, though today people are bilingual in the local language and Lam Nso', the official language of the Nso' chiefdom.

11. See M. Goheen, "*Ideology and Political Symbols in an African Chiefdom,*" Ph.D. dissertation, Harvard University, 1984; and Tabuwe Michael Aletum and Cyprian Fonyuy Fisiy, *Socio-political Integration and the Nso Institutions, Cameroon* (Yaounde: Institute of Human Sciences, 1989).

12. *A* before some words in Lam Nso', the language of the Nso' people, is a noun-class plural prefix, thus *afon* is the plural of *fon*.

13. P. Kaberry, "Retainers and Royal Households in the Grassfields of Cameroon," *Cahiers d'études africaines* 3, no. 10 (1962): 282–98.

14. The category of *kwan*, or slave, while important historically, is not so in the contemporary context.

15. Leopards are believed to possess special powers, and are a royal prerogative. Only the Fon Nso' has the right to pierce a leopard (*too baa*). If a *wirfon* kills a

leopard, the pelt belongs to the *fon,* but if a *mtaar* kills a leopard, the *fon* must return the whole pelt and the head of the animal to the hunter's lineage head (E. Chilver, personal communication).

16. P. Nkwi, *Traditional Diplomacy: A Study of Inter-Chiefdom Relations in the Western Grassfields, Northwest Province of Cameroon* (Yaounde: University of Yaounde, 1987).

17. See Mzeka, *The Core Culture of Nso.*

18. See Mzeka, *The Core Culture of Nso,* 89–91.

19. E. E. Evans-Pritchard, *The Nuer: A Description of the Modes of Livelihood and Political Institutions of a Nilothic People* (Cambridge: Cambridge University Press, 1974).

20. In Kimbo' (Nso' proper) there were three women's societies based in the palace. In addition to *coŋ* there were *lafolir,* which was restricted to royals and retainers, and *kor,* which was viewed as more prestigious than *coə* and much less widespread. There is little information on the organization and composition of *kor.* See Chem-Langhee, Fanso, and Chilver, "Nto' Nso' and Its Occupants."

21. Kaberry, *Women of the Grassfields,* 98–99.

22. Joseph Lafon (Faay Lii Wong), for the Catholic Christian Community, "An Address on the Occasion of the Episcopal Consecration of Rev. Father Cornelius Fontem Esua, First Bishop of Kumbo," photocopy, 1982.

23. See Mzeka, *The Core Culture of Nso,* 71–75, for a detailed discussion of the office of *sheey,* which is much more complex than this bare outline. Aletum and Fisiy (*Socio-political Integration,* 17) suggest that obtaining offices is a major goal for ambitious and successful men in Nso' today; these authors write that "in order to influence traditional policy, any Nso man . . . in possession of the knowledge and/or wealth vie for recognition either by seeking admission into one of the traditional institutions or by vying for a royal decoration." In the late 1970s, the new elite men in Nso' tried unsuccessfully to have a new title created, that of "*shuusheey,*" which would be more prestigious than the title *sheey,* but the *fon* and Nso' traditional government declined to do so.

24. See B. Chem-Langhee, *The Shuufaayship of Bernard Fonlon* (Yaounde: University of Yaounde, 1989). This was a controversial appointment, since Fonlon belonged to the retainer category. More recently, Chem-Langhee has himself been elevated to *shuufaay,* and a new class of retainer nobles was created, which repaired the previous anomaly post hoc.

25. Nkwi, *Traditional Diplomacy.*

26. Mzeka, *The Core Culture of Nso,* 97. There were at one time five houses, or *lavsi,* in the Nso' palace, today the Lav Ndzə'ən has become extinct. The four houses are Lav Nso', Lav Ŋkar, Lav Nshiylav, and Lav Ŋgoran.

27. Mzeka, *The Core Culture of Nso,* 100.

28. For a parallel example regarding the position of the wives of Grassfield *afon* today, see John Mope Simo, "Royal Wives in the Ndop Plains," *Canadian Journal of African Studies* 25, no. 3 (1991): 418–31.

29. Under certain conditions, a man may be installed as lineage head in his mother's lineage. Any successor must, after being installed, take a cock, hen, wine,

and firewood to the head of his mother's lineage, who makes a sacrifice and gives him a new cap and a stick of ebony for use in certain rites. Until this is done a newly appointed *faay*, or lineage head, cannot perform any sacrifices for his own dependents. Classificatory and "real" sisters' sons (*won jemer*) also have a special relationship with the head of their mother's lineage: they have the right and duty to make an investigation if it is believed that he is threatened by witchcraft or sorcery directed against him by one of his agnates. So while membership of lineage and succession to title are normally determined patrilineally, uterine ties are of very great importance (E. Chilver, fieldnotes, "Nso Clans and Nso History").

30. These figures are from a random survey of eight highland Nso' villages in 1980. It did not include Kimbo'. I have no way to speculate about polygyny in Kimbo' itself and thus no way to speculate whether these figures would hold in the more urban areas of Nso'.

31. The population of Bui Division in 1976 was estimated at 142,015. Taking the population growth rate into account, we can estimate the population at about 220,000 today (source: *Recensement général*, 1976, vol. 1, tome 3, p. 96).

32. Phyllis M. Kaberry, "Traditional Politics in Nsaw," *Africa* 29, no. 4 (1959): 366–83. On page 369 she cites information gathered ca. 1850 from a freed slave by the name of Bunngo indicating that Kimbo' was the capital of Nso' by 1825.

33. Scott and Mahaffey (Goheen), *Executive Summary*. While coffee has remained an important import into the 1990s, the lowered world coffee price has forced a downturn in its profitability to the farmer. Even more seriously, the cooperatives did not pay farmers for their coffee harvest for over two years, and many men, justifiably angry, cut down their coffee trees and planted plantains and bananas. Since the devaluation of the FCFA in 1994, coffee prices have risen substantially in local currency. However, as stated, many farmers cut down their coffee because of former low incentives and prices. It remains to be seen whether the value of coffee will be sustained at current values.

34. Kaberry, *Women of the Grassfields*.

35. S. Fjellman and M. Goheen, "A Prince by Any Other Name? Identity Politics in Highland Cameroon," *American Ethnologist* 11, no. 3 (August 1984): 473–86. It can be argued that the nature of overlordship and the discourse about it have changed substantially since precolonial times. "Paramountcy" from some perspectives can be seen as a European concept; the relationship of the subchiefs to the Fon Nso' was ritual and hierarchic ritually, but whether this was paramountcy before the colonialists showed up is open to question.

36. In January of 1992 the final ceremonies to enstool a new Fon Nsə' were completed. The previous *fon* occupied the stool from 1941 to 1991, and is remembered by friends and rivals alike as a "correct somebody," a proper *fon*.

37. See Fjellman and Goheen, "A Prince by Any Other Name?"

Chapter 3. The Forging of Hegemony

1. V. G. Fanso and E. M. Chilver, "Nso and the Germans: In Contemporary Documents and Oral Tradition," unpublished manuscript, 1990.

2. A Royal Niger Company agent, "the Englishman Taylor," estimated the population of Nso' at 50,000–60,000 in 1905, a figure rejected as too high by the Germans in 1906. See Fanso and Chilver, "Nso and the Germans."

3. E. Chilver and P. Kaberry, *Traditional Bamenda: The Precolonial History and Ethnography of the Bamenda Grassfields* (Buea: Ministry of Primary Education and Social Welfare and West Cameroon Antiquities Commission, 1967); P. Nkwi and J-P. Warnier, *Elements for a History of the Western Grassfields* (Yaounde: University of Yaounde, 1982); E. Chilver, "Native Administration in the West-Central Cameroons," in K. E. Robinson and F. Madden, eds., *Essays in Imperial Government* (Oxford: Basil Blackwell, 1963), 89–139; P. Kaberry, *Women of the Grassfields: A Study of the Economic Position of Women in Bamenda, British Cameroons* (London: Her Majesty's Stationery Office, 1952).

4. The reports referred to here were written by Hptm. (Captain) Glauning, the man to whom the Nso' would surrender in 1906, quoted in Fanso and Chilver, "Nso and the Germans."

5. Fanso and Chilver, "Nso and the Germans."

6. E. Chilver, "Nso and the Germans: The First Encounters in Contemporary Documents and Oral Traditions," working notes, 1984. Faay Koŋgir is quoted as telling Ms. Chilver: "Word had come from Babungo that people would be well-advised to hide guns, spears and cutlasses and that it would be unwise to fight the Germans. So the Fon had this announced in the market. When Nso' saw the Germans for the first time they regarded them as spirit beings. Everyone came to stare at them. The Germans did not make presents: they treated the Nso' like monkeys. They went on to Banyo."

7. Hptm. Glauning, *Deutches Kolonialblatt*, quoted in Fanso and Chilver, "Nso and the Germans." Nko, Djoti, and Bebem correspond to Ŋkor and Jottin and possibly the southern Misaje settlement of Ibbim, all west or northwest of Kimbo'.

8. This chapter will detail enough history to make the historical processes analyzed in the remainder of the book more accessible. It is not meant to be a complete history of Nso'. For a more detailed history of Nso', see Chilver and Kaberry, *Traditional Bamenda;* Kaberry, *Women of the Grassfields;* and Nkwi and Warnier, *Elements for a History of the Western Grassfields.* I will draw on these as well as P. Mzeka, *The Core Culture of Nso* (Agawam: Paul Radin, 1980); and Tabuwe Michael Aletum and Cyprian Fonyuy Fisiy, *Socio-political Integration and the Nso Institutions* (Yaounde: Institute of Human Sciences, 1989). I have also used numerous fieldnotes and interviews collected by Elizabeth Chilver and Phyllis Kaberry between 1945 and 1963.

9. Chilver and Kaberry, *Traditional Bamenda;* Nkwi and Warnier, *Elements for a History of the Western Grassfields.* The few documents available regarding population movements in this area record one significant series of events: the invasion of the trans-Mbam region by the Bali (mixed bands of Chamba-led raiders) ca. 1820–45 (if not earlier), the beginnings of Bamum expansion in their wake, the presence of long-distance traders on the northern edge of the trans-Mbam area, and

the existence of well-defined slave-trade routes to Douala and Calabar (Chilver and Kaberry, *Traditional Bamenda*, 149).

10. The charter myths of Nso' have been fluid and varying through time, not least because of a long-standing dispute between the Fon Nso' and his chief councillor, Ndzəəndzəv, which began in 1925, after the death of a famous holder of this office. See Phyllis M. Kaberry, "Traditional Politics in Nsaw," *Africa* 29, no. 4 (1959): 366–83. See also E. Chilver "Ndzeendzev," working notes," 1989. For the version of the charter myth quoted here see Mzeka, *The Core Culture of Nso;* and Aletum and Fisiy, Socio-political Integration. Chilver and Kaberry (*Traditional Bamenda*) quote a different version of the myth in which it is a prince, or a prince accompanied by his mother, not a princess, of Rifəm who founded Nso', the rest of the legend being identical to the Mzeka and the Aletum and Fisiy descriptions, which appear to have gained currency after the reconciliation of Nso' and Bamum in 1964 as a result of the publication of a pamphlet by the Bamum woman journalist Rabiatou Nji Mamboune Njoya.

11. Mzeka, *The Core Culture of Nso,* 8.

12. The first Fon Nso' is called Jing, Le, and Saŋgo in other versions. According to E. Chilver (personal communication) other names culled from a variety of odd sources are Ko'ntum, Yiŋyaŋ, Dzəəni or Ndzəəfon, and Simfon, none of which has any official authority. The Ndzəəndzəv group claims that the prince their ancestor rescued was called Yir, a name unknown to the dynastic lineage and meaning "presence" or "appearance" or, metaphorically, "reign."

13. Aletum and Fisiy, *Socio-political Integration,* 20, claim that the visale (Visaly) accepted Ŋgonso' and her son as their leaders because there was a Visale myth that at one point they would be governed by a woman. When Ŋgonso' came along, she was identified as that mythical woman. The enthronement of her son was just a "logical extension" of the fulfillment of the myth without actually having to enthrone a woman chief. Besides, so the reasoning goes, if Ŋgonso' had been a male, she would have been a prince and maybe a *fon* in Rifəm, so there was no reason when the Visale *fon* died without leaving an heir to the throne that the son of Ŋgonso' could not become *fon*. This story contains the double message we find in Nso' about women. Women are powerful but are entitled to that power by virtue of being mothers. Women create the country to be ruled by men. (The source given by Aletum and Fisiy is the Nso' playwright Sheey Sankie Maimo.)

14. There is an ongoing debate about the authenticity of the claims of the Grassfield chiefdoms to a Tikar origin. Many authors feel this claim is a justification for royal prerogative and solidarity with other large chiefdoms. See especially E. Chilver and P. Kaberry, "The Tikar Problem: A Non-problem," *Journal of African Languages* 10 (1971): 13–14; and David Price, "Who Are the Tikar Now?" *Paideuma* 25 (1979): 89–98; and Ronald K. Engard, "Myth and Political Economy in Bafut (Cameroon): The Structural History of an African Kingdom," *Paideuma* 34 (1988): 49–89.

15. Chilver and Kaberry, *Traditional Bamenda,* 23.

16. Merran McCulloch et al., *The Tikar of the British and French Cameroons*

(London: International African Institute, 1954); and Chilver and Kaberry, *Traditional Bamenda*, 66.

17. E. Chilver, "Nso' History and the Baranyam Raids," working notes, 1984. It is unclear just who was raiding whom at any one point in time. Apart from the official jihad accompanied by rivalries between its protagonists, other groups, displaced by the Fulani advance, engaged in raiding in the Grassfields or sought new territory. Among the participants were raiding confederacies under Chamba leadership, who appear to have preceded the Adamawa Fulani, the clients of the Fulani, including the Wute, and Wiya and the Bamum; who engaged in regular arrival raids.

18. Chilver "Nso and the Germans," p. 2. The early evidence for raids is to be found in the narrations of recaptives and domestic slaves questioned by Koelle in Sierra Leone and Clarke on the coast, and in the words of traders questioned by the explorer Barth in Yola and by Consul Hutchinson on the coast at Calabar.

19. Mzeka, *The Core Culture of Nso*, 11.

20. Kaberry, "Traditional Politics in Nsaw" 376.

21. See B. Chem-Langhee, V. G. Fanso, and E. M. Chilver, "Nto' Nso' and Its Occupants: Privileged Access and Internal Organisation in the Old and New Palaces," *Paideuma* 31 (1985): 151–81.

22. Williams, *Marxism and Literature*.

23. A. Gramsci, *Selections from the Prison Notebooks*, quoted in Williams, *Marxism and Literature*, 108.

24. Here I am using "doxa" after P. Bourdieu, *Outline of a Theory of Practice* (Cambridge: Cambridge University Press, 1977). Doxa, or that which is taken for granted, is the result of the semiperfect fit between the objective structures and the internalized structures present in society, which together organize reality. It is the realm where the established order—cosmological and political—is not perceived as arbitrary, but as the self-evident and natural order which goes without saying and without question. See pp. 159–70.

25. Williams, *Marxism and Literature*, 111.

26. By "discourse" here, following Foucault, I mean the language used to describe gender and other social relationships in Nso' as well as the social institutions and the practices which reproduce and sometimes transform these relationships. Discourse in this sense includes also the ways of thinking about these relationships, institutions, and practices.

27. After the German conquest of Nso', this process was accelerated by the German policy of designating "high chiefs," supporting them against dissidents, and leaving them largely to their own devices, providing that the station's demands were promptly met.

28. E. E. Evans-Pritchard, *The Nuer: A Description of the Modes of Livelihood and Political Institutions of a Nilothic People* (Cambridge: Cambridge University Press, 1974). See also Basil Davidson, *The African Genius: An Introduction to African Culture and Social History* (Boston: Little, Brown, 1969).

29. Mzeka (*The Core Culture of Nso*) and Aletum and Fisiy (*Socio-political Integration*) suggest the number 300 when speaking of the Fon Nso's wives in the

nineteenth century. E. Chilver (personal communication) suggests that this number is too high and is in all likelihood based on 1913 estimates by Father Emonts of "300 souls" in the women's quarter, which may have included babies and toddlers as well as women. In any case, the networks of affinity to the palace were widespread and far-flung and worked to incorporate a significant number of people into centralized politics in precolonial Nso'.

30. See Aletum and Fisiy, *Socio-political Integration*. These authors suggest that Nso' established and maintained hegemony through three factors: the adroit use of affinity; the education and use of palace retainers, who, through close ties to the *fon* and possession of closely guarded secrets and rituals, were able socially to manipulate these specialized forms of knowledge to reinforce centralized power; and the openness of the title system. This last point facilitated the incorporation of ambitious and clever men into the center of Nso' culture—a process which is continuing today. See also B. Chem-Langhee, *The Shuufaayship of Bernard Fonlon* (Yaounde: University of Yaounde, 1989); and M. Goheen, "The Earth Shall Give Judgment," Boston University Working Paper no. 145, Boston University African Studies Center, 1989.

31. Titles and offices in secret societies and other markers of prestige are *representative* of symbolic capital, which is, in effect, the possession or control of those attributes which give one social authority—the power to control the dominant discourse and impose upon others a vision of one's own view of the world as natural, as it ought to be lived, as legitimate. Symbolic capital, then, is a *credit:* it is the "power granted to those who have obtained sufficient recognition to be in a position to impose recognition" (P. Bourdieu, "Social Space and Symbolic Power," *Sociological Theory* 7, no. 1 [Spring 1989]: 23). See also chapter 4 in Bourdieu, *Outline of a Theory of Practice*.

32. Jack Goody, *Technology, Tradition and the State in Africa* (Cambridge: Cambridge University Press, 1979).

33. See E. Chilver, "Thaumaturgy in Contemporary Traditional Religion: The Case of Nso in Mid-century," *Journal of Religion in Africa* 20, no. 3 (1990): 226–47.

34. Chilver, "Thaumaturgy." As Chilver points out, this transformation is perhaps a metaphor, but a powerful and "pregnant" one. See also Mzeka, *The Core Culture of Nso*.

35. Nkwi and Warnier, *Elements for a History of the Western Grassfields*.

36. See M. Rowlands, "Power and Moral Order in Precolonial West-Central Africa," in E. Brumfiel and T. Earle, eds. *Specialization, Exchange, and Complex Societies*, 52–63. (Cambridge: Cambridge University Press, 1987). The ambiguous nature of power and the regulatory society will be discussed in detail in chapter 6. On page 58, Rowlands suggests that "political centralization [in the Grassfield chiefdoms] is . . . only possible by fusing the ambiguous nature of power with the pure legitimacy of ancestral order in the institution of chiefship."

37. M. Rowlands, "Notes on the Material Symbolism of Grassfields Palaces," *Paideuma* 31 (1985): 203–13; and Rowlands, "Power and Moral Order." See also J-P. Warnier, *Échanges, développement et hiérarchies dans le Bamenda*

pré-colonial, Studien zur Kulturkunde, no. 76 (Stuttgart: Franz Steiner for the Frobenius-Gesellschaft, 1985).

38. J-P. Warnier, "La polarité culture-nature entre le chef et Takoengoe à Mankon," *Paideuma* 25 (1979): 21–33.

39. Marcel Mauss, *The Gift: The Form and Reason for Exchange in Archaic Societies* trans. W. D. Halls, (London: Routledge, 1990).

40. P. M. Kaberry, "Fieldnotes: 1940's and 1950's," comp. E. Chilver; and Mzeka, *The Core Culture of Nso,* chapter 7. Sons of the *fon* or other royal princes were not hanged for adultery with the *fon*'s wives but were either sold into slavery or banished from Nso'.

41. Some Nso' people when questioned by Chilver and Kaberry claimed that the word "*kibay,*" meaning "councillor," is derived from a separate root, from "*-bay,*" meaning "thorn," the imagery being that the *fon*'s councillors surround him like a hedge of thorns to protect him. But Mzeka claims that the two are related, writing to Chilver that "the version I had appears to indicate that the word [for councillor] has more or less the same meaning as the *kibay* which is associated with *sem* . . . whereas ordinary people may use their *sem* to transform or produce *kibay* (*vibay*) some of which may do wicked things [unlike the *fon* and his councillors] they cannot transform into powerful beasts such as lion, leopard and buffalo." The meaning of "plant with thorns" was, according to Chilver's notes, given to Kaberry by Shuufaay Lun, who probably had good reason to separate the two forms of *kibay,* since he himself was a *kibay.*

42. Mzeka (*The Core Culture of Nso',* 18) quotes the Banso Assessment Report of February 1927: "The loyalty of the [Nso'] subchiefs is extraordinary and in many cases their attitude is even more Banso than that of the Bansos. The degree of self-government is in pleasant contrast to that allowed by the Balis!" And in *Traditional Bamenda,* Chilver and Kaberry note: unlike the conquered chiefdoms absorbed into Bamum, the subchiefs of Nso', recognizing the paramountcy of the Fon Nso', remained on their original sites, managed their hereditary dynasties, and were allowed autonomy in management of local affairs except in the matter of war and capital punishment. On page 16 of *The Core Culture of Nso',* Mzeka points out that the Nso' quite freely borrowed cultural and political institutions from conquered tribes and suggests that this borrowing helped ensure the loyalty of subjugated peoples.

43. Williams, *Marxism and Literature,* p. 110.

44. Bourdieu, "Social Space and Symbolic Power," 14–25.

45. Williams, *Marxism and Literature,* 37.

46. While the center at Kimbo' became culturally dominant, the subchiefdoms met some of the Nso' demands with resistance. Lam Nso' became the most common language for daily social interaction, and clearly categories of persons and things such as land became those of the Nso' culture. Nevertheless, there has been resistance, especially from the Nooni chiefdoms, who have retained their original language until fairly recently, and from the Limbum-speaking chiefdom of Nsə' as we shall see in chapter 6.

47. The degree to which the Nso' were successful in establishing hegemony

and the current effects of this success are illustrated in the writings of scholars from Nso' today, many of whom have produced excellent descriptions of Nso' culture. These invariably and unambiguously celebrate the collective morality underlying Nso' values and institutions, and stress the moral and sacred aspect of Nso' *fon*ship as entirely natural and unproblematic, while mentioning what would seem to be extremely coercive practices only tangentially and without comment. Although there is a counterhegemony to be found, it has not yet insinuated itself into the works by this generation of Nso' scholars, who are the first to reflect on their own culture and are thus the translators, both literally and figuratively, between Nso' and the outside world. See especially Mzeka, *The Core Culture of Nso;* Aletum and Fisiy, *Socio-political Integration; Chem-Langhee, The Shuufaayship; and D. Lantum,* "Introduction," in Mzeka, *The Core Culture of Nso.*

48. This is, of course, a common pattern in West Africa, a pattern which becomes more pronounced in large hierarchic societies. These groups or networks of women whose marriages are controlled by lineage heads have been referred to as marriage wards; the term has nothing to do with local wards but merely refers to any women, resident or nonresident in a lineage household, over whom the lineage head has rights of disposal in marriage. In Nso' this formerly included rights of disposal in a deferred-exchange marriage, whereby the bride-giver had rights of disposal of the bride's first-born daughter. For a transformational analysis of the Tiv and their neighbors, see Richard Fardon, "Sisters, Wives, Wards and Daughters: A Transformational Analysis of the Political Organisation of the Tiv and Their Neighbors," *Africa* 54, no. 4 (1984): 2–21. See Robert Brain, *Bangwa Kinship and Marriage* (Cambridge: Cambridge University Press, 1972), for a more overtly investment-oriented system. The control of marriage alliance and of reproduction is the basis of structural Marxist arguments regarding the lineage mode of production. See especially P. P. Rey, "Class Contradiction in Lineage Societies," *Critique of Anthropology* 4, nos. 13/14 (1979): 41–60; and C. Meillassoux, *Maidens, Meal and Money: Capitalism and the Domestic Commuity* (Cambridge: Cambridge University Press, 1981; originally published in 1975).

49. M. Rowlands, "Local and Long Distance Trade and Incipient State Formation on the Bamenda Plateau in the late 19th Century," *Paideuma* 25 (1979): 1–20.

50. E. Chilver "Nineteenth Century Trade in the Bamenda Grassfields, Southern Cameroons," *Afrika und Übersee* 45 (1961): 233–58. Here she writes, "A man of substance could buy the fon's market bag . . . with prestigious goods or supplies of food and wine. He received war captives or ivory to sell from the royal stock . . . Profits above fair average prices in terms of cloth, cowries or important beads were kept by the entrepreneur and the balance taken to the palace when the next supply was sought" (pp. 241–42).

51. Bourdieu, "Social Space and Symbolic Power."

52. Marriages of royal daughters and sisters took place on a number of levels. Nso' women married into chiefdoms of equal status: Kom, Bali, and Bafut. Royal women intermarried with related chiefdoms such as Oku and Mbiame. Tributary chiefs gave royal women to the paramount *fon.* P. Nkwi, *Traditional Diplomacy: A Study of Inter-chiefdom Relations in the Western Grassfields, Northwest Province of Cameroon* (Yaounde: University of Yaounde, 1987), 47.

53. E. Chilver, "Women Cultivators, Cows and Cash-Crops: Phyllis Kaberry's *Women of the Grassfields* Revisited," in P. Geschiere and P. Konings, eds., *Proceedings/Contributions: Conference on the Political Economy of Cameroon—Historical Perspectives*, 383–421, Research Report No. 35 (Leiden: University of Leiden, African Studies Centre, 1989).

54. Fanso and Chilver, "Nso and the Germans."

55. Fanso and Chilver, "Nso and the Germans."

56. Fanso and Chilver, "Nso and the Germans."

57. Fanso and Chilver, "Nso and the Germans."

58. Fanso and Chilver, "Nso and the Germans."

59. Jean-François Bayart, *L'état en Afrique: La politique du ventre* (Paris: Librairie Arthème Fayard, 1989); Jean-François Bayart, *L'état au Cameroun* (Paris: Presses de la Fondation nationale des sciences politiques, 1979); Victor Le Vine, *The Cameroon Federal Republic* (Ithaca: Cornell University Press, 1971); Mark DeLancey, *Cameroon: Dependence and Independence* (Boulder: Westview Press, 1989); Willard Johnson, *The Cameroon Federation: Political Integration in a Fragmentary Society* (Princeton: Princeton University Press, 1970); Ndiva Kofele-Kale, *Tribesmen and Patriots: Political Culture in a Polyethnic African State* (Washington, D.C.: University Press of America, 1981); Tambi Engoteyah and Robert Brain, *A History of the Cameroon* (London: Longman, 1974); Chilver and Kaberry, *Traditional Bamenda*.

60. Nkwi and Warnier (*Elements for a History of the Western Grassfields*, 214) comment on this: "It appears that manpower was the greatest asset which reached the coastal firms under German management . . . For most German firms, the major economic potentials of the Grassfields lay in their human resources. When the military station was erected in Bamenda, at the beginning of 1902, its main objectives were to promote and facilitate the flow of manpower to the coastal plantations . . . Chiefs who refused to supply labor were often raided by German patrols; even contracting chiefs were also in conflict with their satellites." See also E. Chilver, "Paramountcy and Protection in the Cameroons: The Bali and the Germans, 1889–1915," in Prosser Gifford and Wm. Roger Louis, eds., *Britain and Germany in Africa*, 479–511 (New Haven: Yale University Press, 1967), for details about labor recruitment in the Grassfields.

61. Fanso and Chilver, "Nso and the Germans."

62. In 1915 British civil administrators took over Bamenda Station. In 1921 the policy of indirect rule, as set out in Lugard's political memoranda of 1918, was officially adopted. This policy aimed to allow traditional rulers to continue governing their territories under their traditional structures, with a British official acting in an advisory capacity. The most important outcome of both German and British colonial policies for the Fon Nso' was the ability to maintain a discrete traditional political organization with strong internal cohesiveness.

63. E. Chilver, "Women Cultivators, Cows and Cash-Crops."

64. We see an example of these elsewhere in the early 1960s in the Grassfields, in the Anlu women's uprising in Kom. Here women protested both an attempt by the colonial government to interfere with their farming techniques and rumors that the men were selling (or planning to sell) land to the Ibo. See Shirley Ardener,

"Sexual Insult and Female Militancy," in S. Ardener, ed., *Perceiving Women* (London: Malaby, 1975). See also Eugenia Shanklin, "ANLU Remembered: The Kom Women's Rebellion of 1958–61," *Dialectical Anthropology* 15, nos. 2–3 (1990): 159–82.

65. The Grassfield *afon* saw themselves as the rightful, or "real," political leaders. They referred to themselves as the natural leaders and to the educated elite as the artificial leaders. In 1958 the Fon Nso' issued a mandate to the nationalist politicians visiting Nso', cogently summarizing the role the *afon* assigned to the educated politicians. The Fon Nso' couched the mandate in a metaphor, telling the new elites to "go forth as his hunting dogs to ensure separation from Nigeria." Clearly the traditional rulers viewed the Western-educated elites as subordinates who must follow the orders of legitimate authority. They were seen by the traditional rulers as the *fon*'s pawns in the nationalist game. See B. Chem-Langhee, "The Origin of the Southern Cameroons House of Chiefs," *International Journal of African Historical Studies*, 16, no. 4 (1983): 653–73. The quotation is from Chem-Langhee, quoted in M. Ndobegang, "Grassfields Chiefs and Political Change in Cameroon, ca. 1884–1966," PhD dissertation, Boston University, 1985. See also Johnson, *The Cameroon Federation*.

66. There is a fairly substantial literature on these movements which raises many issues outside the scope of this chapter. See in particular Bayart, *L'état en Afrique*; Paul Nkwi, "Cameroon Grassfield Chiefs and Modern Politics," *Paideuma* 25 (1979): 99–115; Ndobegang, "Grassfields Chiefs and Political Change"; and Johnson, *The Cameroon Federation*.

67. A. Ahidjo, *Présence africaine* (Paris: Harmattan, 1964), 13.

68. In a personal communication to me in 1983, Elizabeth Chilver wrote, "The *asheey* phenomenon [expanding the title of *sheey*] had not occurred to any marked extent in 1963, but the Fon was considering it [selling titles] to incorporate the new intelligentsia into traditional government."

69. The term "ethnic barons" is from Ndiva Kofele-Kale, "Ethnicity, Regionalism, and Political Power: A Post-Mortem of Ahidji," in M. G. Schatzberg and I. W. Zartman, eds., *The Political Economy of Cameroon* (New York: Praeger, 1986). See also Kofele-Kale, *Tribesmen and Patriots*.

70. The literature on access to the state as a form of accumulation and power is too vast to list here, and the relationship has become a standard part of the African literature. In regard to Cameroon in particular, see N. Kofele-Kale, "Class, Status and Power in Postreunification Cameroon: The Rise of an Anglophone Bourgeoisie, 1961–1980," in Irving Markovitz, ed., *Studies in Power and Class in Africa* (Oxford: Oxford University Press, 1987).

Chapter 4. Female Farmers, Male Warriors: Gendering Production and Reproduction

1. P. Kaberry, *Women of the Grassfields: A Study of the Economic Position of Women in Bamenda, British Cameroons* (London: Her Majesty's Stationery Office, 1952), 150.

2. Kaberry, *Women of the Grassfields*, 152.

3. Kaberry, *Women of the Grassfields.*

4. This is not an argument for talking about male power as public and female power as private or domestic. These categories do not adequately describe Nso' gender relations either historically or today. But there are male and female spheres or domains of power which are well-recognized and which crosscut the public-private distinction.

5. The term "field of possible actions" is from M. Foucault, *Discipline and Punishment,* trans. Alan Sheridan (New York: Vintage, 1979).

6. Kaberry, *Women of the Grassfields.*

7. Jane Guyer, "Household and Community in African Studies," *African Studies Review* 24, no. 2/3 (1981): 87–138, esp. p. 104.

8. Jack Goody, *Production and Reproduction: A Comparative Study of the Domestic Domain* (Cambridge: Cambridge University Press, 1976).

9. The quantitative information on which much of this chapter is based was obtained from a 1981 survey of 72 households in eight villages of Nso'. Each household was surveyed for four days, during which time household fields were measured, nutrition data collected, and separate information on production, labor times, and budgets was elicited from men and women. This information is supplemented by observations and conversations over a two-year period of living with families in Nsə' and Kimbo' from 1979 to 1981 and in 1988, and a duplicate survey conducted over a period of six months in 1991.

10. For a detailed analysis of economic relationships within the Nso' household see M. Goheen, "Land and Household Economy: Women of the Grassfields Today," in Jean Davison, ed., *Women, Lands and Agriculture: The African Experience,* (Boulder: Westview Press, 1988); and M. Goheen, "The Ideology and Political Economy of Gender: Women and Land in Nso, Cameroon," in Christina Gladwin, ed., *Structural Adjustment and African Women Farmers,* 239–56 (Gainesville: University of Florida Press, 1991).

11. Kaberry, *Women of the Grassfields,* 87.

12. Kaberry, *Women of the Grassfields,* 150.

13. Kaberry, *Women of the Grassfields,* passim.

14. Until January of 1994, the FCFA was tied to the French franc at 1:50; today it has been devalued to 1:100. In 1979 US $1 was worth 200 FCFA; in 1991 the FCFA had fallen in value in relation to the dollar, and US $1 was worth 265 FCFA.

15. There is not space in this book to discuss the current crisis in detail. Cameroon, once seen as the model of progressive economics in sub-Saharan Africa, is today beset by a number of economic problems, problems which have their roots in its colonial history. Upon independence, as a supplier of raw materials and an importer of finished products, Cameroon was closely tied to France, which continued to dominate its foreign economic relations. Although to date Cameroon has been mostly self-sufficient in food production, this self-sufficiency is on the decline. In 1987–88, 60 percent of the national investment budget went to foreign debt repayment, leaving little for domestic development and improvement. See Mark DeLancey, *Cameroon: Dependence and Independence* (Boulder: Westview Press,

1989). The effects of the crisis are evident in the routine of daily village life. Currency is tattered, as are women's *lapas*. Signs in the banks admonish people to save against the more disastrous effects of the "Crise economique." Those who have salaried jobs have often not been paid for several months or even longer. Coffee receipts in some cases have not been paid for over two years. Men have switched from drinking bottled beer to palm wine in the bars. Many children have been sent away from school because their parents don't have the cash to pay school fees. In Nso' people are not hungry because they grow virtually all that they eat, but people say, "Chop de, money no de," and wonder what the future will hold for their children. Some see the crisis as a government plot to keep all the national wealth for itself. Women see the crisis in part as a result of men's economic practices and of male spending patterns, which often include a substantial amount of money spent on *mimbo* and socializing while the women till the farms. The suspicions directed towards the central government in Yaounde have not been alleviated by the fact that in 1993 France paid the interest on Cameroon's debt to the World Bank; this further reinforced the idea that the central government is heavily Francophone in orientation and loyalty.

16. Jane Guyer, "Household Budgets and Women's Incomes: Cases and Methods from Africa," paper prepared for the conference Women and Income Control in the Third World, New York, 1982, p. 11.

17. M. Goheen and L. Matt, "Effects of Improved Demand Prospects on Northwest Province Farmers' Production and Food Consumption," USDA/ Nutrition Group Report (Yaounde: United Republic of Cameroon and USAID, 1981).

18. For a full discussion of Benjamin's dilemma and historical conditions within which it was embedded, see S. Fjellman and M. Goheen, "A Prince by Any Other Name? Identity Politics in Highland Cameroon," *American Ethnologist* 11, no. 3 (August 1984): 473–86.

19. For a discussion of witchcraft accusations within the modern state, see Cyprian Fisiy and Peter Geschiere, "Judges and Witches, or How Is the State to Deal with Witchcraft? Examples from Southeastern Cameroon," *Cahiers d'études africaines* 118 (1991): 135–56; and Cyprian Fisiy and Michael Rowlands, "Sorcery and Law in Modern Cameroon," *Culture and History* (Copenhagen) 6 (1990): 63–84.

Chapter 5. *Sum* and *Nsay*: Access to Resources and the Sex/Gender Hierarchy

1. This has been well-documented in Africa. See especially R. Downs and S. Reyna, eds., *Land and Society in Contemporary Africa* (Hanover, N.H.: published for the University of New Hampshire by the University Press of New England, 1988); Jean Davison, ed., *Women, Lands and Agriculture: The African Experience* (Boulder: Westview Press, 1988); and Sara Berry, ed., *Africa: Special Edition 59*, no. 1 (1989).

2. W. Scott and M. Mahaffey (Goheen), *Executive Summary: Agricultural Marketing in the Northwest Province, United Republic of Cameroon* (Yaounde: USAID, 1980).

3. P. M. Kaberry, "Some Problems of Land Tenure in Nsaw, Southern Cameroon," *Journal of African Administration* 11, no. 1 (1959): 21–28; and P. M. Kaberry and E. Chilver, fieldnotes, 1944–63.

4. For the relationship between value and scarcity and the cultural construction of scarcity, see M. Sahlins, *Stone Age Economics* (Chicago: Aldine, 1972), and various Marxist critiques of formalist economics. For land in particular, see H. W. O. Okoth-Ogendo, "Some Issues in the Study of Tenure Relations in African Agriculture," *Africa* 59, no. 1 (1989): 6–17.

5. Okoth-Ogendo, "Tenure Relations in African Agriculture." 11.

6. Sara Berry ("Social Institutions and Access to Resources," *Africa* 59, no. 1 [1989]: 41–55) suggests that this is true for most African land tenure systems.

7. See E. Chilver "Thaumaturgy in Contemporary Traditional Religion: The Case of Nso in Mid-century," *Journal of Religion in Africa* 20, no. 3 (1990): 226–47.

8. Daniel Biebuyck, "Land Tenure: Introduction," in David Sills, ed., *International Encyclopedia of the Social Sciences,* vol. 8, 562–75 (New York: Macmillan, 1968), quote is from pp. 562–63. See also R. Downs and S. P. Reyna, "Introduction," in Downs and Reyna, eds., *Land and Society,* 1–22; and John Bruce, "A Perspective on Indigenous Land Tenure Systems and Land Concentration," in Downs and Reyna, eds., *Land and Society,* 23–52.

9. For a discussion of the social construction of gender, see S. B. Ortner and H. Whitehead, "Introduction: Accounting for Sexual Meanings," in Sherry B. Ortner and Harriet Whitehead, eds., *Sexual Meanings: The Cultural Construction of Gender and Sexuality,* 1–27 (Cambridge: Cambridge University Press, 1981).

10. The current version of "tradition" is the result of a long historical process, one in which Nso' was under colonial rule for over half a century, and one in which cash crops were introduced. It is, of course, a selective version of tradition, and may not replicate the exact precolonial circumstances. I am relying on descriptions of land tenure recorded by Phyllis Kaberry (1952 and 1959) as well as my own interviews conducted from 1979 to 1981 and in 1988. Martin Chanock has argued that many laws interpreted during colonial times as traditional were only selectively so; that is, these interpretations often turned on the version (and vision) that elder males gave to the colonial governments, which then became encoded in law. Chanock argues that, in precolonial Africa, laws were more flexible and open to interpretation and argument, and that women had more say and more rights in court. This may very well be the case in Nso', where rules of customary land tenure reflect the power structure as interpreted by first German and then British colonial governments as "customary law." See M. Chanock, "Making Customary Law: Men, Women and Courts in Colonial Northern Rhodesia," in M. J. Hay and M. Wright, eds., *African Women and the Law: Historical Perspectives* (Boston: Boston University, African Studies Center, 1982).

11. For a discussion of this pertaining to the Grassfields in general, see M. J. Rowlands, "Local and Long Distance Trade and Incipient State Formation on the Bamenda Plateau in the late 19th Century," *Paideuma* 25 (1979): 1–20. A number of theorists have suggested that the elder men of the community controlled mar-

riage alliances as the source of political power in precolonial Africa. See especially P. P. Rey, "Class Contradiction in Lineage Societies," *Critique of Anthropology* 4, nos. 13/14 (1979): 41–60, and C. Meillassoux *Maidens, Meal and Money: Capitalism and the Domestic Community* (Cambridge: Cambridge University Press, 1981; originally published in 1975).

12. Okoth-Ogendo ("Tenure Relations in Africa Agriculture," 11) argues against using the concept of bundles of rights in land in Africa, because he feels this can lead to the "ownership trap into which many scholars have fallen and which has sometimes led to the insistence that a 'communal something' was always present in African land relations if the familiar categories of ownership found in Western society were missing." Instead, he argues for a definition of property in land as consisting in "the value equivalents of the status differentia which a particular category of membership in a production unit carries." While his point is well taken, it seems possible to view particular rights of use, control, access, and administration as associated with specific membership, status, and social category equivalents without falling into the communal argument trap.

13. Downs and Reyna, ("Introduction," in Downs and Reyna, *Land and Society*) make an argument for using these analytic categories for African land tenure systems in general.

14. Chilver and Kaberry (*Traditional Bamenda*) argue that nowhere in the Bamenda Grassfields do lineage heads enjoy as much freedom and power as in Nso', but nowhere else is the succession to office as tightly controlled by the *fon* and the palace.

15. Kaberry, *Women of the Grassfields*.

16. For a more complete discussion, see Kaberry, *Women of the Grassfields*.

17. Kaberry, *Women of the Grassfields*, 31.

18. In a personal communication, Shuufaay Chem-Langhəə writes, "Land disputes between two lineages, between two individuals, or between an individual and a lineage in a particular *ŋvən* [area or 'field' controlled by a *taaŋvən*, or landlord] are settled, ideally, by the *taaŋvəe*, or, when the authority of the *taaŋvən* is no longer respected, by the Fon or the modern court; land disputes between two lineages in two different fields, or *ŋvən si*, between two individuals in two different *ŋvən si*, or between an individual and a lineage in two different *ŋvən si* are settled, ideally, by the two *attaaŋvən* involved, or by the Fon when the two *ataaŋvən* have failed to reach agreement, or by the modern court where traditional authority is no longer respected; land disputes between two *ataaŋvən* are settled by the Fon, or by the modern court where traditional authority is no longer respected; ideally, there should be no land dispute between the Fon of Nso' and any other chieftain or person in Nso' (Bui Division; . . . note that I have not mentioned *ŋweroŋ* vis-a-vis the settlement of land disputes because *ŋweroŋ*, I think, only acts on the Fon's instructions)." This is the ideal pattern—and one could argue "idealized" pattern—of adjudication in land disputes. Others in Nso' told me a slightly different story within which *ŋweroŋ* played a role in conjunction with the *fon*, but always with the option to dispute the *fon*'s interpretation. This letter also shows that the issue of land and the meanings and practices associated with it are constantly

negotiated; it shows as well (and Shuufaay Chem-Langhəə writes this in another part of the letter) that practices regarding the hierarchy of control vary between chiefdoms and village subchiefdoms in Nso'.

19. Marcel Ngue, "Agricultural and Rural Development Statistics," mimeo, USAID, Yaounde, 1979. Later official statistics are not available; however, of almost 60 households surveyed in 1991, all women interviewed were farming on lineage land. It is most likely the case that a substantial amount of lineage land has been alienated for purposes of building, but most land for food crops still remains under lineage control.

20. Sara Berry ("Social Institutions," 49) suggests that this is true for Africa as a whole. People interviewed in Nso' during the early 1980s were already trying to gain access to as much land as possible through traditional means, by buying land outright from landlords willing to sell land, and through channels of access to the modern state.

21. Christine Okali, "Issues of Resource Access and Control: A Comment," *Africa* 59, no. 1 (1989): 56–60.

22. H. S. Maine, *Ancient Law: Its Connection with the Early History of Society, and Its Relation to Modern Ideas* (1861; Boston: Beacon Press, 1963), 25.

23. Kaberry, *Women of the Grassfields*.

24. Cash payments are more often demanded from nonlineage members, and while the prestation of the small portion of the harvest is demanded from women outside the lineage, this may be waived for lineage members. In fact, people say that historically this prestation was asked only of women working on the land who were not family or lineage members, but now the landlord wants to reassert his control over the land and so asks for a symbolic payment from all the women working on his land, even when they are members of his lineage.

25. Regional land use patterns are as follows: cultivated land, 10.6 percent; developed agricultural land, 11 percent; forest reserves, 7 percent; grazing land, 59 percent; other, 12.3 percent. The difference between cultivated land and developed agricultural land lies in the intensity of cultivation and the type of crops cultivated, with some land left fallow. Permanent and cash crop land are considered more developed than land for food crop production. Because of the increasing scarcity of arable farmland, land is left fallow for shorter periods of time, with a consequent decline in soil fertility. The 59 percent of land designated as grazing land has become a major source of dispute, with farmers and herders increasingly competing for land. See Scott and Mahaffey (Goheen), *Executive Summary*.

26. The animal population has grown rapidly over the past two decades; the total livestock count in the early 1980s in the division was 643,155, including cows, sheep, goats, and pigs. Out of these, 373,345 were cattle.

27. Kaberry, "Some Problems of Land tenure in Nsaw," 21–28; E. Chilver, "Women Cultivators, Cows and Cash-Crops: Phyllis Kaberry's *Women of the Grassfields* Revisited," in P. Geschiere and P. Konings, eds., *Proceedings/Contributions: Conference on the Political Economy of Cameroon—Historical Perspectives,* 383–421, Research Report no. 35 (Leiden: University of Leiden, African Studies Centre, 1989).

28. Berry, "Social Institutions," 49.

29. Jane Guyer, *Family and Farm in Southern Cameroon*, African Research Studies no. 15 (Boston: Boston University African Studies Center, 1984). On pages 80–81 Guyer makes this argument regarding inheritance rights to daughters.

30. United Republic of Cameroon, *Land Tenure and State Lands: Ordinances Nos. 74–1, 74–2, 74–3 of 6th July 1974, extract of OGURC No. 1 Supplementary of 5th August 1974 (Yaounde: United Republic of Cameroon, 1974)*.

31. The following categories of land are included under private property: (1) registered lands; (2) freehold lands; (3) lands acquired under the transcription system; and (4) lands covered by final concession. United Republic of Cameroon, *Land Tenure and State Lands*.

32. United Republic of Cameroon, *Land Tenure and State Lands*.

33. Provincial Delegation for Agriculture of the Northwest, "Evaluation of Agricultural Development from 1959/60–80," mimeo, Provincial Agricultural Office, Bamenda, 1979.

34. Members of the land board can include, depending on the nature of the land grant, members from the Surveys Department, the Town Planning and Housing Department, the Department of Agriculture, the Veterinary Department, and the Department of Construction.

35. In a very different part of the world and in a different context, Margaret Rodman makes a similar argument regarding Longana, Vanuatu, in Melanesia. M. Rodman, *Masters of Tradition: Consequences of Customary Land Tenure in Longana, Vanuatu* (Vancouver: University of British Columbia Press, 1987).

36. FONADER, or the National Fund for Agricultural Development, organized specific credit programs such as the Livestock Fattening Program, financed by the World Bank, and provided credit to farmers in conjunction with the cooperative movement. Jua has also argued that the majority of these loans in Cameroon have gone to national bureaucrats and large farmers rather than small villagers. N. Jua, "The Petty Bourgeoisie and the Politics of Social Justice in Cameroon," in P. Geschiere and P. Konings, eds., *Proceedings/Contributions: Conference on the Political Economy of Cameroon—Historical Perspectives*, 737–55 Research Report no. 35 (Leiden: University of Leiden, African Studies Centre, 1989).

37. Scott and Mahaffey (Goheen), *Executive Summary*.

38. Scott and Mahaffey (Goheen), *Executive Summary*.

39. See especially Berry, "Social Institutions"; K. Staudt, "Women Farmers and Inequities in Agriculture," in Edna G. Bay, ed., *Women and Work in Africa* (Boulder: Westview Press, 1982) and various chapters in Davison, ed., *Women, Lands and Agriculture*.

40. John Van Deusan Lewis, ed., *Agricultural Marketing in the Northwest Province, United Republic of Cameroon* (Yaounde: USDA/USAID, 1980); Jane Guyer, ed., *Feeding African Cities: Studies in Regional African History* (Bloomington: Indiana University Press in association with the International African Institute, 1987).

41. Joseph Ntangsi, *The Political and Economic Dimensions of Agricultural Policy in Cameroon* (Washington, D.C.: World Bank, 1987); Jua, "The Petty Bour-

geoisie"; Jean Koopman Henn, "Food Policy, Food Production and the Family Farm in Cameroon," in Geschiere and Konings, eds., *Proceedings/Contributions*, 531–55.

42. Koopman Henn, "Food Policy"; M. Goheen, "The Ideology and Political Economy of Gender: Women and Land in Nso, Cameroon," in Christina Gladwin, ed., *Structural Adjustment and African Women Farmers* (Gainsville: University of Florida Press, 1991).

43. Berry, "Social Institutions"; Sara Berry, "Agrarian Crisis in Africa? A Review and an Interpretation," paper prepared for the Joint African Studies Committee, SSRC and ACLS, presented at the African Studies Association Meetings, Boston, 1983.

44. See Okali, "Issues of Resource Access and Control."

45. A. Landes and A. Marcus, "Marketing of Food Crops in the Northwest Province of Cameroon," a study prepared for the project Promotion of Adapted Farming Systems Based on Animal Traction (PAFSAT), Hamburg, German Technical Cooperation, 1988.

Chapter 6. The *Fon*'s New Leopards, or Sorcerers of the Night? The Articulation of Male Hegemony

1. Tabuwe Michael Aletum and Cyprian Fonyuy Fisiy, *Socio-political Integration and the Nso Institutions, Cameroon* (Yaounde: Institute of Human Sciences, 1989); P. Nkwi and J-P. Warnier, *Elements for a History of the Western Grassfields* (Yaounde: University of Yaounde, 1982).

2. This program was broadcast from Bafut, June 8, 1988. The announcer characterized these societies as having comprehensive responsibilities, including revenue collection, collection for upkeep of local shrines, collection and distribution of tribute, acting as a court of final appeal, and, if need be, acting as a court of impeachment. He described their administrative roles as deciding on the promotion to the rank of quarterhead, acting as a "kingmaker," and supervising and carrying out the orders of the *fon*. He said their religious roles include the purification of the land, the "outlaw of illness," the charge "of the doctrine of rain—they bring and send rain and thunder"; they have a "direct link with the gods of the land." These regulatory societies have been described in the scholarly literature as characteristic of the Grassfield chiefdoms in general and of the more centrally organized ones in particular, where they are associated with the power of the *fon* and at the same time act to remove pollution from him by ordering and carrying out punishments which are viewed as repressive. See M. Rowlands, "Power and Moral Order in Precolonial West-Central Africa," in E. Brumfiel and T. Earle, eds., *Specialization, Exchange, and Complex Societies*, 52–63 (Cambridge: Cambridge University Press, 1987); P. Mzeka, *The Core Culture of Nso* (Agawam: Paul Radin, 1980); E. Chilver, "Thaumaturgy in Contemporary Traditional Religion: The Case of Nso in Mid-century," *Journal of Religion in Africa* 20, no. 3 (1990): 226–47.

3. Rowlands, "Power and Moral Order."

4. E. Chilver and P. Kaberry, *Traditional Bamenda: The Precolonial History*

and Ethnography of the Bamenda Grassfields (Buea: Ministry of Primary Education and Social Welfare and West Cameroon Antiquities Commission, 1967).

5. Rowlands, "Power and Moral Order."

6. For the repressive aspect of Bamileke chiefs, see D. Miaffo, "Role sociale de l'autopsie publique traditionelle chez les Bamileke," Memoire de DES, Department of Sociology, University of Yaounde, 1977, mimeo, quoted in Rowlands, "Power and Moral Order."

7. Chilver, "Thaumaturgy."

8. M. Rowlands, "Notes on the Material Symbolism of Grassfields Palaces," *Paideuma* (1985): 203–13; and Rowlands, "Power and Moral Order"; J-P. Warnier, *Échanges, développement et hiérarchies dans le Bamenda pré-colonial,* Studien zur Kulturkunde, no. 76 (Stuttgart: Franz Steiner for the Frobenius-Gesellschaft, 1985).

9. See Chilver, "Thaumaturgy."

10. Hostile, or foreign, *səm* is talked about as bad winds which can fly over Nso', extracting human and natural fertility and transforming them for use elsewhere; wealth objects detected by *aŋgasəm* (possessors of *səm*) could likewise be extracted and re-created (e.g., Land Rovers were talked about in this way in the 1960s) (P. M. Kaberry and M. D. W. Jeffreys, "Nso Working Notes: The Burial and Installation of the *Afon* of Nso," fieldnotes compiled by E. M. Chilver, 1945–63, copies of which we can be found at the Institute of Human Sciences and the Department of History at the University of Yaounde)

11. See also Rowlands, "Power and Moral Order."

12. See Chilver, "Thaumaturgy."

13. The main titleholders have been described in chapter 1. There are gradations of these titles in the Nso' bureaucracy which have not been described in detail in this book. These are described and explained in Mzeka, *The Core Culture of Nso;* in Aletum and Fisiy, *Socio-political Integration;* and in various publications of Kaberry and Chilver.

14. *Ŋweroŋ* is described in great detail in Mzeka, *The Core Culture of Nso.* See also Aletum and Fisiy, *Socio-political Integration;* P. Kaberry, "Retainers and Royal Households in the Grassfields of Cameroon," *Cahiers d'études africaines* 3, no. 10 (1962): 282–98; and Chilver and Kaberry, *Traditional Bamenda.* These regulatory societies are found throughout the Grassfields in all the major chiefdoms, where they are referred to variously as *ŋkwi'fon, kwifon, kwifo, kwifoyn, ŋgumba, tifwan, ŋgwaase, ŋwarŋgoŋ, əwaruŋ,* and *ŋweroŋ.*

15. See Chilver, "Thaumaturgy."

16. Members could be recruited into *ŋweroŋ* as pages in a variety of ways. Families whose earlier lineage heads had received a princess or royal ward in gift marriage owed boys to the palace in a long-term deferred exchange. Other boys were given as tribute. Sons of refugees were often recruited. Those who wandered, knowingly or unknowingly, into the *ŋweroŋ* quarters in the palace were initiated. Once acquired, the liability to palace service became heritable, though not necessarily activated. Boys were recruited at a young age, 8 or 10, and kept in the palace or in *ŋweroŋ* as servants for a period of nine years. During their period of internment

the boys acted as pages to the *asheey* or officers of *ŋweroŋ* and as interpreters for the *ŋweroŋ* police, who were allowed to speak only by signs and gestures, which were interpreted by a young page. They also acted as escorts for some of the jujus, or masked figures, when they performed at mortuary ceremonies. See Mzeka, *The Core Culture of Nso*, 82.

17. It is interesting to note here that many of the well-educated intelligentsia in Nso' today are from *nshiylav* families. When the *fon*, Ŋga' Bi'fon I, was asked by the Roman Catholic missionaries for sons to send to the school they were starting, he initially sent more pages and sons of palace pages than *won nto*.

18. Mzeka, *The Core Culture of Nso*, 76.

19. Aletum and Fisiy, *Socio-political Integration*.

20. In describing *yee ŋweroŋ*, the inner circle of the regulatory society limited to senior members of *ŋweroŋ*, Mzeka (*The Core Culture of Nso*, 93), writes, "Nowadays, recruitment appears to be at random and many of the provisos [for membership] are overlooked. The . . . Assembly is flooded with 63 members . . . this is the highest enrollment *ŋweroŋ* has ever had . . . 'membership has increased in quantity and decreased in quality.' "

21. Weberian concepts of legitimate authority or legitimate domination are thus difficult to apply to Nso'. The *fonship* has aspects of traditional authority in Weberian terms, but while Nso' legitimate authority appeals to "an eternal yesterday," the legitimacy of the *fon* is much more ambiguous, and less directly centered on religious values than Weberian concepts of traditional authority imply.

22. United Republic of Cameroon, *Land Tenure and State Lands: Ordinances Nos. 74–1, 74–2, 74–3 of 6th July 1974* (Yaounde: United Republic of Cameroon, 1974), 4.

23. Not only are the *fon* and his notables instrumental in allocating land and judging land disputes, but also *ŋweroŋ* has retained its position of imposing injunctions over disputed land, and acts in some instances as a court of appeal within the traditional court system.

24. P. M. Kaberry, *Women of the Grassfields: A Study of the Economic Position of Women in Bamenda, British Cameroons* (London: H.M.R. Stationery Office, 1952).

25. It is hard to interpret the meaning of these statements, since men are supposed to deny any aspirations for traditional lineage office. However, I knew of one young man in Nso' who left for Nigeria rather than become the *faay* of his lineage, and heard rumors of several others who fled the area when chosen for traditional office.

26. Aletum and Fisiy, *Socio-political Integration*, 17. Titles had become so important by the late 1970s that the new elite tried to get the Fon Nso' to create a new title, *shuusheey*, which have higher status than *sheey*, which was becoming widely distributed. The *fon* and his notables declined.

27. It is said that originally there were 7 *ashuufaay* in 1947 there were 13 and by the early 1980s there were more than 20. The number of lineage heads (mostly *afaay*) was between 500 and 550 in 1947 (Kaberry, *Women of the Grassfields*, 118). I do not know how many there are today, but the Nso' population has more

than tripled since that time. If lineage size has remained constant, and we "guesstimate" that at most one-third of the population increase is composed of Fulani and other "outsiders" residing in Nso', then the number of traditional lineage heads has at least doubled.

28. Aletum and Fisiy, *Socio-political Integration*, 17.

29. In 1980 the exchange rate was approximately 200 FCFA to US $1. The amount invested in acquiring titles is fairly substantial, even for those men who earn higher-than-average salaries. In 1980 the average per capita income in Nso' was US $280 per year. The amount required for a *sheey*ship amounted to approximately one month's salary for a schoolteacher (20,000 FCFA).

30. If a titled lineage head is deposed, or destooled, a member of *ŋweroŋ* removes the man's cap and calls his given name, signifying that the titleholder has now become an ordinary man. It is considered an act of treason to call the *fon* by his given name, since to do so would be to "put yourself above the *fon*."

31. The names used in the following profiles are, for reasons of privacy, completely fictitious.

32. J-F. Bayart, "La politique par le bas en Afrique noire," *Politique africaine* 4, no. 1 (1981): 53–83.

33. The dispute is said to have started when members of *ŋgiri* approached the *fon* to ask if they could be allowed to wear the *mbor* leaf, a symbol allowed to be displayed only by members of *ŋweroŋ*. They claim to have offered to pay 5000 FCFA per man for the privilege but say the *fon* demanded 50,000 FCFA, at which time they just appropriated the symbol for themselves. The fight is, of course, not about the leaf itself, but is instead a power struggle between *ŋgiri* and *ŋweroŋ*. The latter has gathered unto itself a great deal of power as a consequence of the coercive duties imposed upon the *fon* in the early period of colonial rule; this was seen by other groups as more power than was "correct." The feud has been exacerbated by the fact that the royal family was not fond of the then-*fon* (who died in late 1993), of whom they (and others) said that he "loves money too much." The royal family says that *ŋgiri* should have more power because they are "brothers of the *fon*." A member of *ŋweroŋ* told me that this is sacrilege because the "*fon* has no brothers; once a royal prince is made *fon* he belongs to *ŋweroŋ* and to the Nso' people and not to his natal family." The dispute is in many ways about control over the political discourse and control over resources in Nso' today, including land, but it is a stark example of the ways in which local politics is carried out utilizing Nso' cultural symbols and institutions.

Chapter 7. Counterhegemony and Dissent on the Periphery: Chiefs, Subchiefs, and the Modern State

1. E. Chilver, "Thaumaturgy in Contemporary Traditional Religion: The Case of Nso in Mid-century," *Journal of Religion in Africa* 20, no. 3 (1990): 226–47.

2. Raymond Williams, *Marxism and Literature* (Oxford: Oxford University Press, 1977), 115–19.

3. See quotation from a pamphlet put out in Nsə' for Nseh Cultural Week in 1977, quoted below in the text.

4. See M. Sahlins, *Historical Metaphors and Mythical Realities: Structure in the Early History of the Sandwich Islands Kingdom* (Ann Arbor: University of Michigan Press, 1981), 7.

5. I have argued this in chapter 3; see also M. Goheen, "Land Accumulation and Local Control: The Negotiation of Symbols and Power in Nso, Cameroon," in R. Downs and S. Reyna, eds., *Land and Society in Contemporary Africa* (Hanover, N.H.: published for the University of New Hampshire by the Press of New England, 1988).

6. E. Chilver and P. M. Kaberry, "From Tribute to Tax in a Tikar Chiefdom," *Africa* 30, no. 1 (1960): 1–19.

7. According to both the *Nseh Cultural Week* pamphlet written in 1977 and to various people in Nsə' and in Nso' proper, the Nsə' aided the Nso' when they were at war with Bamum, Din, Lassin, and Ndu. After Nso' had defeated Bamum, the Fon Nso' took the head of the *fon* of Bamum who, was killed in the war, and the Fon Nsə' took his cutlass, his necklace decorated with frogs, and his cap, which are still in the keeping of the Fon Nsə' today. According to the Nsə', that is why, during the reconciliation of Nso' and Bamum, many of the traditional activities were performed by the Fon Nsə'.

8. It is worthy of note that the *Nseh Cultural Week* pamphlet written and distributed in 1977 does not mention this transaction but instead claims that "the Fon Nseh presented the Germans with 4 bags of salt and one hundred calabashes of honey which he produced by means of witchcraft."

9. As will be recalled from previous chapters, the Lam Nso' word for love (*koŋ*) can be glossed in several ways, one of which means "respect for a ruler." Firewood and food are among the items of tribute traditionally owed by village chiefdoms to the Fon Nso'.

10. See S. Fjellman and M. Goheen, "A Prince by Any Other Name?" *American Ethnologist* 11–13 (August 1984). Two of the important *ashuufaay* of Nso'— Ndzəəndzəv and Lun—are related to Nsə', as are many members of the Do' clan, of which the Fon Nsə' is the head. Regarding *nzəy* medicine, cf. P. M. Kaberry and M. D. W. Jeffries, "The Ve-do'o or Do' Clans: Traditions of Their History and Settlement," fieldnotes compiled by E. Chilver, 1945–63.

11. *Nseh Cultural Week*, 1977, p. 3.

12. Most of the following information was obtained from Chilver and Kaberry, "From Tribute to Tax"; and from Phyllis Kaberry's fieldnotes, 1945–63, which were generously made available to me by Ms. Chilver. The remainder was collected during 1979–81, when I lived in Kimbo' and Nsə' for extended periods of time.

13. These arguments were of long standing; on January 19, 1974, the Fon Nsə' addressed a petition to the governor of the Northwest Province against the Fon Nso' regarding their dispute over land. He alleged that the Fon Nso' had seized some of the Nsə' lands in Kuylov, Luv, Mbo'fum, Taakov, Vituvenyam, Toom-Nsə', Bashi, and Bokviya. He gave the history of the Nsə' people in this document and added that, as Cameroonians, anyone should have the right to live in any part of the country. He decried the payment of taxes by Nsə' people to the Fon Nso' as well as the "ill treatment my children have received in the above named locations."

Following is a quote from one section of the petition: "The Fon of Nso has seized hoes personally from women in the disputed areas. He has even opened his farms in this land without my knowledge by force. Again the Fon Nso has imprisoned a woman by name Yaayi for encroaching in Kuvluv land which he considers to be Nso land, neglecting Nso-Nseh."

14. P. Kaberry, fieldnotes, 1945–63; also P. M. Kaberry, "Report on Farmer-Grazier Relations and Changing Patterns of Agriculture in Nsaw," 1959, mimeo, Buea National Archives.

15. The Fon Nsə' has directed Nsə' lineage heads not to lend out land to people from Kimbo'. One lineage head who did so anyway was destooled and fined 12 goats, 12 fowls, and 12 calabashes of palm wine.

16. Important to the meaning is its dependence also on the configuration of the relationship of symbols to each other within varying interpretations of history, or as Rabinow argues, "Meaning is not found on the cultural level alone but in the partial and imperfect relation of symbols to the particular historical conditions in which they are situated." Paul Rabinow, *Symbolic Domination: Cultural Form and Historical Change in Morocco* (Chicago: University of Chicago Press, 1975).

17. For an excellent analysis of power, legitimacy, and moral order in the Grassfields, see Michael Rowlands, "Power and Moral Order in Precolonial West-Central Africa," in E. M. Blumfiel and T. M. Earle, eds., *Specialization, Exchange, and Complex Societies,* 52–63 (Cambridge: Cambridge University Press, 1987).

18. The traditional council is composed of a number of people elected (or appointed) by the *fon* and his councillors. The president must be "an objective man who knows about traditional law and is over thirty-five years old." If he "goes wrong" he can be dismissed by the *fon*. The *fon* also appoints a secretary or scribe for council decisions and, in conjunction with members of the rural council (government-instituted council members), appoints members from various quarters. All quarters in Nso' are represented. The *afaay* and *ashuufaay* are also members. If the matter to be discussed concerns women's rights, there is a *yaa,* or queen, who sits on the council. The *fon* holds right of veto, and may make the decision to send the case to the magistrate's court. Councillors are briefed on what kinds of cases to try. The traditional court handles land cases, witchcraft accusations, debt cases, and cases regarding marriage payments, but not murder cases. There has to be a quorum of half of the members in order to try a case.

19. In 1980 there were said to be 39 landlords in Nso' proper and 16 in Nsə'.

20. The most common land cases taken beyond traditional or local decision-making bodies are those in which educated young men dispute the right of inheritance by a family head or an uncle. The magistrate's court in these instances will be inclined to decide in the young man's favor, referring to inheritance laws of the state rather than to traditional rules of inheritance. These cases are occurring less commonly now that it is becoming the norm for a male heir rather than the lineage head to inherit.

21. I have previously argued that, in order to understand individual acts and decisions in Nso' today, it is necessary to understand Nso' history. See Fjellman and

Goheen, "A Prince by Any Other Name," American Ethnologist, 11, no. 3 (1984): 473–86.

22. The ways in which various peoples conceptualize the self have been the subject of much interest in recent literature. Several of these recent studies have sought to place more emphasis on the individual in societies where previous studies had stressed the societal and relational aspects to the exclusion of an autonomous self or awareness of the self as an individual actor. (E. McHugh, "Concepts of the Person among the Gurungo of Nepal," *American Ethnologist* 16, no. 1 [February 1989]: 75–86). Others have dealt with cross-cultural variation in concepts of the self (C. Geertz, "From the Native's Point of View," in R. A. Shweder and R. A. LeVine, eds., *Cultural Theory: Essays on Mind, Self, and Emotion* [Cambridge: Cambridge University Press, 1984]; F. Errington and D. Gewertz, *Cultural Alternatives and a Feminist Anthropology: An Analysis of Culturally Constructed Gender Interests in Papua New Guinea* [Cambridge: Cambridge University Press, 1988]; R. A. Shweder and E. J. Bourne, "Does the Concept of the Person Vary Cross-Culturally?" in Shweder and LeVine, eds., *Culture Theory*).

23. This is a common pattern in modern African states, one which is more pronounced among men in bureaucratic jobs who have moved to the cities. See M. Rowlands and J. P. Warnier, "Sorcery, Power, and the Modern State in Cameroon," *Man* 23, no. 1 (1988): 130: "Urban dwellers earning a salary are compelled to house and feed young relatives from the village who come to town to attend school and to take advantage of city life. Members of the urban elite are also expected to put their positions in the State apparatus or in the party to good use, to provide their villages with roads, a school, a dispensary, etc. . . . and their kin with salaried jobs."

24. Williams, *Marxism and Literature*.

Chapter 8. Conclusion: Gender, Protest, and New Forms of Stratification

1. In a survey on six villages and 50 households in Nso' surveyed in October 1990–January 1991, between one-half and two-thirds contained unmarried women who had children. The majority of these young women were engaged in wage or salaried jobs or were attending school. Susan Diduk (personal communication, 1990) reports a similar phenomenon for villages around Bamenda. When I interviewed older women they all emphasized the fact that young women today do not want to get married, and although there were differing views and opinions about this, most older women agreed that there was no reason for women to get married to unemployed men with no real prospects. The ability to remain unmarried and have children who are raised in one's parents' compound has long been an option for women in Cameroon. Jane Guyer (*Family and Farm in Southern Cameroon*, African Research Studies no. 15 [Boston: Boston University African Studies Center, 1984] reports a growing trend among the Beti in this direction in the late 1970s; although it was not seen as particularly desirable to have children and remain unmarried, it was an acceptable option. The number of women choosing this option has increased substantially in Nso'; in a survey I conducted of nine highland villages in Nso' in 1981, very few women were single mothers, whereas today a substantial number of women are choosing to have children and not get married.

2. See *Le messager,* no. 010 (Friday, November 2, 1990): 15; *Le combattant* no. 439 (Monday, October 29, 1990): 10; and *The Activator* (the newsletter of the Association for Creative Teaching) 4/1 (January 1990), especially "The Cameroonian Woman in Development," by Bernadette Wendi, pp. 16–17.

3. Wendi, "The Cameroonian Woman in Development," 16–17.

4. Women's Cameroon National Union (WCNU) 1982, *Integration of the Cameroon Women in the Economic Development Processus* [sic] (Yaounde: United Republic of Cameroon, 1982), 96.

5. Donald Donham, *History, Power, Ideology: Central Issues in Marxism and Anthropology* (Cambridge: Cambridge University Press, 1990), 203.

6. *Le combattant,* no. 439 (Monday, October 29, 1990): 10.

7. It is evidently not only elite women in Kenya who choose not to get married. Jean Ensimiger in a 1990 article ("Co-opting the Elders: The Political Economy of State Incorporation in Africa," *American Anthropologist* 92, no. 3: 662–75) argues that in 1987 among the Orma pastoralists in northwest Kenya there was frequent refusal by young women to accept arranged marriages and by widows to accept prescribed leverate marriages.

8. In a recent survey of 50 households in Nso', between one-half and two-thirds contained unmarried mothers and their children living with the mother's parents; many of these unmarried mothers were either working at clerical jobs, or engaged in petty trade, or attending secondary or technical training school. This trend is also widespread in Bamenda and seems to be becoming at least a provincewide phenomenon. In a personal communication in July 1990, Susan Diduk wrote to me that the phenomenon of unmarried women with children is widespread in Bambui, Kedjom Keku, and Kom, adding, "The twenty-four such women in the quarter where we lived [Kedjom Keku] all live at home and have no plans to do otherwise."

9. See Raymond Williams, *Marxism and Literature* (Oxford: Oxford University Press, 1977), 123–24.

10. P. Bourdieu, "Social Space and Symbolic Power," *Sociological Theory* 7, no. 1 (Spring 1989): 14–25.

11. For reasons of personal privacy, the names of the young women in the following descriptions have been changed, and their identities have been changed as much as possible while still keeping the ethnographic facts undistorted.

12. See M. Goheen, "Land and the Household Economy: Women of the Grassfields Today," in Jean Davison, ed., *Women, Lands and Agriculture: The African Experience* (Boulder: Westview Press, 1988).

13. I am using "distinctive" here in Bourdieu's sense of the term. That is, social groups are created and create themselves by assuming particular symbols and relationships in social life which are different from those around them. Thereby they generate differences which function as distinctive signs that separate the social space they create into symbolic spaces of lifestyles and status groups which characterize them as separate from their nonelite kin and neighbors.

I am using "middle class" and "elite" somewhat interchangeably in this discussion, since in Nso' the two are used as simultaneous markers of status. The Nso' elites live a distinctively middle-class lifestyle, as all but a very small number of national elites do, and even the lifestyles of those few that one is tempted to label as upper class do not deviate qualitatively from the middle-class norm as described here.

14. J. Goody and S. J. Tambiah, *Bridewealth and Dowry* (Cambridge: Cambridge University Press, 1973).

15. Again, names have been changed and identities disguised as much as possible to preserve the privacy of the people involved.

16. P. Bourdieu, *Distinction: A Social Critique of the Judgement of Taste*, trans. Richard Nice (Cambridge: Harvard University Press, 1984).

17. See Donham *History, Power, Ideology*, 69; and Pierre Bourdieu, *Outline of a Theory of Practice* (Cambridge: Cambridge University Press, 1977), 159–71, quoted in Donham, *History, Power, Ideology*.

18. The term "ethnic barons" is used by Ndiva Kofele-Kale in "Ethnicity, Regionalism, and Political Power: A Post-Mortem of Ahidjo," in M. G. Schatzberg and I. W. Zartman, eds., *The Political Economy of Cameroon* (New York: Praeger, 1986), 41, and is elaborated upon by Nantang Jua, "Power, Ethnicity and Counterdiscourse in Post-colonial Cameroon, 1982–1990," paper presented at the Black Studies Seminar Series, Amherst College, April 29, 1991.

19. For documentation of local and regional protests see E. Chilver, "Women Cultivators, Cows and Cash-Crops: Phyllis Kaberry's *Women of the Grassfields* Revisited," in P. Geschiere and P. Konings, eds., *Proceedings/Contributions: Conference on the Political Economy of Cameroon—Historical Perspectives*, 383–421, Research Report no. 35 (Leiden: University of Leiden, African Studies Centre, 1989); Eugenia Shanklin, "ANLU Remembered: The Kom Women's Rebellion of 1958–61," *Dialectical Anthropology* 15 nos. 2–3 (1990): 159–82; and Susan Diduk, "Women's Agricultural Production and Political Action in the Cameroon Grassfields," *Africa* 59, no. 3 (1989): 338–56. Given the importance of gender, the centrality of women's labor in sustaining current hierarchies of power, and the history of women's protests, it is rather surprising that more attention has not been focussed on gender as a political issue in the literature on the state in Cameroon. Gender as such has largely been ignored in recent political analyses of Cameroon. In his study of civil society and popular modes of political action, J. F. Bayart ("Civil Society in Africa," in Patrick Chabal, ed., *Political Domination in Africa: Reflections on the Limits of Power*, 109–25 [Cambridge: Cambridge University Press, 1986] argues, almost as an afterthought, that women seek to utilize the economic and political resources of the state to achieve individual or familial but rarely collective progress. Mark DeLancey in his recent comprehensive work on the Cameroonian state mentions women only at the end, stating that ". . . growing inequalities between different sections of the population also include the increasing awareness of women of their second-class status in the Cameroon polity and economy" (Mark DeLancey, *Cameroon: Dependence and Independence* [Boulder: Westview Press, 1989], 169). Yet throughout the literature on Cameroon as well as in popular belief women are acknowledged as the backbone of the economy. Jean-François Bayart in the Forward to *L'état en Afrique: La politique du ventre* (Paris:

Librairie Artheme Fayard, 1989 stresses the position of women as "the very substance of wealth," and any honest person, male or female, will tell you that the very
fabric of society is held together by women; the ability of people to survive within
the current economic crisis rests squarely on women's shoulders.

20. Jean-François Bayart, "La politique par le bas en Afrique noire,"
Politique africaine 4, no. 1 (1981): 53–83.

21. Sharon Stichter and Jane Parpart, eds., *Patriarchy and Class: African
Women in the Home and the Workforce* (Boulder: Westview Press, 1988); Kathleen
Staudt, "Women's Politics, the State, and Capitalist Transformation in Africa," in
I. L. Markovitz, ed., *Studies in Power and Class in Africa*, 193–231 (New York:
Oxford University Press, 1987); Christine Gailey, *Kinship to Kingship: Gender
Hierarchy and State Formation in the Tongan Islands* (Austin: University of Texas
Press, 1987); C. Gailey, "Putting Down Sisters and Wives: Tongan Women and
Colonization," in M. Etienne and E. Leacock, eds., *Women and Colonization:
Anthropological Perspectives*, 294–322 (New York: Praeger, 1980); Karen Sacks,
Sisters and Wives: The Past and Future of Sexual Equality (Westford, Conn.: Green-
wood Press, 1979); M. Etienne and E. Leacock, "Introduction," in M. Etienne and
E. Leacock, eds., *Women and Colonization*, 1–24; Sherry B. Ortner, "Gender and
Sexuality in Hierarchical Societies," in S. Ortner and H. Whitehead, eds., *Sexual
Meanings: The Cultural Construction of Gender and Sexuality, 359–409* (Cambridge: Cambridge University Press, 1981). Unlike the other authors, Ortner makes
the argument that in some instances hierarchic societies tend towards but do not
achieve, gender equality, since within hierarchies inequalities are often based on
distinctions other than gender, such as control over property.

22. Stichter and Parpart, *Patriarchy and Class*.

23. Jean-François Bayart, *L'état au Cameroun* (Paris: Presses de la Fondation
nationale des sciences politiques, 1979).

24. This point has been argued by C. Meillassoux, G. Rubin, P-P. Rey, and S.
Stichter and J. Parpart, among others. C. Meillassoux, *Maidens, Meal and
Money: Capitalism and the Domestic Community* (Cambridge: Cambridge Uni-
versity Press, 1981; originally published in 1975); and C. Meillassoux, " 'The
Economy' in Agricultural Self-sustaining Societies: A Preliminary Analysis," in
David Seddon, ed., *Relations of Production: Marxist Approaches to Economic
Anthropology* (London: Frank Cass, 1978; originally published in 1960); Pierre-
Philippe Rey, "The Lineage Mode of Production," *Critique of Anthropology* 3,
no. 11 (Spring 1975): 27–79; Gayle Rubin, "The Traffic in Women: Notes on the
'Political Economy' of Sex," in R. Reiter, ed., *Toward an Anthropology of
Women*, 157–210 (New York: Monthly Review Press, 1975); Stichter and
Parpart, *Patriarchy and Class;* M. Goheen, "Les Champs appartiennent aux
hommes, les récoltes aux femmes: Accumulation dans la région de Nso," in P.
Geschiere and P. Konings, eds., *Itinéraires d'accumulation au Cameroun*, 241–71
(Paris: Éditions Karthala, 1993).

25. The term "popular mode of political action" is from Bayart, "Civil Society in Africa."

26. M. M. Bakhtin, "Discourse in the Novel," in Michael Holquist, ed. *The

Dialogic Imagination: Four Essays, 259–422 (Austin: University of Texas Press, 1981).

27. Bayart (*L'état au Cameroun*) eschews the notion of class as relevant to the African context and instead advocates using only vague categories such as *dominants* or *dominés*. As Geschiere has pointed out ("Hegemonic Regimes and Popular Protest: Bayart, Gramsci and the State in Cameroon," in Wim van Binsbergen, F. Reyntjens, and G. Hesseling, eds., *State and Local Community in Africa* [Brussels: Centre d'Etude et de Documentation africaines, 1986], 319), the vagueness of these terms creates problems for Bayart's analysis of the hegemonic project in Cameroon, since he does not relate this project to a clear social group. Bayart emphasizes the fact that political relations in Cameroon have been based on a fusion of old and new relations of domination; therefore, it is essential that these relations be described in detail. I am arguing that in performing such a detailed analysis of the articulation of power between local and national arenas one can also discern the outlines of what Bourdieu has referred to as the distinctive symbolic space which demarcates social class.

Bibliography

The Activator. (Newsletter for the Association for Creative Teaching.) 4/1 (January 1990).

Ahidjo, A. *Présence africaine.* Paris: Harmattan, 1964.

Aletum, Tabuwe Michael, and Cyprian Fonyuy Fisiy. *Socio-political Integration and the Nso Institutions, Cameroon.* Yaounde: Institute of Human Sciences, 1989.

Anderson, Benedict Richard O'Gorman. *Imagined Communities: Reflections on the Origin and Spread of Nationalism.* London: Verso Editions and NLB, 1983.

Ardener, Shirley. "Sexual Insult and Female Militancy." In Shirley Ardener, ed., *Perceiving Women,* London: Malaby Press, 1975.

Ariza-Nina, Edgar, et al. *Consumption Effects of Agricultural Policies: Cameroon and Senegal.* Ann Arbor: University of Michigan Center for Research on Economic Development, 1982.

Bakhtin, Mikhail Mikhailovich. 1981. "Discourse in the Novel." In Michael Holquist, ed., *The Dialogic Imagination: Four Essays,* 259–422. Austin: University of Texas Press, 1981.

Bay, Edna G., ed. *Women and Work in Africa.* Boulder, Colo.: Westview Press, 1982.

Bayart, Jean-François. "Civil Society in Africa." In Patrick Chabal, ed., *Political Domination in Africa: Reflections on the Limits of Power,* 109–25. Cambridge: Cambridge University Press, 1986.

Bayart, Jean-François. *L'état au Cameroun.* Paris: Presses de la Fondation nationale des sciences politiques, 1979.

Bayart, Jean-François. *L'état en afrique: La politique du ventre.* Paris: Librairie Arthème Fayard, 1989.

Bayart, Jean-François. "La politique par le bas en Afrique noire." In *Politique africaine* 4, no. 1 (1981): 53–83.

Berry, Sara S. "Agrarian Crisis in Africa? A Review and an Interpretation." Paper prepared for the Joint African Studies Committee, SSRC and ACLS, presented at African Studies Association Meetings, Boston, 1983.

Berry, Sara S. "Social Institutions and Access to Resources." *Africa: The Journal of the International African Institute* 59, no. 1 (1989): 41–55.

234

Berry, Sara S., ed. *Africa: Special Edition* 59, no. 1 (1989).

Biebuyck, Daniel. "Land Tenure: Introduction." In David Sills, ed., *International Encyclopedia of the Social Sciences*, vol. 8, 562–75. New York: Macmillan, 1968.

Bourdieu, Pierre. *Distinction: A Social Critique of the Judgement of Taste*, trans. Richard Nice. Cambridge, Mass.: Harvard University Press, 1984.

Bourdieu, Pierre. *Outline of a Theory of Practice*. Cambridge: Cambridge University Press, 1977.

Bourdieu, Pierre. "Social Space and Symbolic Power." *Sociological Theory* 7, no. 1 (1989): 14–25.

Brain, Robert. *Bangwa Kinship and Marriage*. Cambridge: Cambridge University Press, 1972.

Bruce, John. "A Perspective on Indigenous Land Tenure Systems and Land Concentration." In Richard Downs and Steven P. Reyna, eds., *Land and Society in Contemporary Africa*, 23–52. Hanover, N.H.: published for the University of New Hampshire by the University Press of New England, 1989.

Champaud, Jacques. *Commentaire des cartes: Atlas regional, Ouest II*. Yaounde: ORSTROM, 1973.

Chanock, Martin. "Making Customary Law: Men, Women and Courts in Colonial Northern Rhodesia." In Margaret J. Hay and Marcia Wright, eds., *African Women and the Law: Historical Perspectives*. Boston: Boston University, African Studies Center, 1982.

Chem-Langhee, Bonfen. "The Origin of the Southern Cameroons House of Chiefs." *International Journal of African Historical Studies* 16, no. 4 (1983): 653–73.

Chem-Langhee, Bonfen. *The Shuufaayship of Bernard Fonlon*. Yaounde: University of Yaounde, 1989.

Chem-Langhee, Bonfen. "Southern Cameroons Traditional Authorities and the Nationalist Movement, 1953–1961." *Africka Zamani* 1, nos. 14–15 (1984): 147–63.

Chem-Langhee, Bonfen, Verkijika G. Fanso, and Elizabeth M. Chilver. "Nto' Nso' and Its Occupants: Privileged Access and Internal Organisation in the Old and New Palaces." In *Paideuma: Mitteilungen zur Kulturkunde* 31 (1985): 151–81.

Chilver, Elizabeth M. "Native Administration in the West-Central Cameroons." In K. Robinson and F. Madden, eds., *Essays in Imperial Government*, 89–139. Oxford: Basil Blackwell, 1963.

Chilver, Elizabeth M. "Nineteenth Century Trade in the Bamenda Grassfields, Southern Cameroons." *Afrika und Übersee*. 45, no. 25 (1961): 233–58.

Chilver, Elizabeth M. "Ndzeendzev." Working notes, 1989.

Chilver, Elizabeth M. "Nso and the Germans: The First Encounters in Contemporary Documents and Oral Traditions." Working notes, 1984.

Chilver, Elizabeth M. "Nso Clans and Nso History." Fieldnotes written 1945–63.

Chilver, Elizabeth M. "Nso' History and the Baranyam Raids." Working notes, 1984.

Chilver, Elizabeth M. "Paramountcy and Protection in the Cameroons: The Bali and the Germans, 1889–1915." In Prosser Gifford and Wm. Roger Louis, eds. (with the assistance of Alison Smith), *Britain and Germany in Africa*, 479–511. New Haven: Yale University Press, 1967.

Chilver, Elizabeth M. "Thaumaturgy in Contemporary Traditional Religion: The Case of the Nso in Mid-century." *Journal of Religion in Africa* 20, no. 3 (1990): 226–47.

Chilver, Elizabeth M. "Women Cultivators, Cows and Cash-Crops: Phyllis Kaberry's *Women of the Grassfields* Revisited." In Peter Geschiere and Piet Konings, eds., *Proceedings/Contributions: Conference on the Political Economy of Cameroon—Historical Perspectives*, 383–421. Research Report no. 35. Leiden: University of Leiden, African Studies Centre, 1989.

Chilver, Elizabeth M., and Phyllis M. Kaberry. "From Tribute to Tax in a Tikar Chiefdom." *Africa: Journal of the International African Institute* 30, no. 1 (1960): 1–19.

Chilver, Elizabeth M., and Phyllis M. Kaberry. "The Tikar Problem: A Non-problem." *Journal of African Languages* 10, part 2, (1971): 13–14.

Chilver, Elizabeth, M., and Phyllis M. Kaberry. *Traditional Bamenda: The Precolonial History and Ethnography of the Bamenda Grassfields*. Buea: Ministry of Primary Education and Social Welfare and West Cameroon Antiquities Commission, 1967.

Cohen, Ronald, and John Middleton, eds., *From Tribe to Nation in Africa: Studies in Incorporation Processes*. Scranton, Pa.: Chandler Publishing Company, 1970.

Comaroff, Jean. *Body of Power, Spirit of Resistance: The Culture and History of a South African People*. Chicago: University of Chicago Press, 1985.

Comaroff, John. "Dialectical Systems, History and Anthropology: Units of Study and Questions of Theory." *Journal of Southern African Studies* 8, no. 2 (1982): 143–72.

Le combattant. No. 439. Monday, October 29, 1990; p. 10.

Corrigan, Philip, and Derek Sayer. *The Great Arch: English State Formation as Cultural Revolution*. New York: Basil Blackwell, 1985.

Davidson, Basil. *The African Genius: An Introduction to African Cultural and Social History*. Boston: Little, Brown and Company, 1969.

Davidson, Jean, ed. *Women, Lands and Agriculture: The African Experience*. Westview Special Studies on Africa. Boulder: Westview Press, 1988.

DeLancey, Mark W. *Cameroon: Dependence and Independence*. Profiles: Nations of Contemporary Africa. Boulder: Westview Press, 1989.

Diduk, Susan. "Women's Agricultural Production and Political Action in the Cameroon Grassfields." *Africa: Journal of the International African Institute* 59, no. 3 (1989): 338–56.

Dirks, Nicholas. *The Hollow Crown: Ethnohistory of an Indian Kingdom*. Cambridge: Cambridge University Press, 1987.

Donham, Donald L. *History, Power, Ideology: Central Issues in Marxism and Anthropology*. Cambridge: Cambridge University Press, 1990.

Downs, Richard, and Steven P. Reyna. "Introduction." In Downs and Reyna, eds.,

Land and Society in Contemporary Africa, 1–22. Hanover, N.H.: published for the University of New Hampshire by the University Press of New England, 1988.

Downs, Richard, and Steven P. Reyna, eds. *Land and Society in Contemporary Africa.* With a foreword by John Middletown and an epilogue by Francis Mading Deng. Hanover, N.H.: published for the University of New Hampshire by the University Press of New England, 1988.

Durkheim, Émile. *Professional Ethics and Civic Morals,* trans. Cornelia Brookfield. London: Routledge and Paul, 1957; originally published in French in 1904.

Eagleton, Terry. *Ideology.* London: Verso, 1991.

Emonts, Johannes, SCJ. *Ins Steppen und Bergland Innerkameruns.* Aachung: Xaverius, 1927.

Engard, Ronald K. "Myth and Political Economy in Bafut (Cameroon): The Structural History of an African Kingdom," *Paideuma* 34 (1988): 49–89.

Engoteyah, Tambi, and Robert Brain. *A History of the Cameroon.* London: Longman, 1974.

Ensminger, Jean. "Co-opting the Elders: The Political Economy of State Incorporation in Africa." *American Anthropologist* 92, no. 3 (1990): 662–75.

Errington, Frederick K., and Deborah Gewertz. *Cultural Alternatives and a Feminist Anthropology: An Analysis of Culturally Constructed Gender Interests in Papua New Guinea.* Cambridge: Cambridge University Press, 1988.

Etienne, Mona, and Eleanor Leacock. "Introduction." In Etienne and Leacock, eds., *Women and Colonization: Anthropological Perspectives,* 1–24. New York: Praeger, 1980.

Evans-Pritchard, E. E. *The Nuer: A Description of the Modes of Livelihood and Political Institutions of a Nilotic People.* Cambridge: Cambridge University Press, 1974.

Fanso, Verkijika, and Elizabeth Chilver. "Nso and the Germans: In Contemporary Documents and Oral Traditions." Unpublished manuscript, 1990.

Fardon, Richard. "Sisters, Wives, Wards and Daughters: A Transformational Analysis of the Political Organisation of the Tiv and Their Neighbours." *Africa* 54, no. 4 (1984): 2–21.

Fisiy, Cyprian Fonyuy. "Power and Privilege in the Administration of Law." Doctoral dissertation, University of Leiden, African Studies Center, 1992.

Fisiy, Cyprian, and Peter Geschiere. "Judges and Witches, or How Is the State to Deal with Witchcraft? Examples from Southeastern Cameroon." *Cahiers d'études africaines* 118 (1991): 135–56.

Fisiy, Cyprian, and Michael Rowlands. "Sorcery and Law in Modern Cameroon." *Culture and History* (Copenhagen) 6 (1990): 63–84.

Fjellman, Stephen M., and Miriam Goheen. "A Prince by Any Other Name? Identity Politics in Highland Cameroon." *American Ethnologist* 11, no. 3 (1984): 473–86.

Foster-Carter, Aidan. "The Mode of Production Controversy." *New Left Review* 107 (1978): 47–77.

Foucault, Michel. *Discipline and Punishment: The Birth of the Prison,* trans. from French by Alan Sheridan. New York: Vintage Books, 1979.

Gailey, Christine Ward. *Kinship to Kingship: Gender Hierarchy and State Formation in the Tongan Islands.* Austin: University of Texas Press, 1987.

Gailey, Christine. "Putting Down Sisters and Wives: Tongan Women and Colonization." In Mona Etienne and Eleanor Leacock, eds., *Women and Colonization: Anthropological Perspectives,* 294–322. New York: Praeger, 1980.

Gaillard, Philippe. *Le Cameroun.* Paris: L'Harmattan, 1989.

Geertz, Clifford. "From the Native's Point of View." In Richard A. Shweder and Robert A. LeVine, eds., *Culture Theory: Essays on Mind, Self, and Emotion.* Cambridge: Cambridge University Press, 1984.

Gerth, Hans Heinrich, and C. Wright Mills, eds. *From Max Weber.* New York: Routledge and Kegan Paul, 1948.

Geschiere, Peter. "Hegemonic Regimes and Popular Protest: Bayart, Gramsci and the State in Cameroon." In Wim M. J. van Binsbergen, Filip Reyntjens, and Gerti Hesseling, eds., *State and Local Community in Africa.* Brussels: Centre d'Etude et de Documentation africaines, 1986.

Geschiere, Peter. *Village Communities and the State: Changing Relations among the Maka of Southereastern Cameroon.* London: Kegan Paul International, 1982.

Goheen, M. "Les champs appartiennent aux hommes, les récoltes aux femmes: Accumulation dans la region de Nso" [Men own the fields, women own the crops: Gender and accumulation in Nso]. In Peter Geschiere and Piet Konings, eds., *Itinéraires d'accumulation au Cameroun,* 241–71. Paris: Éditions Karthala, 1993.

Goheen, Miriam. "The Earth Shall Give Judgment." Boston University Working Paper no. 145. Boston: Boston University African Studies Center, 1989.

Goheen, Miriam. "The Ideology and Political Economy of Gender: Women and Land in Nso, Cameroon." In Christina H. Gladwin, ed., *Structural Adjustment and African Women Farmers,* 239–56. Center for African Studies, University of Florida. Gainesville: University of Florida Press, 1991.

Goheen, Miriam. "Ideology and Political Symbols in an African Chiefdom." PhD dissertation, Harvard University, 1984.

Goheen, Miriam. "Land Accumulation and Local Control: The Negotiation of Symbols and Power in Nso, Cameroon." In Richard Downs and Steven P. Reyna, eds., *Land and Society in Contemporary Africa.* Hanover, N.H.: published for the University of New Hampshire by the University Press of New England, 1988.

Goheen, Miriam. "Land and the Household Economy: Women of the Grassfields Today." In Jean Davidson, ed., *Women, Lands, and Agriculture: The African Experience.* Westview Special Studies on Africa. Boulder: Westview Press, 1988.

Goheen, Miriam, and Lisa Matt. "Effects of Improved Demand Prospects on the Northwest Province Farmers' Production and Food Consumption." USDA/Nutrition Group Report. Yaounde: United Republic of Cameroon and USAID, 1981.

Goody, Jack. *Production and Reproduction: A Comparative Study of the Domestic Domain.* Cambridge Studies in Social Anthropology 17. Cambridge: Cambridge University Press, 1976.

Goody, Jack. *Technology, Tradition and the State in Africa.* Cambridge: Cambridge University Press, 1979.

Goody, Jack, and Stanley J. Tambiah. *Bridewealth and Dowry.* Cambridge Studies in Social Anthropology 7. Cambridge: Cambridge University Press, 1973.

Gramsci, Antonio. *Selections from the Prison Notebooks,* trans. and ed. Quintin Hoare and Geoffrey N. Smith. New York: International Publishers, 1971.

Guyer, Jane I. *Family and Farm in Southern Cameroon.* African Research Studies Paper no. 15. Boston: Boston University African Studies Center, 1984.

Guyer, Jane I. "Food, Cocoa, and the Division of Labor by Sex in Two West African Societies." *Comparative Studies in Society and History* 22, no. 3 (1980): 355–73.

Guyer, Jane I. "Household and Community in African Studies." *African Studies Review* 24, nos. 2/3 (1981): 87–138.

Guyer, Jane I. "Household Budgets and Women's Incomes: Cases and Methods from Africa." Paper prepared for the conference Women and Income Control in the Third World, New York, 1982.

Guyer, Jane I., ed. *Feeding African Cities: Studies in Regional African History.* Bloomington: Indiana University Press in association with the International African Institute, 1987.

Hyden, Goren. *Beyond Ujamaa in Tanzania: Underdevelopment and an Uncaptured Peasantry.* Berkeley: University of California Press, 1980.

Hyden, Goren. *No Shortcuts to Progress: African Development Management in Perspective.* Berkeley: University of California Press, 1983.

Johnson, Willard. *The Cameroon Federation: Political Integration in a Fragmentary Society.* Princeton: Princeton University Press, 1970.

Jua, Nantang. "The Petty Bourgeoisie and the Politics of Social Justice in Cameroon." In Peter Geschiere and Piet Konings, eds., *Proceedings/Contributions, Conference on the Political Economy of Cameroon—Historical Perspectives,* 737–55. Leiden: University of Leiden, African Studies Centre, 1989.

Jua, Nantang. "Power, Ethnicity and Counterdiscourse in Post-colonial Cameroon, 1982–1990." Paper presented at the Black Studies Seminar Series, Amherst College, April 29, 1991.

Kaberry, Phyllis M. "Fieldnotes: 1940's and 1950's," comp. Elizabeth M. Chilver.

Kaberry, Phyllis M. "Report on Farmer-Grazier Relations and Changing Patterns of Agriculture in Nsaw." Mimeo, Buea National Archives, 1959.

Kaberry, Phyllis M. "Retainers and Royal Households in the Grassfields of Cameroon." *Cahiers d'etudes africaines* 3, no. 10 (1962): 282–98.

Kaberry, Phillis M. "Some Problems of Land Tenure in Nsaw, Southern Cameroon." *Journal of African Administration* 11, no. 1 (1959): 22–28.

Kaberry, Phyllis M. "Traditional Politics in Nsaw." *Africa: Journal of the International African Institute.* 29, no. 4 (1959): 366–82.

Kaberry, Phyllis M. *Women of the Grassfields: A Study of the Economic Position of*

Women in Bamenda, British Cameroons, with a preface by Daryll Forde. London: Her Majesty's Stationery Office, 1952.

Kaberry, Phyllis M., and M. D. W. Jeffreys. "Nso Working Notes: The Burial and Installation of the *Afon* of Nso." Fieldnotes comp. by E. M. Chilver, 1945–63, reposited at the Institute of Human Sciences and the Department of History, University of Yaounde, Cameroon.

Kaberry, Phyllis M., and M. D. W. Jeffreys. "The Ve-do'o or Do' Clans: Traditions of Their History and Settlement." Fieldnotes compiled by E. Chilver, 1945–63.

Kofele-Kale, Ndiva. "Class, Status and Power in Postreunification Cameroon: The Rise of an Anglophone Bourgeoisie, 1961–1980." In Irving Leonard Markovitz, ed., *Studies in Power and Class in Africa.* New York: Oxford University Press, 1987.

Kofele-Kale, Ndiva. "Ethnicity, Regionalism, and Political Power: A Post-Mortem of Ahidjo." In Michael G. Schatzberg and I. William Zartman, eds., *The Political Economy of Cameroon.* New York: Praeger, 1986.

Kofele-Kale, Ndiva. *Tribesmen and Patriots: Political Culture in a Polyethnic African State.* Washington D.C.: University Press of America, 1981.

Koloss, H. J. "Kwifon and Fon In Oku." In Erna Beumers and H.J. Koloss, eds., *Kings of Africa,* 33–42. Maastricht: Foundation Kings of Africa, 1992.

Koopman, Henn, Jeanne. "Food Policy, Food Production and the Family Farm in Cameroon." In Peter Geschiere and Piet Konings, eds., *Proceedings/Contributions, Conference on the Political Economy of Cameroon—Historical Perspectives,* 531–55. Leiden: University of Leiden, African Studies Centre, 1989.

Lafon, Joseph. "An Address on the Occasion of the Episcopal Consecretation of Rev. Father Cornelius Fontem Esua, First Bishop of Kumbo." Photocopy, 1982.

Landes, A., and A. Marcus. "Marketing of Food Crops in the Northwest Province of Cameroon." Study prepared for the project Promotion of Adapted Farming System Based on Animal Traction (PAFSAT). Hamburg: German Technical Cooperation, 1988.

Lantum, D. "Introduction." In P. Mzeka, ed., *The Core Culture of Nso.* Agawam: Paul Radon, 1980.

Le Vine, Victor T. *The Cameroon Federal Republic.* Ithaca: Cornell University Press, 1971.

Lewis, John Van Deusan, ed. *Agricultural Marketing in the Northwest Province, United Republic of Cameroon.* Yaounde: USDA/USAID, 1980.

MacCormack, Carol P., and Marilyn Strathern. *Nature, Culture and Gender: A Critique.* Cambridge: Cambridge University Press, 1980.

McCulloch, Merran, et al. *The Tikar of the British and French Cameroons.* London: International African Institute, 1954.

McHugh, Ernestine L. "Concepts of the Person among the Gurungo of Nepal." *American Ethnologist* 16, no. 1 (1989): 75–86.

Maine, Henry James Sumner. *Ancient Law: Its Connection with the Early History of Society, and Its Relation to Modern Ideas.* With an introduction and notes by Frederick Pollard. Preface to the Beacon paperback edition edited by Raymond

Firth. Beacon Series in Classics of the Law. Boston: Beacon Press, 1963. Originally published in 1861.

Mauss, Marcel. *The Gift: The Form and Reason for Exchange in Archaic Societies,* trans. W. D. Halls. Foreword by Mary Douglas. London: Routledge, 1990.

Mbembe, Achille. "Provisional Notes on the Postcolony." *Africa* 62, no. 1 (1992): 3–37.

Meillassoux, Claude. " 'The Economy' in Agricultural Self-sustaining Societies: A Preliminary Analysis." In David Seddon, ed., *Relations of Production: Marxist Approaches to Economic Anthropology,* 127–57. London: Frank Cass, 1978.

Meillassoux, Claude. *Maidens, Meal and Money: Capitalism and the Domestic Community.* Cambridge: Cambridge University Press, 1981.

Meillassoux, Claude, ed. *The Development of Indigenous Trade and Markets in West Africa,* with an introduction by Claude Meillassoux, Foreword by Daryll Forde. Studies presented and discussed at the Tenth International African Seminar at Fourah Bay College, Freetown, December 1969. London: Oxford University Press for the International African Institute, 1971.

Le messenger. No. 010. Friday, November 2, 1990, p. 15.

Miaffo, D. "Role sociale de l'autopsie publique traditionelle chez les Bamileke." Mimeo, Memoire de DES, Department of Sociology, University of Yaounde, 1977.

Moore, Sally Falk. *Social Facts and Fabrications: "Customary" Law on Kilimanjaro, 1880–1980.* Cambridge: Cambridge University Press, 1986.

Mzeka, N. Paul. *The Core Culture of Nso.* Agawam: Paul Radin, 1980.

Ndobegang, M. "Grassfields Chiefs and Political Change in Cameroon, ca. 1884–1966." PhD dissertation, Boston University, 1985.

Ngayap, Pierre Flambeau. *Cameroun, qui governes? De Ahidjo a Bija: L'heritage et l'enjeu.* Paris: Harmattan, 1983.

Ngue, Marcel. "Agricultural and Rural Development Statistics." Mimeo, USAID, Yaounde, 1979.

Nkwi, Paul Nchoji. "Cameroon Grassfield Chiefs and Modern Politics." *Paideuma: Mitteilungen zur Kulturkunde* 25 (1979): 99–115.

Nkwi, Paul Nchoji. *Traditional Diplomacy: A Study of Inter-chiefdom Relations in the Western Grassfields, Northwest Province of Cameroon.* Yaounde: University of Yaounde, 1987.

Nkwi, Paul Nchoji, and Jean-Pierre Warnier. *Elements for a History of the Western Grassfields.* Yaounde: University of Yaounde, 1982.

Ntangsi, Joseph. *The Political and Economic Dimensions of Agricultural Policy in Cameroon.* Washington D.C.: World Bank, 1987.

Okali, Christine. "Issues of Resource Access and Control: A Comment." *Africa: Journal of the International African Institute* 59, no. 1 (1989): 56–60.

Okoth-Ogendo, H. W. O. "Some Issues in the Study of Tenure Relations in African Agriculture." *Africa: Journal of the International African Institute* 59, no. 1 (1989): 6–17.

Ong, Aihwa. *Spirits of Resistance and Capitalist Discipline.* Albany: State University of New York Press, 1987.

Ortner, Sherry B. "Gender and Sexuality in Hierarchical Societies." In Sherry Ortner and Harriet Whitehead, eds., *Sexual Meanings: The Cultural Construction of Gender and Sexuality.* Cambridge: Cambridge University Press, 1981.

Ortner, Sherry B. "Theory in Anthropology since the Sixties." *Comparative Studies in Society and History* 26, no. 1 (1984): 126–66.

Ortner, Sherry B., and Harriet Whitehead. "Introduction: Accounting for Sexual Meanings." Ortner and Whitehead, eds., *Sexual Meanings: The Cultural Construction of Gender and Sexuality,* 1–27. Cambridge: Cambridge University Press, 1981.

Price, David. "Who Are the Tikar Now?" *Paideuma: Mitteilungen zur Kulturkunde* 25 (1979): 89–98.

Provincial Delegation for Agriculture of the Northwest. "Evaluation of Agricultural Development from 1959/60–80." Mimeo, Provincial Agricultural Office, Bamenda, 1979.

Rabinow, Paul. *Symbolic Domination: Cultural Form and Historical Change in Morocco.* Chicago: University of Chicago Press, 1975.

Recensement general. Vol. 1, Tome 3, p. 96. United Republic of Cameroon: Yaounde, 1980.

Reed-Danahay, Deborah. "The Kabyle and the French: Occidentalism in Pierre Bourdieu's Theory of Practice." In James G. Carrier, ed., *Occidentalism,* 21–42. Cambridge: Cambridge University Press, forthcoming.

Rey, Pierre-Philippe. *Les alliances de classes.* Paris: Maspero, 1973.

Rey, Pierre-Philippe. "Class Contradiction in Lineage Societies." *Critique of Anthropology* 4, no. 13–14 (1979): 41–60.

Rey, Pierre-Philippe. "The Lineage Mode of Production." *Critique of Anthropology* 3, no. 11 (1975): 27–79.

Robertson, Claire, and Iris Berger, eds. *Women and Class in Africa.* New York: Holmes and Meier, 1986.

Rodman, Margaret. *Masters of Tradition: Consequences of Customary Land Tenure in Longana, Vanuatu.* Vancouver: University of British Columbia Press, 1987.

Rowlands, Michael J. "Local and Long Distance Trade and Incipient State Formation on the Bamenda Plateau in the Late 19th Century." In *Paideuma: Mitteilungen zur Kulturkunde* 25 (1979): 1–20.

Rowlands, Michael J. "Notes on the Material Symbolism of Grassfields Palaces." *Paideuma: Mitteilungen zur Kulturkunde* 31 (1985): 203–13.

Rowlands, Michael J. "Power and Moral Order in Precolonial West-Central Africa." In Elizabeth M. Brumfiel and Timothy K. Earle, eds., *Specialization, Exchange, and Complex Societies,* 52–63. Cambridge: Cambridge University Press, 1987.

Rowlands, Michael. "Prestige of Presence: Negotiating Modernisation through Tradition." Paper prepared for the ASA Bicentennial Conference, Oxford University, 1993.

Rowlands, Michael J., and Jean-Pierre Warnier. "Sorcery, Power, and the Modern State in Cameroon." *Man* 23, no. 1 (1988): 118–32.

Rubin, Gayle. "The Traffic in Women: Notes on the 'Political Economy' of Sex." In
    Rayna R. Reiter, ed., *Toward an Anthropology of Women*, 157–210. New
    York: Monthly Review Press, 1975.
Rubin, Jeffrey. "The Ambiguity of Resistance." Unpublished paper, 1993.
Sacks, Karen. *Sisters and Wives: The Past and Future of Sexual Equality*. Westport,
    Conn.: Greenwood Press, 1979.
Sahlins, Marshall David. *Historical Metaphors and Mythical Realities: Structure
    in the Early History of the Sandwich Islands Kingdom*. ASAO Special Publica-
    tions no. 1. Ann Arbor: University of Michigan Press, 1981.
Sahlins, Marshall David. *Stone Age Economics*. Chicago: Aldine, 1972.
Scott, James C. *Weapons of the Weak*. New Haven: Yale University Press,
    1985.
Scott, William, and Miriam Mahaffey (Goheen). *Executive Summary: Agricultural
    Marketing in the Northwest Province, United Republic of Cameroon*. Yaounde:
    USAID, 1980.
Shanklin, Eugenia. "ANLU Remembered: The Kom Women's Rebellion of 1958–
    61." *Dialectical Anthropology* 15, nos. 2–3 (1990): 159–82.
Shweder, Richard A., and Bourne, E. J. "Does the Concept of Person Vary Cross-
    Culturally?" In Richard A. Shweder and Robert A. LeVine, eds., *Culture
    Theory: Essays on Mind, Self, and Emotion*. Cambridge: Cambridge University
    Press, 1984.
Simo, John Mope. "Royal Wives in the Ndop Plains." *Canadian Journal of African
    Studies* 25, no. 3 (1991): 418–31.
Staudt, Kathleen A. "Women Farmers and Inequities in Agriculture." In Edna G.
    Bay, ed., *Women and Work in Africa*. Westview Special Studies on Africa. Boul-
    der: Westview Press, 1982.
Staudt, Kathleen A. "Women's Politics, the State, and Capitalist Transformation in
    Africa." In Irving Leonard Markovitz, ed., *Studies in Power and Class in Africa*
    Oxford: Oxford University Press, 1987.
Stichter, Sharon B., and Jane L. Parpart, eds. *Patriarchy and Class: African Women
    in the Home and the Workforce*. African Modernization and Development Se-
    ries. Boulder: Westview Press, 1988.
United Republic of Cameroon. *Land Tenure and State Lands: Ordinances Nos.
    74–1, 74–2, 74–3 of 6th July 1974*. Extract of OGURC No. 1 Supplementary of
    5th August 1974. Yaounde: United Republic of Cameroon, 1974.
United Republic of Cameroon. *Nseh Cultural Week*. Pamphlet. Yaounde: United
    Republic of Cameroon, 1979.
Warnier. Jean-Pierre. "La polarité culture-nature entre le chef et Takoengoe à
    Mankon." *Paideuma: Mitteilungen zur Kulturkunde* 25 (1979): 21–33.
Warnier, Jean-Pierre. *Échanges, développement et hiérarchies dans le Bamenda
    pré-colonial*. Studien zur Kulturkunde, no. 76. Stuttgart: Franz Steiner for the
    Frobenius-Gesellschaft, 1985.
Wendi, Bernadette. "The Cameroonian Woman in Development." *The Activator*,
    newsletter for the Association for Creative Teaching, Northwest, 4/1 (January
    1990): 16–17.

Williams, Raymond. *Marxism and Literature*. Oxford: Oxford University Press, 1977.

Women's Cameroon National Union. *Integration of the Cameroon Women in the Economic Development Processus* [*sic*]. Yaounde: United Republic of Cameroon, 1982.

Index